How to Launch a Token

An Essential Guide for the Uninitiated

Alexander Rees-Evans

How to Launch a Token: An Essential Guide for the Uninitiated

Alexander Rees-Evans
La Pounche, France

ISBN-13 (pbk): 979-8-8688-0532-5   ISBN-13 (electronic): 979-8-8688-0533-2
https://doi.org/10.1007/979-8-8688-0533-2

Copyright © 2024 by Alexander Rees-Evans

Managing Director, Apress Media LLC: Welmoed Spahr
Acquisitions Editor: Malini Rajendran
Development Editor: James Markham
Coordinating Editor: Gryffin Winkler

Cover designed by eStudioCalamar

Cover image by Freepik (www.freepik.com)

Distributed to the book trade worldwide by Apress Media, LLC, 1 New York Plaza, New York, NY 10004, U.S.A. Phone 1-800-SPRINGER, fax (201) 348-4505, e-mail orders-ny@springer-sbm.com, or visit www.springeronline.com. Apress Media, LLC is a California LLC and the sole member (owner) is Springer Science + Business Media Finance Inc (SSBM Finance Inc). SSBM Finance Inc is a **Delaware** corporation.

For information on translations, please e-mail booktranslations@springernature.com; for reprint, paperback, or audio rights, please e-mail bookpermissions@springernature.com.

Apress titles may be purchased in bulk for academic, corporate, or promotional use. eBook versions and licenses are also available for most titles. For more information, reference our Print and eBook Bulk Sales web page at http://www.apress.com/bulk-sales.

Any source code or other supplementary material referenced by the author in this book is available to readers on GitHub (https://github.com/Apress). For more detailed information, please visit https://www.apress.com/gp/services/source-code.

If disposing of this product, please recycle the paper

To my beloved partner Manon and son Sandro,
who helped make this possible.

Table of Contents

About the Author

After working in various other roles, **Alexander Rees-Evans** moved into the world of crypto as a strategic partner of a trading platform for high value assets, Idoneus. One of his successes was convincing the French royal family to accept cryptocurrency as a method of payment for their champagne "Heritage." Since then, he has headed up large sales teams, private placement platforms, produced weekly newsletters, and hired new staff at large crypto platforms, exchanges, and a high-level token management platform known as Kaizen Finance. Furthermore, Alexander was a mentor in firms such as Techstars, GeniusX, and AVio. Today, Alexander is an internationally renowned advisor in this space, spending the majority of his time advising tier 1 clients for the Code Craft group encompassing Dverse, Inferno labs, Community3, and Lux labs while also presiding over the blockchain and cybernetic commission of the World Business Union.

Acknowledgments

A special thank-you to the European Blockchain Association, World Business Union, and the Dubai Blockchain Center.

Introduction

In the rapidly evolving world of cryptocurrency, this comprehensive guide offers a deep dive into the intricacies of launching and successfully managing a cryptocurrency token. Spanning 12 chapters, the book begins with the fundamentals, explaining the different types of tokens and the core concepts of crypto projects, guiding readers through the critical decision-making process about the necessity and role of a token in their venture. As the narrative progresses, readers are taken on a journey through the life cycle of a crypto project. The book meticulously covers every aspect, from structuring the project and transforming an idea into a reality to the detailed construction of a Minimum Viable Product (MVP). It emphasizes the importance of a well-thought-out roadmap, a compelling pitch deck, and the crucial process of assembling a skilled team. Diving deeper, the book explores the complex world of tokenomics, offering insights into various economic models behind tokens and how to tailor them to specific projects. It also sheds light on market conditions and cycles, teaching readers how to identify the best times to launch their tokens. A key aspect of this guide is its focus on go-to-market strategies, including targeting the right audience, effective marketing techniques, and the vital role of community building. Additionally, it addresses the essentials of fundraising in the crypto space, highlighting the types of investors to approach and strategies for engaging them effectively. Security and stability are paramount in the crypto world. The book provides a detailed analysis of the storage and custody of funds, comparing centralized and decentralized mechanisms and emphasizing the importance of robust security measures. Market makers and exchanges, both decentralized and centralized, are thoroughly examined, offering strategies for negotiation and partnership. This is crucial for ensuring liquidity and accessibility of the token in the market. The guide culminates with a focus on the launch day, detailing the preparation, organization, and key considerations to ensure a successful token launch. The final chapter looks beyond the launch, discussing strategies for maintaining the health and longevity of a token, thereby ensuring its long-term success and sustainability in the market.

This book is an indispensable resource, providing invaluable insights and practical advice, ensuring that you are well-equipped to navigate the complex and exciting world of cryptocurrency token launches.

CHAPTER 1

Introduction to Launching a Token

So, you're thinking about launching a token (Glossary 1)? But how do you avoid becoming another statistic of failed launches? What blockchain do you launch on and why? How do you build your team and raise funds? Do you launch on a CEX (Glossary 2) or DEX (Glossary 3)? How do you choose your Market Maker? How come thousands of tokens launch but the majority fail? You may have read my book on "So You Want to Work in Crypto," as you can see, this one is very different. However, you may not know the exact secret sauce necessary to successfully launch your own token and crypto project. In this book you will learn your tips, tricks, and hacks to ensure a successful launch. There are thousands of reasons on why you should launch a token and hundreds of thousands of problems you'll encounter along the way. We'll even explore how to create a uniquely powerful ecosystem, providing your token with exceptional use cases for all of your community members and investors.

When one embarks on a journey into the heart of the digital revolution – the creation of cryptocurrency tokens isn't just a technological feat; it's a strategic maneuver increasingly embraced by savvy institutions worldwide. From startups to corporate giants, the allure of tokenization is reshaping the financial and technological landscape as we speak. This section offers a panoramic view of why launching a token is becoming an indispensable tool in the arsenal of modern business strategy.

© Alexander Rees-Evans 2024
A. Rees-Evans, *How to Launch a Token*, https://doi.org/10.1007/979-8-8688-0533-2_1

What Are Tokens?

Tokens are more than digital assets; they represent a new frontier in utility and functionality. To start, we'll explore the myriad ways in which tokens are being used – from simplifying transactions and streamlining supply chain processes to democratizing investments and fostering community engagement. It's a journey through the multifaceted utility tokens can bring to various industries when deployed wisely.

The narrative of cryptocurrency tokens is witnessing a pivotal shift as major financial institutions and corporate entities dive into this deep crypto pool. It's a testament to the growing recognition of tokens as viable, valuable instruments in the global market. In a world where digital transformation is the mantra, tokenization has emerged as a strategic imperative. When done correctly, launching a token can offer businesses a competitive edge, unlock new revenue streams while providing a universal platform for groundbreaking innovation.

What Is Tokenization?

At its core, tokenization is the process of converting and fractionalizing rights of an asset into a digital token on a blockchain (Glossary 4). Imagine a world where anything of value, real estate to artwork, from shares in a startup to loyalty points, or even the unearthed precious metals and rocks can be tokenized. This ability to digitize and fractionalize assets democratizes access to individuals all over the world by granting them the opportunity to invest very small amounts, if needed, from wherever they may be on the planet. As you launch your own token, it is important to keep in mind the individuals, backing your token financially.

Always remember that the funds you obtain aren't yours. They come from investors and retail traders entrusting you greatly. Once your token is tradable, the risk of losing your investors' funds is very real. Not only will this massively impact your reputation and credibility for your future endeavors, but many people having trusted you with their funds will be at a real loss. It is noteworthy to remember this section, as your project's direct success can indeed change people's lives, for better or for worse. Always consider this when making any token/business related decisions. Of course, they're aware of the risks involved, it's just important to be aware of the responsibility involved in launching your own token. For bad execution or simple lack of structure can lead to legal repercussions too. The financial regulators and governments around the world take the entire crypto market seriously, even if they have not yet come to a global consensus on how to deal with everything emerging from it. Some, however, are starting to lead the way such as the "Securities and Exchange Commission" (SEC) in the United States, to the "Market In Crypto Assets" (MICA) in Europe or even the "Financial Conduct Authority" (FCA) in the UK. Increasingly stringent rules and regulations are being constantly laid down, imposing you to be even more cautious with your client's funds. On August 28, 2024, the ex-founder of FTX, the second largest exchange in the world, was sentenced to 25 years of prison for mismanaging client funds. Much like Eduard John Smith, captain of the Titanic, you have not just a moral duty, but also an ethical duty toward your investors. Be the honorable person, act with dignity and steadfastness on your principles, as your reputation and values can help you transcend any stormy weather you may face. Abiding by these principles will resonate with your community and build further trust within.

Tokenization really does break down traditional barriers to entry in investment and asset ownership. By fractionalizing assets, it allows individuals to own portions of assets that would otherwise be out of reach. A piece of prime real estate, a rare piece of art, or equity in a high-potential startup can now be owned in fractions and transferred in a few seconds without banks, making them more accessible to a broader audience. This increased accessibility not only democratizes wealth creation but also injects enhanced liquidity into markets, paving the way for a more dynamic and responsive economic landscape. Yet, it remains a big pain point for the majority of them also. For those of you who don't remember, Porsche released a collection of Non Fungible Tokens (NFTs) (Glossary 5) that failed miserably and it was quite an embarrassment for the prestigious company as a whole. Imagine if they launched a tradable token on an exchange? Far more people watch the traditional altcoin charts rather than follow NFT charts, launching a traditionnal token means much more visual exposure, hence amplifying successes, but also making extremely visible the failures. The risk of launching a token with the intention to be listed on exchanges differs far more than launching an NFT collection per se as there are more variables and higher visibility from the entire crypto community, noting that there's approximately 360,000 NFT holders in the world as of 2023 (How Many NFTs Are There in 2023? • NFT Statistics (mymillennialguide.com)). On the other hand, there's 420 million cryptocurrency users in the world as of 2023 (How Many Crypto Users Are There in 2024? (Updated Statistics) (coinweb.com)). Evidently, the cryptocurrency market dwarfs that of NFTs, coincidentally amplifying the risk/reward ratio across all boards. Any entity looking to launch their own token must be aware of such facts as the two markets are very different in all ways possible, including structure, community, technology, trends, and pitfalls. Over half of the new crypto projects that launch in this industry don't make it past their first year. In 2014, around 75% of the 793 tokens released that year failed (Dead coins: How many cryptocurrencies have failed? | CoinGecko) (Charting the Number of Failed Crypto Coins, by Year (2013–2022) (visualcapitalist.com)) (How Many Cryptos Have Failed? List of Dead Coins That Went Bust (hedgewithcrypto.com)) (Number of cryptocurrencies 2013–2023 | Statista). It may not be the norm to put graphs on the first pages of a book, but the failure rate of token launches is so staggering, I have to do this.

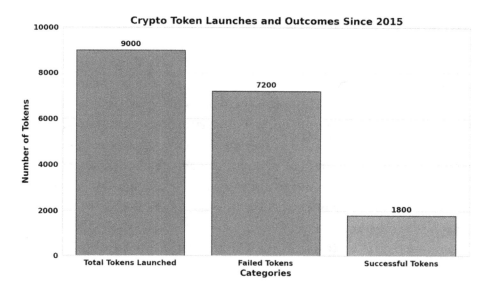

Never think you're too cool for school, stay humble. Even if you raise millions of dollars, keep your eye on the goal: Having a successful token launch.

Starting your journey of successfully launching your token, you'll need to build a solid foundation which your launch will rely on. What type of token should you launch and what type of tokens actually exist? In order to give you the full scope of choice, let's take a look through our kaleidoscope of crypto tokens.

Utility Tokens: The Fuel of the Crypto Ecosystem

Utility tokens are far more than digital assets; they represent access, utility, and participation within their native ecosystems. Think of them as multifunctional keys, unlocking a diverse range of services and experiences in the digital world. These tokens are integral to the functionality of numerous blockchain-based applications, serving as the cornerstone for a wide array of platforms. In essence, utility tokens are the fuel for decentralized applications (dApps). Whether it's a gaming platform, a decentralized exchange, or a content-sharing network, these tokens grant users access to specific functionalities. For example, in a blockchain-based gaming environment, a utility token could be used to purchase in-game items, unlock special features, or even used as an in-game currency.

This not only enhances the user experience, but also creates an internal economy within the ecosystem, driving engagement and retention, hence offsetting selling pressure and encouraging buying pressure. Moreover, utility tokens can play a pivotal role in governance and decision-making processes within decentralized projects such as Decentralised Autonomous Organisations (DAOs) (Glossary 6). Token holders might have the ability to vote on key decisions, propose changes, or contribute to the project's development like ReddCoin, one of the oldest altcoins out there still alive today. This democratizes the governance process, aligning it closely with the ethos of decentralization that underpins the blockchain space. Beyond their immediate functionality, utility tokens are often a means for projects to raise funds through Initial Coin Offerings (ICOs) (Glossary 7) or other token sale models. Investors purchase these tokens with the expectation that their utility within the platform and/or project's ecosystem will increase their demand, and consequently, their value. However, it's crucial for token creators to clearly articulate the use case and value proposition of their utility tokens to potential investors and users, as these factors significantly influence the token's success and adoption.

Security Tokens: Digitizing Traditional Investment Instruments

Security tokens are a groundbreaking blend of traditional investment instruments and cutting-edge blockchain technology. They represent an ownership stake in an asset, be it equity in a company, a share of real estate, or participation in an investment fund, for example. These tokens digitize securities, making them more accessible, divisible, and easier to trade in. Imagine the impact on real estate investment, where traditionally high barriers to entry have limited access to only a select few. Security tokens enable fractional ownership of real estate, allowing investors to purchase a part of a property. This not only democratizes access to this asset class but also provides enhanced liquidity, as these tokens can be traded on secondary markets much like stocks or bonds. In the corporate finance domain, security tokens offer an innovative way for businesses to raise capital. By tokenizing shares, companies can reach a global pool of investors, bypassing some of the traditional hurdles of equity fundraising. This method also presents an opportunity for more transparent and efficient shareholder management through the blockchain's immutable ledger. However, the issuance and trading of security tokens are subject to stringent regulatory requirements, as they fall under securities law in most jurisdictions. Navigating this regulatory landscape is crucial for the legitimacy and success of security tokens. Adherence to regulations not only ensures compliance but also builds investor confidence in the token's credibility. Security tokens are set to revolutionize traditional finance by enhancing accessibility, liquidity, and transparency. They indeed present a compelling use case for blockchain technology, extending its benefits to a broader financial context and bridging the gap between the traditional and digital economies.

Stablecoins: The Pillars of Stability in a Volatile Market

In the often turbulent waters of the cryptocurrency market, stablecoins stand as beacons of stability. Pegged or tethered to more stable assets like fiat currencies or commodities, these tokens mitigate the volatility typically associated with cryptocurrencies. This stability makes them ideal for everyday transactions, trading, and as a safe haven for investors during market downturns. Consider the role of stablecoins like USDT (Tether), which is pegged to the US Dollar. In a market where most cryptocurrencies experience significant price fluctuations, stablecoins provide a much-needed anchor. The Stablecoin is only as strong as the anchor itself and liquidity made available. This stability is crucial for businesses and individuals who want to leverage the benefits of blockchain technology without the risk of extreme volatility. It's also often used to purely stock and safeguard value without moving into fiat until the owner makes their next crypto investment. Stablecoins also play a critical role in the decentralized finance (DeFi) ecosystem. They provide a stable medium of exchange and store of value, essential for various DeFi applications like lending, borrowing, and yield farming (Glossary 8). This stability is key to the functioning and growth of the DeFi space, offering users and community members a uniquely reliable way to participate in these financial services. It's important to note that the mechanisms used to maintain the peg (Glossary 9) of stablecoins vary also. Some are backed by reserves of the asset they are pegged to, while others use algorithms to manage supply and demand to maintain their value. Regardless of the method, the goal is the same: to provide a stable, reliable digital currency that can be used in a wide range of financial contexts.

Non-Fungible Tokens (NFTs): Revolutionizing Digital Ownership and Creativity

Non-Fungible Tokens (NFTs) may not be the primary suspect for launching a token; however, it's in the name, they're tokens! When first created, it led to a huge explosion in the digital scene, redefining the concept of ownership within the digital realm. Each NFT is unique, representing ownership of a specific item or piece of content, such as digital art, music, videos, or even tweets. Unlike other cryptocurrencies, NFTs are not interchangeable, with each token holding its distinct value and characteristics. Now NFTs aren't just pictures of silly monkeys or pixelated images of degens (Glossary 10) selling for millions of dollars. The impact of NFTs on the creative industry has been monumental. Artists and creators can now tokenize their work, ensuring authenticity and ownership while reaching a global audience. This has opened up new avenues for monetizing digital creations, enabling artists to sell their work directly to collectors without intermediaries. NFTs also introduce a novel concept in digital rights management. Through blockchain technology, NFTs can ensure that ownership and transaction history are transparent and immutable. This not only protects the rights of creators but also provides buyers with verifiable proof of authenticity and provenance! The world of NFTs is not limited to art and creativity. They are being used to represent a wide array of digital assets, including virtual real estate, collectibles, and even identity documents. Today, some of them actually have even more utility that companies like DVerse and Kaizen Finance help take to the next level such as when we created a new form of NFTs for the national stock market of Hong Kong, hence enhancing the security and fluidity of stock transfers. As this technology evolves, the potential applications of NFTs continue to expand, offering endless possibilities in the digital world, leading to an interesting option for project founders.

DeFi Tokens: Fueling the Decentralized Finance Revolution

DeFi tokens are painted with a bit of a broad brush, they're a sub-class of either Utility tokens or Security tokens at the heart of the decentralized finance (DeFi) movement, a paradigm shift in the world of finance. These tokens often represent a stake in DeFi platforms, allowing users to participate in decentralized lending, borrowing, trading, and yield-farming activities. DeFi tokens are more than just digital assets; they are the engines driving a new financial ecosystem that operates without traditional financial intermediaries. In the DeFi space, tokens can serve various purposes. They can be used as collateral for loans, as a medium of exchange in decentralized trading, or as a way to earn interest on deposits. Some DeFi tokens also confer governance rights, allowing holders to vote on changes to the platform, similar to governance tokens. The rise of DeFi tokens signifies a shift toward a more open, inclusive, and transparent financial system. It offers opportunities for financial participation and innovation previously unavailable to a large segment of the global population. This democratization of finance is not just a technological achievement but also a social and economic breakthrough. DeFi tokens have also introduced new economic models in the crypto space which the traditional financial sector lacks. Yield farming, liquidity mining (Glossary 11), and staking (Glossary 12) are concepts that have emerged from the DeFi movement, offering token holders innovative ways to generate returns on their holdings.

Meme Coins: The Playful Yet Risky Mavericks of the Crypto World

This is going to be a long one guys, there's so much hype around these tokens that do nothing, yet some of them have market caps of hundreds of millions, if not billions of dollars! To top that, one of the best performing tokens of 2023 was PEPE coin (How the Pepe coin, "fueled by pure memetic power," soared past a $1.6 billion market cap in 3 weeks—and then tumbled | Fortune Crypto), literally the picture of a right-wing frog with a sense of humor! We're going to dive into just what on earth is going on with this very bizarre class of tokens. Even if they're classed as utility tokens for the majority of them, Meme coins are often born out of Internet jokes and viral phenomena, having carved a unique niche in the cryptocurrency landscape. These tokens, while initially not taken seriously by many, have garnered immense popularity and market capitalization, often driven by a strong community presence and social media influence. Meme coins typically originate from Internet culture, embodying a sense of humor and light-heartedness that contrasts with the other more serious and utility-focused cryptocurrencies. The most famous example, Dogecoin, started as a parody of Bitcoin, featuring the Shiba Inu dog from the "Doge" meme as its mascot. Despite its humorous beginnings, Dogecoin and its ilk have attracted a massive following, leading to significant market activity and wealth to early holders. The true power of meme coins lies in their communities.

These tokens often don't possess the utility or backing of more established cryptocurrencies but thrive on the strength of their community support and viral marketing. Social media platforms, particularly Twitter and Reddit, play a crucial role in building and sustaining the hype and enthusiasm around meme coins. Celebrity endorsements and social media influencers have also significantly impacted the popularity and, consequently, the market value of meme coins. High-profile figures like Elon Musk tweeting about Dogecoin have led to substantial market reactions, showcasing the influence of social dynamics in the valuation of these tokens. It's important to note that they're also characterized by high volatility and are often subject to huge speculative trading. Unlike traditional cryptocurrencies, the value of meme coins can skyrocket or plummet based on social media trends, celebrity comments, or community sentiment, rather than underlying technological developments or adoption. This volatility makes meme coins a high-risk, high-reward venture for investors. While some traders have reaped substantial gains from meme coin investments, others have faced significant losses, especially those who join during the hype without understanding the market's speculative nature. Meme coins have had a much broader impact on the cryptocurrency world than initially expected. They have introduced a new demographic to crypto trading, attracting individuals drawn to the fun and community aspect rather than the technical or financial side of cryptocurrencies. This has helped in further popularizing the concept of digital currencies. Furthermore, meme coins have sparked discussions about the value and nature of cryptocurrencies. They challenge traditional notions of asset valuation, highlighting the role of community sentiment and cultural phenomena in determining value in this new digital era.

SoulBound Tokens: Once You Have It, It Sticks to You like Glue

Imagined by none other than the founder of Ethereum, Vitalik Buterin describes soulbound tokens as the ultimate vehicle for digital identity. Souldbound tokens get that name for a reason, once you have one, you can't transfer it. It literally will be "bound to your soul," in the digital realm, of course. The use cases for these non-transferable NFTs are endless, and to give a spectrum of thought, what better example than Vitalik's: the digital identity of a person. This identity could not be transferred, stolen, misplaced, or even forged due to the very nature of the supporting blockchain technology. Such rigid technology can provide great value if used in the appropriate manner.

Always think wisely and carefully about what type of token you want to launch beforehand as this will heavily impact how you will build your project and develop your go-to-market strategy.

This leads us to touch briefly upon crypto projects themselves.

Crypto Projects

In the vast, uncharted territories of the digital world, crypto projects are at the very heart of every token launch. These projects are not mere ventures in coding and finance; they are comprehensive ecosystems that blend technology, community, economics, and vision into a cohesive whole which you will need to master. Every crypto project begins with an idea, but not just any idea. Much like a traditional business, it's an idea that seeks to solve a problem, fill a gap, or create something entirely new, but in the digital realm. This idea is the seed from which the project grows, encompassing everything from a new way to transact value to a complete overhaul of traditional systems using blockchain technology. Think of it as the inception point, where vision meets potential.

Blockchain Technology

At the heart of every crypto project is blockchain technology. This revolutionary technology provides the foundation upon which all projects are built. It's the canvas where ideas are painted and the stage where innovations play out. Whether it's a public blockchain like Ethereum or a private one tailored for specific needs, this underlying technology defines the project's potential and limitations.

Tokens are often the lifeblood of crypto projects, serving various roles from utility to value exchange. In some projects, tokens are a means of participating in the ecosystem – buying, selling, or accessing services. In others, they represent a stake in the project, aligning the interests of the holders with the project's success. The design and functionality of these tokens are critical, as they can significantly influence the project's adoption and sustainability.

Smart Contracts

Another crucial part of your crypto project token launch are the Smart contracts (Glossary 13) originally created by Ethereum. These are the automated enforcers of the crypto world. These self-executing contracts with predefined rules are what make decentralized projects truly autonomous. From facilitating transactions to governing interactions within the ecosystem, smart contracts ensure that the operations of a crypto project are transparent, efficient, and trustless.

Audits

It's important to note that audits of Smart contracts aren't a guarantee of quality, this is one of the biggest myths in the industry. Watch out, especially those audited by Certik and Hacken. Literally every single token that's crashed has been audited by one or the other. When you go for audits, do some research on what the founders of the company actually did before Web3, research projects audited by them months after they've launched and don't get fooled by them putting millions into marketing. Look for a strong cyber security background like the audit firm DeuSsec, for example.

Community

Another capital point of all crypto projects is the community. As we discussed during the explanations of Meme Coins, a crypto project's community is its heartbeat, pumping energy, support, and vitality into the ecosystem. These communities are not just groups of investors and users; they are often active participants in the project's development, governance, and advocacy. A strong, engaged community can be the difference between a project's success and obscurity, so it's important to give each member extra special treatment. Often you can keep them engaged by giving them voting power or forms of governance. Crypto communities are about decision-making and direction; you can fully include them in many ways and forms. How a project is governed – whether through a centralized team, a Decentralised Autonomous Organisation (DAO), or a hybrid model – greatly impacts its development and adaptability.

Effective Governance Structures

Effective governance structures are crucial for navigating the challenges and opportunities that come with running a decentralized project.

Apart from Meme Coins, an important measure of a crypto project's success lies in its use cases. These are the real-world applications of the technology – how it solves problems, improves systems, or creates new opportunities. From finance to supply chain management, healthcare to entertainment, the potential applications of crypto projects are vast and varied. Developing such a project requires resources – both human and financial. Funding these ventures often involves innovative methods like ICOs, STOs (Glossary 14), or Venture Capital (VC) funding, each with its own set of challenges and advantages that we'll explore later on in this book. The development process itself is a complex journey, requiring a blend of technical expertise, strategic planning, and adaptability. On your journey to launch a token, the legal and regulatory landscape for crypto projects is also a maze of complexity and variability. Navigating this landscape is crucial, as it can impact everything from a project's structure, development time to its global reach.

Compliance

Compliance and foresight in legal matters are not just necessary for survival; they are imperative for credibility and trust as we saw with Binance in 2023. Even if you leave these matters to once you have deep pockets, regulators will eventually catch up and cost you big. Another often overlooked point for your crypto project to thrive on is it must be adopted. This requires strategic marketing, clear communication, and often, a bit of evangelism without pushing it too far. How a project presents itself to the world, attracts users, and builds partnerships is integral to your token's growth and success. Remember that every dollar people spend on the idea of your token, they speak to their friends about it. If you neglect them in your socials, they'll start to think it's a scam or purely just want you to fail as they've lost respect for you, your project and before you know it, word has spread like wild fire... As you're building out your project and preparing your token launch, cherish every person and entity participating, however small they may seem. Make them feel special.

Strategic Considerations

At its heart, deciding to introduce a token in your crypto project is a strategic move. It's about aligning your project's objectives with the functionalities and opportunities that a token can offer. Does your project aim to create a decentralized ecosystem? Are you looking to incentivize user participation? Or is your goal to raise funds? The answer to these questions can guide you in determining the role a token could play in your project. While fundraising is often a primary driver behind tokenization, particularly through mechanisms like ICOs or STOs, the utility of tokens extends far beyond just capital generation for Start-Ups. Tokens can be a powerful tool for user engagement, community building, and creating a decentralized governance model. They can represent voting rights, access to services, or even a share in the project's future revenues, among much more!

One of the key considerations in tokenizing your project is understanding your target market and audience. Will your potential users be familiar with cryptocurrency? This is why GameFi projects are very complex to actually make successful as the Web3 community's generally interested in speculating on the token, whilst the game is often too poor a quality for the Web2 users to engage in. The success of a token heavily relies on its acceptance and utilization by its intended audience.

Regulatory Environments

The decision to launch a token must also be made taking into account the context of the current regulatory environment. Different jurisdictions have varying regulations regarding the issuance and trading of tokens, especially if they are deemed securities. Navigating these legal waters is essential, not only to ensure compliance but to protect your investors and your project from future regulatory challenges. The technical infrastructure and Security when creating a token doesn't necessarily require a solid technical foundation. However, you need to have a solid understanding of how tokenization and the industry work. This includes choosing the right blockchain platform, ensuring the security of the token, developing smart contracts, and much more. The technical aspect of tokenization is critical and it must align with your project's needs and be executed with precision and security in mind.

Economic Model (Tokenomics)

A crucial aspect of introducing a token is designing its economic model, or tokenomics (Glossary 14). This involves determining the token's supply, distribution mechanism, use cases, and how it will retain or appreciate in value over time. A well-thought-out tokenomics model is key to ensuring the long-term viability and success of the token. Launching your token also involves a significant marketing effort. It's about communicating the value and utility of the token to potential users and investors. Building a strong community around the token can drive engagement, foster loyalty, and create a network of advocates and supporters. This will provide the trading volume and buying pressure required to absorb the selling pressure of your token. Like the US Dollar, as so many countries use it for international trade, the US Dollar always has buying pressure, which enables them to print trillions of dollars out of thin air without damaging the price too much (inflation). If a currency from a smaller country printed the same amount of money out of thin air, the value of that currency would drop dramatically as there's more people selling that currency than buying it. In our case, regardless of your token supply, you need more people buying your token than people selling it. This is the main driver of positive price action and your token longevity. Deciding whether to incorporate a token into your project is a decision that requires careful consideration of various factors – strategic, regulatory, technical, economic, and beyond. It's about understanding the unique dynamics of your project and weighing the potential benefits against the challenges and responsibilities that come with tokenization. As we continue to explore the multifaceted world of blockchain and cryptocurrency, the decision to tokenize remains a significant and defining choice for any digital venture, one that could set the course for its future in the burgeoning digital economy.

CHAPTER 2

Project Structure

In the exhilarating odyssey of the crypto universe, every token launch starts with an idea. The idea of great innovation combined with relentless passion pushing through the wonders of your imagination. Spearheaded by massive action, your idea is the seed of which you plant and nourish until it blooms into a top-trending token. Regardless of how revolutionary your idea may be, if you're not able to articulate it properly, seldom will it work. The structure of your crypto project is akin to a masterfully charted map, guiding a venture through the turbulent seas of digital innovation and market uncertainties. This introduction marks the first step in our exploration of a successful crypto project structure, a journey that delves into the intricate art of melding visionary ideas with meticulous planning. It's a narrative about launching not just a token but a legacy in the crypto world.

Every great saga in the crypto realm begins with a spark – an idea with the potential to disrupt, innovate, and redefine. Yet, the metamorphosis of this spark into a blazing flame of success hinges on a solid structure. This structure is a tapestry woven from vision, strategy, and relentless execution. It is the foundation upon which ideas transform into impactful realities. Throughout history, at the very core of every big success is a Vision – the guiding star that navigates the entire venture. This vision is more than a goal; it's a beacon that illuminates the path, encapsulating the aspirations, values, and purpose of the project. It's what makes a project resonate with its audience, instilling a sense of belief and anticipation. The realization of this vision is propelled by its community and team. This

© Alexander Rees-Evans 2024
A. Rees-Evans, *How to Launch a Token*, https://doi.org/10.1007/979-8-8688-0533-2_2

diverse crew of visionaries, technologists, strategists, believers, brand advocates, and creators is the driving force behind the project. Each member brings a unique set of skills and perspectives, united by a shared commitment to the project's mission. Their synergy is the alchemy that turns your vision into a tangible reality.

Like all quests, none of them have been embarked upon without a map, and in the world of crypto, this map is the Roadmap (Glossary 16). A well-crafted roadmap outlines the milestones, the timelines, and the strategic goals of the project. It's a dynamic blueprint, one that is adaptable yet focused, guiding your project through development phases, market launches, and beyond. Every project founder should devise four main documents: A private roadmap, a public pitch deck, an investor deck, and a whitepaper. Your private roadmap is to help you structure not just the token launch but your entire crypto project. Think of it as your checklist but with a timeline so you may quantify your progress. The public pitch deck is destined for your community and investors as a first approach. The investor deck is designed solely for advanced discussions with investors. The final document you'll need is of course your Whitepaper, encapsulating all of the explanations and details on what exactly you're building. During this chapter, we'll explore all but the investor deck as we'll delve into this one during Chapter 7. As of now, let's focus on creating your private roadmap. For starters, here are a few pointers you'll definitely want to remember:

> Idea: Make sure you spell out exactly what your idea
> is in great detail and give yourself leeway. The crypto
> environment changes very fast so the last thing you
> want is to spend three years building an idea based
> on a trend that has become obsolete by the time you
> launch. Keep the doors open and stay flexible without
> modifying the core of your idea too much. Plus, bear in
> mind that you're going to have to convince early team

members and advisors to join your venture by selling
them on nothing more than your dream and the future
value of promised tokens.

Business model: It's not because you have an
interesting idea that your token will become top tier and
held by individuals from all sides of the globe. Make
sure that you have a flexible strategy so that integrating
a token in your ecosystem truly does provide extra value
and you have a solid plan on how to monetize this.

Once the above is meticulously combed over, the next step is to
develop your private roadmap. Beyond its allure, the private roadmap
serves as a compass, guiding your project to fruition. It crystallizes the
vision and strategy, ensuring that every team member, from developers
to marketers, share a unified direction and goal. It's a tool that aligns
ambitions with actions, moreover, dreams with deliverables:

Idea Conceptualization:

Identifying and emphasizing the market problem or
opportunity

Identifying and emphasizing the market solution or
opportunity

Validating the idea with potential users and
stakeholders

Team Formation:

Assembling a skilled and diverse team with expertise in
blockchain, legal, marketing, fundraising and business

Defining the clear roles and responsibilities of each
team member

Establishing effective leadership, communication
structures, and delegating priorities

Token Design (Tokenomics):

> Creating a token model that supports the project's goals and incentives

> Deciding on token supply, distribution, vesting (Glossary 17), cliff periods (Glossary 18), and usage

> Planning for long-term economic sustainability and growth

Minimum Viable Product (MVP):

> Determining what you can build in accordance with your level of funding

> Starting development of the product in accordance with your level of funding

> Sharing your MVP with friends, family, and fixing bugs upon feedback

Legal Compliance:

> Determining what company structure and jurisdiction you will use

> Implementing compliance measures to protect the project and its users

> Pre-organizing the company structure and paperwork so you're ready to raise funds

Fundraising:

> Calculating the company valuation and fundraising rounds

> Identifying and approaching popular lead investors and Venture Capitalists (VCs)

> Pre-sale of the Simple Agreement of future tokens (SAFTs) (Glossary 19)

Community Engagement:

> Building and nurturing a strong community around the project

> Engaging with users, investors, and supporters through various channels and socials

> Gathering feedback and fostering a sense of ownership and involvement within the community

> Transforming your community into brand advocates

> Allowing your community to participate in your pre-sale rounds

Product Development:

> Developing the core product or service of the project

> Releasing the first version (Beta) of your product to your community and investors

> Iterating on the product based on user input and market trends

Marketing Efforts:

> Choosing the right marketing company as a partner

> Creating and executing a marketing strategy to promote the project

> Utilizing various channels for outreach and visibility

> Building brand awareness and credibility in the market

> Creating calculated hype around your Pre-sales

> Creating calculated hype around your token launch

> Creating calculated hype post token launch

Token Launch:

> Determining your listing strategy (which Centralized or Decentralized Exchange you'll list on and when)

> Choosing your Market Maker and strategy

> Organizing your liquidity based on anticipated buying and selling pressure with the expected token price fluctuations

> Planning the launch to meet regulatory, technical, and market requirements

Continuous Improvement:

> Regularly updating and improving the project based on community insights

> Staying adaptable and responsive to market changes and challenges

> Innovating while staying ahead of industry trends and competitors

Scaling Operations:

> Expanding your project's reach and capabilities

> Developing partnerships

> Scaling up operations and company personnel to meet growing user demand and market opportunities

> Managing resources effectively for sustainable growth

Adapting to Market:

> Monitoring market trends and user behavior

> Adapting the project's strategy and offerings to stay relevant and competitive

> Being proactive in responding to market shifts and opportunities

As a project founder, the above points are capital to draft before you start reaching out to build your team or fundraise. It's imperative you maintain an omniscient view to keep on top of your priorities as you start progressing. Very often, you'll pivot, turn, and change strategies as you go along. This of course is healthy and paramount to finding the perfect market fit for your project. Having this private roadmap beforehand will enable you to witness the ripple effect of every change in your plan, thus allowing you to strategically amend each one, helping maintain the core of your project. Without this, you can find yourself losing complete track of your initial goal and token launch.

As for your public roadmap, this is what you will make available for all to see. It will be in your pitch deck, on your website, and traveling through social media channels thanks to your community and Key Opinion Leaders (KOLs). This deck is composed of the points from your private roadmap apart from "Idea conceptualization" and "Team formation."

Now that we've completed your public roadmap, it's imperative to draft your public pitch deck. In the pulsating heart of the cryptocurrency and blockchain arena, the public crypto pitch deck emerges as a beacon, boasting to all the fundamentals, goals, and deliverables of your crypto project. This isn't just a presentation; it's a narrative, a compelling story that unfolds the potential, vision, and ambition of your crypto venture. It's the canvas upon which entrepreneurs paint their dreams and aspirations, hoping to captivate investors, partners, and enthusiastic community members. At its core, the public crypto pitch deck is a retail investor magnet. It's crafted to allure, persuade, and convince potential retail investors of the project's merit. By weaving a story that highlights market opportunities, technological novelties, and financial prospects, it aspires to transform skeptics into believers, and observers into backers. This deck isn't just sharing information; it's pitching a future, a vision of what could be, backed by solid data and a clear roadmap.

Professionalism and preparation are the undercurrents of a successful pitch deck. It's a testament to the project team's dedication and credibility. A well-executed deck indicates thorough market research, a deep understanding of the blockchain ecosystem, and a solid commitment to navigating the project to success. As much as it is a beacon for investors, the pitch deck is also a bridge. It connects your project with potential partners, collaborators, and early adopters. It's an invitation to join your journey, to be part of something potentially revolutionary. By clearly articulating the project's value and benefits, it opens doors to collaborations that could be pivotal in scaling the venture. Where brand resonance is paramount, the pitch deck doubles as a marketing arsenal. It's also a platform to showcase the project, to build brand identity, and to foster a community. It's not just presenting facts; it's telling a story that resonates, that sticks with the audience long after the presentation has ended. However, I can't stress enough on this next point. In the crypto world, where community eyes are ever-watchful, your public pitch deck underscores a commitment to transparency and regulatory compliance.

It reflects a project's understanding of the legal landscape, showcasing its readiness to operate within the bounds of regulation, thus building much needed trust and credibility.

A great structure for your pitch deck is simple and concise, with some elegant graphics matching your company brand, colors, and logo organized as follows:

Overview Cover Page:

Picture This: The first glance, the initial handshake, the opening note of your project's symphony. The overview cover page is the grand entrance, setting the stage for what's to unfold. It's not just a title page; it's a promise, an allure, a glimpse into the soul of your crypto venture. This page, adorned with your project's name, a captivating tagline, and a visual that speaks a thousand words, is your first chance to charm, to intrigue, to beckon the audience into your world.

Company Introduction:

Here lies the narrative of your genesis, the story of your inception. In the Company Introduction, you weave the tale of your company's birth, its mission, its vision, and the values that are its beating heart. This is where you share your journey – from the spark of an idea to the entity it is today. It's a narrative that builds more than understanding; it builds emotional connections, setting a tone of trust and belief in your project's purpose.

The Global Problem:

> In this section, you're not just outlining a problem; you're setting a scene on a global stage. This is where you articulate the challenges, inefficiencies, or gaps that your project is poised to tackle. It's about painting a picture of a world that needs your solution, a narrative that stretches beyond borders, resonating with a universal audience. Here, you're not just presenting a problem; you're framing a compelling reason for your project's existence.

The Specific Problem:

> Now, zoom in from the global vista to the specifics. The specific problem section is where you dissect the broader issue, presenting the unique challenge that your project directly addresses. This is your chance to highlight the nuanced understanding of the issue at hand, showcasing your project's relevance and necessity in the intricate tapestry of the crypto world.

The Goal:

> The goal is a key component of your deck. What are you aiming to achieve? How will you redefine, disrupt, or contribute to solving the above problems? This is where your aspirations are crystallized, presenting a clear, measurable, and achievable vision that shows the reader why your project is necessary.

The Solution:

> The solution is where your vision takes form. Here, you unveil how your project elegantly solves the identified problem. This section is the heart of your pitch, showcasing the uniqueness, innovation, and feasibility of your solution. It's more than a description; it's the revelation of your project's essence, the answer to the "why you?" in the vast crypto universe.

Product Overview:

> In the product overview, you provide a window into your offering. Detail the features, functionalities, and the user experience of your product. This section is about tangibility, transforming concepts into perceivable, relatable elements. Illustrate how your product stands in the real world, its interaction with users, and its place in the crypto ecosystem.

Market Demand:

> Understanding the market demand is about aligning your project with the pulse of the market. Here, you present research, statistics, and trends that demonstrate a clear demand for your product. It's about backing your vision with data, showing that there's not just a need, but a craving for what you offer in the marketplace.

Competitive Advantage:

> In the competitive advantage section, you delineate what sets you apart. It's a showcase of your edge over others, be it through technology, strategy, innovation, or market positioning. Often, this is

where a table with ticks and crosses comparing and showing the parts your competitors have and the extra ones that you bring to the table. This is where you assert why your project isn't just another drop in the ocean but a unique wave creating its own ripple in the crypto world.

Traction:

Traction is the proof of your journey's momentum. Within it, you must illustrate your achievements, growth metrics, user base, or any milestones reached. It's evidence of your progress, a testament to your project's viability, and the faith the market has in your vision. This will entice more people to join the journey and further grow your community while reassuring potential investors.

Timing:

Timing is about seizing the moment. Explain why now is the ideal time for your project, be it due to market readiness, technological advancements, or a shift in consumer behavior. This section underlines the timeliness of your venture and why the market is ripe for your solution, at this very juncture.

Tokenomics:

Tokenomics are the blueprint of your project's economic model. Here, you break down the token structure, utility, distribution, and the economic mechanics that ensure the viability and sustainability of your token. It's a crucial section that provides transparency and trust in your project's financial foundation.

Team:

> Here, you introduce the team members and
> the advisors behind your project. Make sure
> you highlight the experience, expertise, and the
> credibility of your team members. It's about
> presenting a group that's not just capable but
> passionate, a team that's equipped to turn your
> vision into a reality. This page will be the window
> for a lot of individuals to judge your capacities to
> follow through and launch your token successfully.

Public Roadmap:

> Your public Roadmap is providing transparency
> and a timeline to all. Lay out the plan, the main
> milestones, and the future aspirations of your
> project. No need to dive into all of the details of
> your private roadmap as here, the readers will
> want to know the relevant information. This
> section is about showing direction, progress, and
> commitment. It's a visual and narrative timeline
> that says, "We know where we're going, and here's
> how we'll get there."

Partnerships:

> In partnerships, unveil the alliances that strengthen
> and validate your project. Highlight collaborations,
> supporters, or any affiliations that lend credibility
> and support to your venture. Show that your project
> isn't in isolation, but is already trusted by a network
> of powerful industry leaders.

Contact information:

> Finally, the contact information is your open door.
> It's an invitation for dialogue, for connections,
> for opportunities. Provide clear and accessible
> contact details, ensuring that anyone inspired by
> your pitch knows exactly how to reach you, start a
> conversation, and begin a partnership to partake in
> your journey.

Now that we have the content in place, it's time for the graphics. Even if you don't have the resources to hire a graphic designer, Canva is a great and cheap tool you can use here. In the realm of crypto pitch decks, graphics aren't just adornments; they are storytellers, they are the silent narrators that amplify your narrative. Picture this: a deck not laden with overbearing graphics, but adorned with visuals that harmonize with your story, enhancing, not eclipsing, the essence of your project. This is the art of crafting graphics for a pitch deck – a delicate balance of elegance and simplicity, clarity and impact. Imagine graphics as the subtle background score of a movie, setting the tone, not overpowering the dialogue. The graphics in your pitch deck should also be simple, yet evocative. They should not scream for attention but rather whisper, complementing the information being presented. It's about choosing visuals that resonate with your project's ethos, be it minimalist icons, crisp charts, or lucid diagrams. They serve as guides, leading the viewer's eye through the story, enhancing understanding, not causing distraction.

Envision a dance between words and visuals, each step calculated, each move in sync. The graphics should flow seamlessly with the text, creating a visual rhythm that makes the complex world of crypto feel more approachable. It's about creating a visual hierarchy where the eye is naturally drawn to key points, aided by graphics that contextualize and clarify. Each image, chart, or icon is there for a reason, to make a point clearer, to underscore a statistic, or to bring a concept to life.

Your choice of colors is paramount to the positive impact upon a reader. Color is emotion, mood, and identity. The color scheme of your graphics should be a reflection of your brand's personality. Whether it's the vibrancy of innovation, the serenity of trust, or the intensity of passion, let your colors speak. However, it's crucial to avoid a carnival of hues; instead, opt for a palette that's coherent, consistent, and complementary to your textual content. Let your colors tell your story in tones and shades that resonate with your project's identity.

In the world of crypto, where data is king, how you present your numbers, trends, and statistics is pivotal. This is where data visualization comes into play. Charts and graphs should be more than just tools of representation; they should be windows into insights. Opt for clear, readable, and straightforward data visuals. Let your graphs narrate the growth, the potential, the trajectory of your project. Remember, the goal is to make data accessible, not to showcase your prowess in complex chart-making.

Consistency in your graphics is another stronghold of your deck's success, the thread that weaves your pitch deck into a cohesive narrative. It's about maintaining a uniform style, be it in iconography, typography, or imagery. This consistency extends beyond just aesthetics; it's about creating a comfortable and predictable visual journey for your audience. When each slide feels part of a larger whole, your story unfolds with a fluidity that will engage and captivate.

As we draw the curtains on the creation of your crypto pitch deck, let's envision it as a masterful performance, where the graphics and narrative harmonize to tell a compelling story. It's akin to a beautifully orchestrated piece, where each note and lyric plays its part in delivering a mesmerizing experience. This pitch deck is not just a presentation; it's an art form where the simplicity and elegance of graphics interweave with the depth and clarity of your narrative. Picture your pitch deck as a gallery where each slide is a canvas, and on this canvas, your story elegantly unfolds before the reader. The graphics are the brushstrokes that add color and life to the tale you're weaving. They're not there to overshadow your message but to illuminate it, to give it depth, to make it resonate. With each slide, the harmony between your words and visuals captivates the audience, guiding them through the essence of your crypto venture, your dreams, your challenges, and your triumphs. As you conclude your deck, remember that it's the equilibrium that creates the magic. It's a delicate dance between the vibrancy of visuals and the power of words, between the intricate details of your project and the overarching narrative of your mission. Your deck is a journey, a path that leads the viewer through the landscape of your vision, painted with the hues of your brand, and narrated with the voice of your passion. In the world of crypto, where innovation intersects with opportunity, your pitch deck is more than an introduction; it's your story, your manifesto. It's a testament to the uniqueness of your project, a showcase of its potential, and a reflection of your team's dedication and ingenuity. As you meld your graphics with your narrative, your pitch deck transforms into an experience, one that doesn't just inform but inspires, not just presents but persuades.

Let your pitch deck be the final chord that resonates with your audience, the memorable blend of vision and artistry that leaves a lasting impression. As you stand at the intersection of creativity and strategy, let your deck be the beacon that shines brightly, illuminating the path to success in the dynamic and ever-evolving world of cryptocurrency.

After speaking with thousands of crypto projects looking to have a successful token launch, you start to see patterns indicating which token launches will be successful and which ones will fail beforehand. These patterns show up very early so I thought it useful to share the traits of a good core team with you. All investors and community members will or will not believe and trust your project, depending on the quality of this core team. In the labyrinthine world of cryptocurrency, building a project is comparable to assembling a crew for a daring voyage across uncharted waters. Your team is your greatest asset, the collective force driving your project toward success. But who do you bring aboard this ambitious journey? Let's delve into the art of choosing and structuring your team, ensuring each member plays a pivotal role in navigating the complex seas of the crypto universe.

The Crypto Expert:

> Imagine a ship without a seasoned captain, adrift amidst the tumultuous waves. In your crypto venture, this captain is your crypto expert. This individual is not just an advisor; they understand the underbelly of the industry and don't fall for the fluff of marketing from big brands with no substance. They possess the unique blend of technical prowess, network, and strategic foresight, essential to not get scammed or crash the token. This expert doesn't merely follow trends; they anticipate and navigate through the evolving crypto landscapes, ensuring your project remains cutting-edge, compliant, and alive.

The Serial Entrepreneur:

> In the realm of crypto, where uncertainty and opportunity dance together, you need a seasoned, steady business hand, a serial entrepreneur with a track record of multiple successful exits. This person is your beacon in the foggy world of startups, bringing invaluable experience, business acumen, and a knack for turning visions into reality. They've been through the trials and triumphs of entrepreneurship, learning lessons that only the trenches of startup life can teach. With their strategic guidance and entrepreneurial spirit, your project will not just sail, but soar.

The Marketeer:

> Your marketing maestro, the Key Opinion Leader
> (KOL) with a massive following and a profound
> understanding of crypto marketing. In the digital
> age, where attention is currency, this individual
> wields immense power. They are not just an
> influencer; they are a trendsetter, community
> builder, and your bridge to a vast audience.
> With their deep insights into market dynamics
> and consumer behavior, they craft captivating
> narratives, turning your project into a name that
> resonates across the crypto community. Their role
> is pivotal in building brand presence, trust, and
> excitement around your venture.

The Legal Luminary:

> As you navigate the murky waters of regulations
> in the crypto world, a legal expert with a profound
> understanding of law and compliance is
> indispensable. They are your shield, safeguarding
> your project against legal pitfalls and ensuring
> adherence to the ever-evolving regulatory
> frameworks. With their expertise, your venture
> isn't just innovative; it's resilient and trustworthy,
> standing firm amidst the legal complexities of the
> crypto industry.

Fundraising Wizard:

> Without funds, you're not going anywhere. This
> individual is capital for propelling your project
> off the ground. They need to have an excellent
> and verifiable track record of raising funds for

other crypto projects. Usually they have a strong background in the Venture Capitalist (VC) realm and can help not only with fundraising, but also the company and token initial valuations while helping structure the fundraising rounds from Pre-seed to series A.

Choosing Advisors:

Advisors in the crypto world can be a double-edged sword. On the one hand, they bring expertise, connections, and credibility. On the other hand, the crypto sphere is riddled with advisors who offer little beyond their names. Choosing advisors is an exercise in discernment. More often than not, they know very little about how the industry actually works and have just a few connections. The really big advisors also can charge anywhere from 1%–3% of the total token supply just to put their face on your deck! Seek those who bring tangible value, not just past successes or high-profile names. Look for advisors who are actively engaged, who understand the nuances of your project, and who can offer you value your core team can't.

It's one thing to put an impressive team together, it's another to make them work efficiently. As we draw the blueprint for placing your team members in roles that maximize their potential, remember, this is the art of orchestrating a symphony where each musician's skill is leveraged for the most harmonious output. In the dynamic landscape of cryptocurrency, how you align your team's talents and roles is not just a matter of organizational structure; it's about creating a living, breathing ecosystem that thrives on synergy, innovation, and shared vision.

First and foremost, understand and appreciate the unique strengths and experiences each team member brings. Like a chess grandmaster, place each individual where their skills can make the most impact. The crypto expert doesn't have to be a coder, but a visionary who can anticipate and navigate future and current industry landscapes. Once you've raised funds, you can hire a Chief Technical Officer (CTO) and delegate the building of the tech to companies specializing in this exact job. The entrepreneur should not merely oversee operations, but infuse the project with strategic direction and business acumen. Encourage a culture where collaboration is the norm, and cross-pollination of ideas is encouraged. The intersection of diverse skills – where the marketer's creativity meets the crypto expert's logic, where the legal expert's precision meets the entrepreneur's vision is where true innovation blossoms. Regular team meetings, brainstorming sessions, and open channels of communication are key in fostering this collaborative spirit. In the fast-evolving crypto world, adaptability is crucial. Team members should be ready to pivot roles and take on new challenges as the project evolves. This flexibility not only keeps the team agile and responsive to market changes but also contributes to a dynamic and engaging work environment where learning and growth are constant. It's very important to regularly revisit and align team roles with the overarching goals of the project. As your venture scales and evolves, so should your team's structure and roles. This alignment ensures that every team member is not just functioning in their individual capacity, but is actively contributing to the collective vision of the project.

Empower your team members with autonomy in their roles, don't micromanage. While guidance and oversight are necessary, giving individuals the freedom to innovate, make decisions, and lead in their

respective domains fosters a sense of ownership and accountability.
A great management style would be SCRUM. We dive deeply into this
management style in my other book "So You Want to Work in Crypto."
In essence, SCRUM makes each person responsible and accountable for
the tasks they were delegated. They're free to make their own plans and
modifications to accomplish the attributed task. This empowerment is
crucial in building a team that's not only skilled but also deeply invested
in the project's success. Strategically placing your team members in roles
where they can shine is akin to setting the sails of a ship for a successful
voyage. It's about leveraging individual talents for a unified purpose,
encouraging collaboration, ensuring flexibility, and maintaining alignment
with your project's goals. With solid private and public roadmaps, a team
structured to complement and elevate each other's skills and a well-
constructed pitch deck, your crypto project is well-equipped to navigate
the exciting, yet challenging environment leading to a successful token
launch. This is not just launching a token; it's crafting a powerhouse of
innovation, commitment, and excellence that will propel your project to
new heights.

CHAPTER 3

Tokenomics

In this inexorable chapter, tokenomics will be the focal point and epicenter of the conversation. This simple but often omitted and neglected segment of crypto projects hides behind a word derived from both "token" and "economics." In short, Tokenomics (Glossary 23) is the study of the economic system governing a blockchain token. As we've now understood the many shapes and forms tokens may take, we must not forget that at its core, a token is a cryptocurrency. It's in that very word, "currency." Like all currencies around the world, such as the US Dollar, the Euro, and the British Pound, tokens also must have a clever economic model backing them. As we've seen time and time again all around the world, native currencies of countries are prone to fluctuations and manipulation, with even more devastating effects than the crashing of a cryptocurrency. Around 2009, Zimbabwe was struck by hyperinflation due to very poor political and economic decisions, hence driving the value of the native currency down so much that they decided to print dollar notes with "100 trillion Zimbabwe dollars" written on them! The goal of this is to not shift a wheelbarrow filled to the brim of bank notes around to the local shop to buy a loaf of bread. More recently, in 2015, we saw this exact phenomenon with the inhabitants of Greece after the country defaulted, making it one of the first ever developed countries to experience such a disaster. Contributory to more problems with traditional currencies is that of corruption, and the possibility to print an infinite amount of bank notes and coins. Given that the value of a bank note is dependent on the chosen asset or assets backing it, in a perfect world, there would be a ratio which

A. Rees-Evans, *How to Launch a Token*, https://doi.org/10.1007/979-8-8688-0533-2_3

41

would be respected. For example, when banknotes were first created, they were purely a receipt stipulating how much gold that person had in the bank. Instead of moving the actual gold to make a transaction, the individual could simply leave his precious asset safeguarded in the bank, and hand over the piece of paper (akin to a deed or title of ownership) to the counterparty of the transaction. This method is far more practical than moving grams, kilos, or even tons of a heavy asset, thus making it one of the first forms of modern currency. Being such a practical measure, more and more people started using this chequebook-like feature and gradually stopped requesting to withdraw the gold in the bank. Soon, the banks noticed this and started to write out more banknotes than they had gold in the vault. Of course, when a major event happens and many people wish to withdraw their actual assets from the bank, major problems occur. Today, in the United States, to limit such a problem, there is an obligatory ratio of funds kept in the bank, to funds they're supposed to have in the bank, known as the "reserve requirement." As we know, banks make money by loaning out peoples' deposits. A reserve requirement means they must keep a percentage of deposited funds in the bank, usually around 10%. In my view, it still is a very high risk, and moreover not normal. It's not normal that they can use the remaining 90% of funds deposited by ordinary people, who deposit in the bank their hard-earned money. (Bank Reserves: Definition, Purpose, Types, and Requirements [investopedia.com]). Again, we can see how the traditional financial world leverages currencies for the benefit of a select few. This is a reason why Bitcoin was so revolutionary, forever changing the landscape and possibilities for currencies worldwide. With Bitcoin, there's no corruption, just as importantly as there's no, and never can be, any inflation, thanks to its fixed total supply. There can never be one more, nor can there ever be one less. This is where the art of tokenomics forced itself into the spotlight, providing real technique and a much larger array of economic features designed to fashion the perfect economy for your token. It encompasses everything from the total supply of tokens, the release schedules, and the mechanisms driving the use and demand for these tokens within the respective ecosystems. As one engages in such an endeavor, it is highly recommended to reach out to experts in this field such as MHL Solutions or Findaas to help you create the most favorable economy for your token. However, understanding tokenomics is pivotal for any individual or entity looking to launch a token, as it influences the entire longevity of a token-based protocol (Glossary 24).

Tokenomics serves as the foundation of any blockchain project, shaping the token's value, utility, and use cases. Tokenomics is, however, not an established science, solely focused on creating hype or artificially inflating token prices. Instead, it aims to encourage positive behavior while promoting price stability and growth. Tokenomics also dictates how participants within the ecosystem are motivated to participate in buying and selling your token. For instance, rewarding users for positive behaviors, further contributing to network growth, fostering active community engagement. Or even punishing users negatively impacting the token price by selling, by implementing sales taxes, hence pushing participants not to sell but to hold.

To further define, let us now touch upon two critical elements that each tokenomics model must have to strive for success: token metrics and token economy.

Token Economy:

> A token economy refers to a structure that utilizes tokens within a blockchain-based ecosystem. This system incentivizes participants to contribute to the growth and development of the network through various means and ways, often incentive based.

> The entire ecosystem is powered by financial incentives revolving around your token. This is precisely what a token economy represents, a fascinating system built upon blockchain

technology, designed to incentivize constant participation and contribution from its participants. Each participant within the network plays a pivotal role in driving growth and development, commonly known as "Community driven economies." The native tokens of a project are used as rewards for community contributions such as sharing posts on socials, providing feedback all the way up to validating transactions as do miners or stakers depending on the protocol, thus creating a real community-driven economy, with tangible financial rewards for all active participants.

Utility:

Another underlying aspect of all tokens is its utility and purpose within the endemic crypto ecosystem. This refers to the specific function that a token serves and answers the crucial question: "Why should I hold this token?" For example, one could hold the token to pay for transaction fees, to obtain access to specific services, features, platforms, or even in hope of the token price increasing over a very long period of time, like Bitcoin. The bespoke incentives must supersede the financial rewards of selling the token. A prime live case study is Uniswap, a decentralized exchange that utilizes their native token "UNI" as a utility token. Holders can participate in governance, propose changes, and vote on protocol upgrades, aligning with the platform's decentralized nature while providing unique powers and control to participants from all over the world.

Secondly, a token's use case refers to the specific purpose for which it is utilized within a crypto project's ecosystem. It essentially answers the fundamental question, "What is this token used for?" As an example, it can be used as a medium of exchange, used to purchase in-game items or merchandise, used to pay for subscriptions, etc. A clear example would be the platform Travala, where you can actually book a vacation paying directly with cryptocurrencies, the use of cryptocurrencies is still heavily correlated with what you can actually do with them in the real world. Dogecoin offers users to transfer from wallet to wallet with low fees, making it an excellent medium of exchange with a very high potential of long-term price increase thanks to a community of Brobdingnagian proportions.

Forbye the above, governance should not be seen as utility, but rather treated as a use case. Governance incentivizes users to hold or stake (Glossary 26) the token during a voting process. However, once the voting concludes, holders often tend to sell their tokens so you need to provide something extra. To address this very issue, mechanisms such as locked staking and vote escrows have been implemented over the past few years. Curve Finance is well-known for introducing such mechanisms, offering a multiplier based on your staked token plan, thereby increasing your voting power. By participating in voting, your community not only exercises in important voting rights but also receives rewards for doing so. An interesting case-study is MakerDAO, employing their native token "MKR" as a governance token, enabling holders to participate in voting on proposals that impact the stablecoin DAI's stability and functionality.

Our second segment of tokenomics will establish the much needed token metrics, providing quantitative data that enable investors and community alike to evaluate the token's present and future potential. Before the actual launch of your token, these metrics will allow you to gain valuable insights into how the token will evolve in terms of its financial stability and sustainability. This climacteric is crucial for showcasing the longevity and viability behind your token launch, fashioning the solidity of your project and impacting investment decisions from across the board.

Token metrics encompass a wide range of factors such as:

- Max supply (number of tokens that will ever exist)
- Total supply (tokens minted [Glossary 27]) – token burned (Glossary 28)
- Circulating supply (tokens circulating in the market)
- Market capitalization (price of the total quantity of tokens composing the circulating supply)
- Fully diluted valuation (price of the total quantity of tokens composing the max supply)
- Distribution Mechanisms (staking, fair launch (Glossary 29), token sale, etc.)
- Trading volume
- Token distribution and emission
- Vesting schedule
- Liquidity levels
- Network activity statistic
- Technological advancements within the project ecosystem
- Price ($USD)
- Price history/action

Once you've elaborated a detailed picture of an adequate form of token economy and metrics for your project, you must then determine which model of tokenomics you wish to base yours upon. There exist many styles, each boasting different advantages and mechanisms, pre-determining very different financial outcomes and strategies for your token's life span.

In this segment, we will now dive into the main tokenomics models, noting that tokenomics are an ever-evolving methodology and can be tweaked or modified in accordance with one's needs.

What better model to start with than the precursor, the trailblazer, having brought one of the direct value propositions of Bitcoin, the fixed supply model. The fixed supply tokenomics model has become increasingly popular, especially with the rise of ICOs and IDOs in recent years. But what makes them so appealing to investors? The answer lies in predictability topped by scarcity. Cryptocurrencies with a fixed supply, such as Bitcoin (with a maximum supply of 21,000,000,000 BTC), offer a level of unparalleled growth potential thanks to the "supply and demand"-driven economics. Tokenomics based on a fixed supply are also easy to forecast because they have a predetermined emission rate. For example, Bitcoin currently issues 6.25 BTC per block (Glossary 30), and this reward is halved every 210,000 blocks. This means that by the year 2140, all 21,000,000,000 Bitcoins will have been minted. This unique bond between predictability and scarcity of an asset cannot be overstated, allowing investors to develop realistic investment plans based on unchanging data in a world where volatility is the norm.

Following suit is the deflationary model. Probably one of the most widespread variants of tokenomics models out there, they have gained significant attention due to their unique approach on countering inflation and increasing the value of each token over time. One of the most common traits of these models is token burning, which directly involves permanently removing a portion of circulating tokens from supply, which may never be recovered, hence the term "burn."

Token burning serves multiple purposes within deflationary systems, such as reducing the overall supply, thus creating scarcity, intended to drive the demand. Burning also promotes long-term holding by decreasing the ownership share, while finally helping stabilize or increasing token prices by decreasing the token supply.

As one ponders on selecting an appropriate tokenomics model, there are multiple key factors to take into careful consideration. The very nature, goals, and structure of your crypto project play a significant role in helping determine the appropriate tokenomics model. Moreover, aligning the tokenomics model with the sundry of incentivization mechanisms you need to include is crucial to nurture, then foster, desired user behaviors within your ecosystem. For example, participation in governance of the project can be encouraged through granting voting rights and providing decision-making power to token holders, enhancing their overall desire to hold and not sell your tokens.

Remember, always check regulatory implications as your tokenomics model can be heavily influenced depending on your jurisdiction and legal obligations in regard to your token. Having a deep understanding and seeking legal opinion are not only important to avoid penal charges, but also for getting your tokens listed on CEXs. Thoroughly check and cross reference with different law firms just to be on the safe side, as many of them still aren't up to date but remain very expensive on an hourly basis. If worst comes to worst, you can always structure your company as a DAO to simplify. Feel free to approach some reputable law firms well versed in this space such as Law Beam, Taylor Wessing, Gunnercooke, Scale-Up legal or even Hassans in Gibraltar.

Additionally, do analyze current market trends as they dictate what investors are interested in at that given time hence determining the success of your fundraise. Forbye the market trends, successful project founders spend time researching similar projects and competitors across different industry sectors, helping tailor their tokenomics. This research will help you identify useful patterns that could fashion designs and incentives, or even use elements from these existing frameworks to help save time. Remember, Tokenomics is far from being one-size-fits-all, instead it necessitates thoughtful planning tailored specifically toward achieving alignment between strategic goals of your project and the tangential economic systems.

Besides designing the economic and metric components of your tokenomics, another salient element, just as important as both of the above, must be established. Psychology and human behavior are both non-negligible components, necessitating careful consideration and tactical deployment. Involving complex economic models, influenced by how people think and act, these connections will play a big role in shaping your tokens and how they're to be managed. Factors like how people see a token's value based on brand perception, community trust, and overall market sentiment are all angles to be appraised. You must also include clever ways to build and keep community trust from day one, to years beyond. Transparent governance, community involvement, and good communication strategies are all vital in not just creating, but maintaining trust in your ecosystem.

Generally speaking, community members are really motivated by incentives, and tokenomics must leverage them as much as possible. Regardless of the design, you must always include rewards, be they native tokens, NFTs, Stablecoins, or even special access or perks to encourage positive behavior for your token. Supplementary token incentives may include staking, airdrops, and governance, etc. They're purposely crafted to match the desires of participants and the community's major goals. Knowing what drives your own community is key to crafting bespoke incentives that will work and last.

Other important market behaviors one must contemplate when designing tokenomics are fueled by emotions such as fear, greed, and FOMO (Glossary 31) and have a big impact and part to play in tokenomics. The thick sheet of unpredictability, gently swathing the crypto market indirectly pre-determines a degree of resilience and malleability one must adopt in their own model. Your tokenomics must be future proof and able to handle swift market changes or community swings. Moreover, you must prepare strategies for distribution while keeping enough assets available in case of liquidity requirements for Market Making, market cycles, or even the theft of a percentage of your supply. Noting that very few crypto projects anticipate these things, it aims to lessen the impact of irrational market moves and events, making your token future-proof.

Another way to incentivize your community is by tainting your tokenomics and overall utility with social proof, socialFi, and network effects, each affixing the psychological aspect. The best tokenomics models nattily invigorate individuals to join, build communities, and make partnerships to grow the network. These happen by requiring people to sign up to your socials, pass KYC, use your protocol for a defined time or even simply by sharing a Twitter/X post you deployed! You must make the tasks easy enough for community members to complete, but important enough for the completed task to have a beneficial impact on your ecosystem. Human psychology is part of how decentralized governance works in tokenomics. In a similar manner, contrivances like how people think, group decisions, and emotions all play an important role that should be thought through thoroughly prior to your token launch. The goal is to have governance that's fair, effective, and provides value to native token holders. Taking a few days to bulk up on the subject of psychology, even reading a few books on the matter can definitely help enhance your perspective on this topic. Be sure to equip yourself with as much relevant knowledge as possible to help you better articulate your tokenomics and incentives design. In order for your tokenomics to work well, user experience and engagement are key. You may even post surveys in your social channels to find out how community members feel. Gather feedback on the new interface, and recover precious metrics as you build and further develop your product. Open communication channels with your users to learn how they're experiencing your project from the inside so you may tweak and adapt your tokenomics accordingly. Never forget that trust is your most valuable asset when launching a token, nurture this by promoting transparent tokenomics and by creating a reassuring environment. Behavioral tokenomics is a young and blooming field blending psychology, decision-making, and economics. To master such complexities, one must better understand human interactions and how to maximize leveraging them. There's also a focus on circular economic models, demonstrating how this mix of psychology, human behavior, and tokenomics, are in a perpetual state of dynamic, constant evolution.

Having solid tokenomics is pivotal for the success of a token launch, whether it's an Initial Coin Offering (ICO) or an Initial Dex Offering (IDO). (*For more info:* $https://www.patreon.com/posts/ep-2-crypto-91072895$) The primary goal of any initial token/SAFT sale is to secure funds, to establish further product development and marketing prior to launch. In order to have a well structured sale, you must try to keep about 70% of supply under the project's control so that you may develop the ecosystem as your project grows. Secondly, the vesting and cliff of your tokens must be favorable towards the community, it's not rare to see founding team members not be able to start selling their tokens until 12 months after the initial token launch! Beforehand you must gaze into the future, anticipate buying and selling pressure while taking into consideration the token price fluctuations. If you solely base your tokenomics on a fixed price of your token, for example, the price when you list it on an exchange, you will have problems not just further on down the road but even for getting your project funded. First of all, you're not giving any interesting financial incentives to early adopters or investors; secondly, if too many tokens are released at a specific time, this may create unwanted selling pressure, therefore creating a significant drop in your token price, leading in some cases to the crash of your token. Also, you must consider the fundraising rounds too, for instance, you must calculate the amount of tokens you're willing to exchange for funding correlating with the price per token for each specific fundraising round. Not focusing on building a sustainable and fair ecosystem with a focus on reducing selling pressure can without a doubt lead to your token's demise. Not having the right amount of liquid tokens available for your ecosystem can also lead to low treasury, hence leaving you with a short runway for your business. Appropriate tokenomics should look something like this:

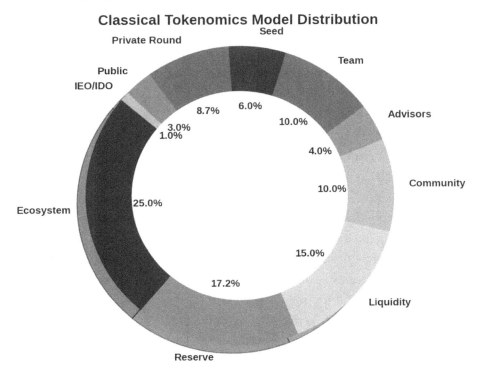

Deciding how tokens are distributed among the team, investors, and other segments is always a challenge and subject to modifications depending on investors, market sentiment, and trends. Please take this into consideration when reviewing the Pie Chart above. Now, we will view a real case called "AIWorld" AI.W following this model.

First in line are the "Sale details"

AI Worlds($AIW) Sale Details

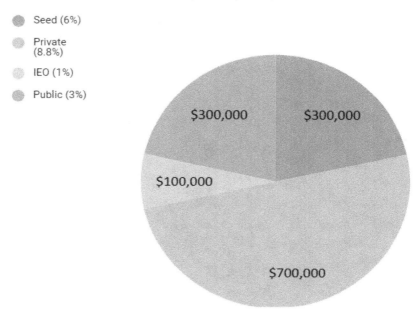

- Seed (6%)
- Private (8.8%)
- IEO (1%)
- Public (3%)

$300,000 · $300,000 · $100,000 · $700,000

Presenting the financial value of your fundraising rounds provides investors with an overview of the total funding involved per round. Bringing a structured vision to the table, hence enhancing comprehension and understanding.

In parallel, you will need to present the token allocation by itself in a similar fashion:

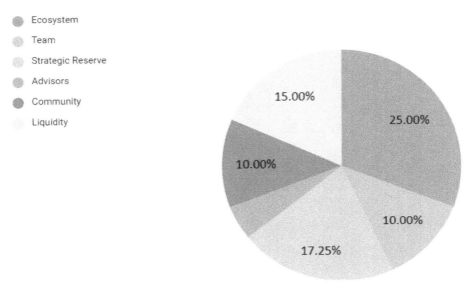

The goal here is to provide a visual understanding to investors and community members, who's getting what piece of the pie. What percentage of the total token supply will go to the concerned parties such as the team or advisors of the project. Investors and community members pay special attention to this one as it provides a brief financial report. Usually, the percentage of team tokens never exceeds 20% of the total token supply and 8% for the percentage allocated to advisors.

Following suit are the capitalization tables, starting with the summary:

Summary

Company	AI Worlds
Token	$AIW
Total Raise (USD)	$1,400,000
Total Token Supply	200,000,000
Tokens for Public Sale	3.00%
Initial Circulating Supply	5,550,000
Initial Circulating Supply %	2.78%
Public Sale Token Price	0.0500
Initial Market Cap (USD)	**$277,500**

Here, you must provide all of the important tokenomics numbers. Bestow the layout and global overview of your project's details upon Investors and community alike.

Next on the list is the written format of the sale summary:

Sale Summary

Amount to be raised	$1,400,000
Tokens to be sold	37,500,000
% Supply	18.75%
Initial Market Cap (USD)	$277,500
Fully Diluted Market Cap (USD)	$10,000,000

Bring forth the information correlating between the funds you're looking to raise, your token, and company valuation in a simple yet concise written format.

One must also showcase the full table of the token sale allocations as follows:

Token Sale Allocations

Investor Type	% of the Total Raise	Total Raise by Value ($)	Round Token price ($)	Fully Diluted Valuation	Tokens issued in Round	% Total Supply issued in Round	Unlocked % @TGE	% of circulating supply @TGE
Seed (6%)	21.43%	$300,000	$0.025	$5,000,000	12,000,000	6.00%	5.0%	0.30%
Private (8.8%)	50.00%	$700,000	$0.040	$8,000,000	17,500,000	8.75%	10.0%	0.88%
IEO (1%)	7.14%	$100,000	$0.050	$10,000,000	2,000,000	1.00%	100.0%	1.00%
Public (3%)	21.43%	$300,000	$0.050	$10,000,000	6,000,000	3.00%	20.0%	0.60%
Total Sale	100.00%	$1,400,000	$0.0396	$10,000,000	37,500,000	18.75%	2.78%	2.78%
Private	78.57%	$1,100,000			31,500,000	15.75%	0.30%	2.18%
Public	21.43%	$300,000	$0.0500	$10,000,000	6,000,000	3.00%	20.00%	0.60%

Within this table lies the mathematics melding your tokenomics together. You need to make this section as clear and precise as possible as this segment dictates the financial aspect of your token launch and rounds in full detail. Boasting such a refined piece of tokenomics promotes understanding, thus reassuring the investors of your capabilities.

Another capital table you must include is that of the token allocations:

Total Token Allocations

Token Allocation	Total Tokens (%)	Token Amount	USD Value
Ecosystem	25.00%	50,000,000	2,500,000
Team	10.00%	20,000,000	1,000,000
Strategic Reserve	17.25%	34,500,000	1,725,000
Advisors	4.00%	8,000,000	400,000
Community	10.00%	20,000,000	1,000,000
Liquidity	15.00%	30,000,000	1,500,000
Non-Sale Tokens	81.25%	162,500,000	8,125,000
All Tokens	100.00%	200,000,000	9,525,000

Concerning primarily investors and VCs, they will scrutinize every aspect and run some calculations themselves to confirm what is written here. Illustrate the full financial value attached to each segment of token dispatches. They want to know what your tokens are actually worth and how that wealth is being shared.

Finally, the table of funds:

Use of Funds

Token Allocation	Total Tokens (%)	USD Amount
Marketing	45%	630,000
Development	35%	490,000
Networking	10%	140,000
Operations	5%	70,000
Others	5%	70,000
All Tokens	**100%**	**1,400,000**

Exemplify the use of funds you are seeking to raise. Transparency is key to persuading investors and VCs to invest in your project. Remember, the nature of investing is to get an ROI then scale investments. Investors must be certain you will use their funds wisely.

The calculation of this must be self-determined in regard with one's needs.

As you develop your tokenomics, it's imperative to keep selling pressure in mind. Selling pressure is the worst enemy of all token launches. Gradually eating away your liquidity provisions and crashing many projects a few days after the token has been made live and tradable on exchanges. Do not be fooled by simply creating tokenomics based on the anticipated selling pressure. Due to your raise rounds, cliff and vesting periods, you must calculate the "initial selling pressure." This initial selling pressure is calculated by adding the combined US Dollar value of all of the tokens that can be unlocked and sold on the day of your launch, hence IDO/IEO. Generally speaking, this selling pressure gravitates around US$100,000 to US$300,000. This value is, however, based on the price of your token at which you will list it. More often than not, founders take these numbers as fixed and predict that they will be able to offset this by injecting liquidity provisions through the market maker. This is one of the biggest mistakes you can make as the general strategy for providing such liquidity is to sell off tokens, or to use investor or market maker funds.

Noting that the real initial selling pressure you will encounter will be much higher and fluctuate in accordance with the token price, buying pressure, and selling pressure.

Imagine your initial token price is US$0.20 with an initial selling pressure of US$300,000 and you've reserved a portion of your funds raised to cover this. The problem is your actual initial selling pressure is directly correlated with your token price, and will fluctuate in symbiosis. Your community isn't selling US$300,000, they're selling US$300,000 worth of your native tokens, which means that if you do a simple 2 x on your initial price, your initial selling pressure doubles instantly. For most launches, the token price does a 10 x in the first couple of hours, thus transforming your initial US$300,000 selling pressure into US$3,000,000 selling pressure. The problem is the USDT funds you reserved to cover this are still equivalent to US$300,000, barely making a dent, even if you inject it all at once! As one realizes this, the first solution that comes to mind is to sell off some native tokens as they intricately hold the same value fluctuation. Making your initial token price 10 x too. The problem here is that the order book will already be congested due to all of the token holders placing sales orders, it may take hours or even days to facilitate such an order (even with the help of your market maker) and if you can actually make it happen, you will be creating an extra US$3,000,000 of selling pressure, totaling US$6,000,000, far from the original US$300,000 you thought you initially had. Now, if the selling pressure and token price rise and drop in perfect symbiosis, and you're able to liquidate the appropriate amount of tokens during a large buying spike, you may be able to buy back some tokens being sold by your community for a couple of hours. The real problems start exactly after this first pump (Glossary 34) when not just the selling pressure but also buying pressure is high. Once the pump is over, the buying pressure drops immensely, but your selling pressure increases. Your token price is directly affected by this by dropping down to a 2 x or 3 x. On the other hand, your selling pressure frequency has accelerated so will de-peg itself from the token price drop and will remain around the 5 x or 6 x range. This

58

means that you will have to sell off approximately twice as many tokens to cover the selling pressure, noting that your order book is more congested than ever due to transaction time increasing as there's simply more people selling than buying.

Often, it's at this fatal moment that projects crash as they don't have enough liquidity provisions to keep buying back the tokens being sold to fluidify trades. As you take longer and longer to fulfill orders, community members trying to sell find themselves waiting. While they wait for abnormal amounts of time, they check the trading charts and see that the token price action is starting to look like a candle, with the token price constantly dropping, this is the beginning of the real dump. Panicking, they will run to your official social media groups and share the fear and problems they're encountering to sell your tokens. More and more community members will engage with this and even if some didn't consider selling your token at that stage, they will try just to see if they actually can. As they will experience the very same problems for themselves, they will also panic and spread the word and fear. Before you know it, a snowball effect of negative press will smother the hype of your launch day, creating skepticism that encourages the sale of your token from all holders. The dump has now taken place and cannot be stopped. Unfortunately, the only end from this point on, no matter what positive marketing or PR you try to spin, is the distrust from your once loving community, leading to the total crash of your token.

Understanding, then creating your token's economy and utility is vital prior to designing the fundraising campaign. Poor token design can result in fundraising struggles, poor community retention and high selling pressure once the token is live. Always remember, the goal is to have more buying pressure than selling pressure, design your tokenomics with this philosophy in mind. Your project will be unique, and there's no one-size-fits-all formula for designing your tokenomics. However, understanding the mechanics can help avoid mistakes and drastically increase the chances of success.

The most successful tokenomics builds trust, encourages long-term commitment, while fostering juicy community incentives. Always showcase clear community incentives in your tokenomics documents, helping them make a split decision to invest and hold. As you're doing this very thing, be careful not to oversell and always be sure to deliver. It's better to remove a feature straight from the start which you might not deliver than promising to the community something that might not happen at all. This can lead to skepticism, short-term speculation, and the potential dump of your token altogether (Glossary 33). Unrealistic expectations, unfair distribution, and a lack of long-term incentives may even discourage investor participation, thus preventing your token launch from ever taking place at all.

CHAPTER 4

Market Cycles

As captivated as you may be by the spellbinding charm of launching your own token, timing is paramount to doing this successfully. Much like all businesses in this world, if you have the right product but you release it at the wrong time, it can be an instant failure, even if your product is great. When one launches a token, such endeavors must be taken into consideration. The timing and strategy of your token launch can significantly influence and, in some cases, pre-determine its success. This is particularly true when considering the dynamic and fluctuating nature of the industry to begin with. For example, if you launch a token linked to Artificial Intelligence (AI) once the trend of AI has become obsolete, it probably won't work or have the same success and hype as initially planned. Moreover, an even larger aspect of influence is the market cycle. These cycles aren't endemic to the crypto industry, they exist in the traditional financial markets also, further shaping global economies, political decisions, and dragooning new government policies. As unconventional as it may be, we're going to explore the main cycles and market conditions that not just influence, but fashion the state of the crypto market, creating favorable and unfavorable moments to launch your token. As you will be stipulating an approximate date of your token launch in your Roadmap and other various documents, you must not only know but understand every market-changing aspect. Mastering these fluctuations will enable you to swiftly raise funds, prioritize company tasks, and anticipate all favorable launch dates months ahead, assuring the best possible conditions to generate as much buying pressure as possible.

© Alexander Rees-Evans 2024
A. Rees-Evans, *How to Launch a Token*, https://doi.org/10.1007/979-8-8688-0533-2_4

As a primary step toward understanding these bespoke market fluctuations, we will first explore two of the most infamous of cycles, commonly known as the Bear Market (Glossary 20) and the Bull market (Glossary 21). Not only are these market conditions clever opposites with interesting names, they are the Greek titans dominating the industry from the mountains, dictating value and investments as they govern from afar. Far from being mere words, the industry shakes and shifts at the very mention of these two words!

In the crypto industry, a bear market is defined by prolonged price declines of cryptocurrencies (especially Bitcoin and Ethereum) and is endowed with an overall wisp of investor pessimism. Additionally, the trading volumes of exchanges, both centralized and decentralized, diminish then dwindle to extreme lows. Although the value of digital assets plummets, the high volatility remains the same, producing a very tough-to-navigate environment for all investors alike. During these down times, the predominating sentiment is one of despondency and circumspection, sometimes even leading to a halt of investor-related activities. Once in motion, this cyclonic phenomenon feeds off itself, creating a self-reinforcing cycle of declining prices, helping maintain prices low, and the market sentiment sparse. Such market conditions often result from factors such as regulatory crackdowns, negative press, or broader economic downturns. In 2022 and 2023, we experienced a multitude of the above such as tremendous regulatory pressure from the Securities and Exchange Commission (SEC) in the United States, the downfall of large crypto protocols such as Celcius and TerraLuna, or even the demise of the second largest exchange in the world, FTX. With such a large quantity of negative events happening in this short period of time, the industry experienced a tremendous devolution in value, negatively impacting the price of Bitcoin and Ethereum. As the vast majority of crypto investor's wealth is held in both of these cryptocurrencies, when the value diminishes, so does the investment capacity. With Bitcoin and Ethereum losing over 50% of their value at one point, the industry hence lost over 50% of investment potential. With only half of investment capital left over, the entire industry is sucked dry of necessary funding to keep the ecosystem running. Much like a drought, this hostile environment leads to a domino effect in the entire food chain, where only the fittest survive. Being a start-up-fueled industry, seldom do all of them make it through this cycle. This negative sentiment, combined with an even higher risk of projects failing due to low buying pressure, drive VCs to reduce investments even more. Sometimes in extreme cases, investors and VCs can freeze all investments until market conditions recover, even if it takes years. During bear markets, active investors are typically more cautious, focusing on preserving capital and minimizing risk, eliciting even harsher conditions for projects to launch in.

This said, for the brave renegades willing to persevere and of which are already funded, bear markets can also be a benison. With careful planning and strategy that we'll discuss soon, launching your token in a Bear market will make you a bigger fish in a smaller pond. Due to fewer tokens launching, as the majority prefer to wait for better market conditions, it's easier to stand out and get your token in the spotlight of traders around the world. Other advantageous factors of launching in these conditions are heavy price reductions on outsourced needs such as technology providers, service providers, and even listing fees on Exchanges. All of the above are in dire need of funds so they usually drop their prices and sometimes conditions. It's not unusual to obtain big discounts, extra perks, flexible payment plans, small down payments, or even more lenient listing conditions. However, in a bear market, being funded and building investor trust are paramount to launching in this cycle. You should emphasize solid fundamentals, including a clear use case, a well-developed product, a strong team, and a transparent use and return of funds. If you decide to launch in such conditions, you must also have an engaged community that can help sustain buying pressure. Don't try to launch if you don't have at least 20,000 followers on X (Formally Twitter) and 10,000 people in your Telegram channel, for your launch to be successful; in this belligerent environment, you must have your own, solid, engaged, and active community. Focusing on your core audience and brand advocates who understand and believe in your project's potential is crucial during a Bear market.

One must also be prepared to re-evaluate one's market cap and token valuation, to align them with the reality of the market conditions. These parameters vary considerably within the bi-lateral movement of market conditions and must remain up-to-date. In such a market cycle, this precisely translates as directly decreasing the value of your project and tokens to stay realistic. Imagine you have a valuation of US$27,000,000 in reasonable market conditions, expect to divide this in half during a Bear market. But why would you launch if this means losing half of your project's value? The simple answer is because as market conditions get better, your valuation increases. Due to the fact that your token would have already been tradable for a while, it will gain a solid reputation and many traders will view it as a safe investment option, noting that your token would have proven itself by launching and surviving the Bear market, further adding to your token's credibility. We all know that it's hard to find a solid project which isn't a scam, retail traders know this more than anyone. If launched correctly during a bear market and your token survives, the reputation will supersede all others and inspire confidence from all. Moreover, as you keep body and soul together during this period, when the market picks up, your token really will have the potential to "moon"!

Now, the moment all investors and creators alike dream of, the Bull market.

A crypto bull run, a term that conjures images of skyrocketing prices and frenetic market activity! Much more than just an upward trend in cryptocurrency prices, this positive extremely favorable market cycle represents a complex interplay of market dynamics, Venture Capitalists' psychology, and an overall positive vibe for investing. It is the moment we go over the bull market with a fine tooth comb, learning the nuances and how to best leverage these conditions for your token launch. Unlike the Bear Market or fleeting price spikes, bull runs in the crypto market typically sustain positive price action over a long period of time. Such duration allows the market to build upward momentum, drawing in more investors and sparking further general interest in cryptocurrencies. This enthusiasm leads to a ripple effect across the entire crypto market providing an almost "safe environment" for any token launch if executed correctly. Another major advantage is the speed and acceleration with which investments and community adoption happen. What may take a year to accomplish in a Bear Market could take only a few weeks to attain in the Bull Market, promising a swift Return On Investment (ROI). Your newly launched token could even receive heightened interest and value appreciation in some cases, directly benefiting you and your project.

Several factors can trigger a bull run, some traits to observe indicating one are technological breakthroughs in blockchain, positive regulatory developments like the approval of the Bitcoin ETF in early 2024 by the SEC, or continuous positive talk of cryptocurrencies by the mainstream media, all playing a significant role in shaping public perception during a bull run. Such positive news and events can amplify investor interest, while negative news can dampen enthusiasm, slowly dragging out into a Bear market if it persists for too long.

Much like we discovered how behavioral tokenomics affect community's interest in a project, the same can be said for investors. Investor psychology in a bull run oscillates between greed and fear, both smothered with high-paced decision-making. Knowing the market's on the rise but won't last forever, the desire for high returns drives investors toward aggressive investment strategies, while the fear of missing out (FOMO) can lead to irrational market behavior in some cases. Due to the very nature of this favorable market condition, it often attracts new and diverse groups of investors, from seasoned traditional investors from the corporate world, to individuals who just got lucky; each with different strategies and tolerance levels for risk join the chase.

If there's a bull run when you decide to make your move, it will provide an ideal backdrop for your token launch. Investors will also be more inclined to taking risks, making them more receptive to investing in new and untested tokens. Unlike the Bear market, the favorable conditions of a bull run also mean increased competition. Among the frantic environment, numerous other projects besides your own will be seeking investor attention, necessitating even more unique value propositions and robust marketing strategies on your behalf. Where investor attention spans are short and competition is fierce, the ability to craft a compelling and outstanding narrative around your token becomes crucial. Because money is plentiful in a Bull market, navigating these complexities can be accomplished by injecting funds strategically into areas like social media, marketing, crypto conferences for networking and even splashing out on some expensive KOLs can significantly boost your visibility and attractiveness to potential investors. However, the exuberance of a bull run can lead to overvaluation of assets, delusional speculation, and messy investments. For the sake of your project's longevity, it's vital that you remain grounded and realistic about your token's potential and market positioning. Many founders take their eye off the ball due to the new attention and success; much like Icarus, who flew too close to the sun, they too experience the quietus wrath of falling from a great height. To prevent this, ensure that your token is not just sustainable in favorable market conditions, but champion's sustainability, practicality, and utility beyond the bull run. Depending on market euphoria alone is a very risky, and seldom sustainable, long-term strategy.

Having emphasized many times on the benefits of launching in a Bull run, one must not do this blindly. Timing is paramount as trends must be considered. If, for example, your token involves GameFi, but the current hot trend is AI, you may not take advantage of all of the perks a Bull run has to offer by launching immediately. Regardless of market conditions, trends are just as important and can be determined by simply inquiring of people working in the industry about them. With the majority of Web3 companies, anyone can book a free 30min call. Be sure to continuously build and nurture your community too. May it be a Bear market or a Bull run, your community is your most powerful weapon, and if treated graciously, they can provide support and stability, thus helping sustain interest and value as the market cycles shift.

Even if the bull run presents a very good setting for token launches, it still possesses inherent challenges. While it offers the potential for rapid growth and high returns, it also requires extra vigilance from you and your team to avoid the pitfalls of overvaluation and short-term thinking. The Bear market, on the other hand, is often a token killer due to the low levels of engagement and funding, but also offers an exceptional spotlight to those who dare. This said, it's recommended that your project be relatively well funded to maximize chances of a successful launch.

Following suit, we must talk about another major event within the crypto industry which heavily impacts not only the decision of whether or not to launch, but the actual capacity of Web3 VCs and the direct price of the industry's blood flow, Bitcoin. This preeminent event is more commonly known as the Bitcoin halving. For it is not a contingency with some possible effects roughly every four years, it is a guaranteed occurrence promoting change at the very core. But if this only affects the price of Bitcoin, why is this such an important affair for launching your token, you may ask yourself? Well, to understand, we first need to take a few steps back and unravel the intricacies of Bitcoin and its vital role in the full crypto ecosystem.

As we all know, Bitcoin is the first and most well-known cryptocurrency which revolutionized the entire thought process and landscape of the concept of money and finance as we knew it back when Bitcoin was introduced in 2009. The very creation of Bitcoin marked the beginning of a new era in not just digital currency and blockchain technology but the global economy. But what sets it apart from traditional currencies, and why does it continue to be a significant and influential player in the world of cryptocurrency?

The inception of Bitcoin begins with its enigmatic creator, known only by the pseudonym Satoshi Nakamoto. In 2008, Nakamoto published the Bitcoin whitepaper, presenting the concept of a decentralized digital currency outside the boundaries of the classical banking governance system. The whitepaper itself is titled *Bitcoin: A Peer-to-Peer Electronic Cash System.* This revolutionary publicly available document, introduced the idea of a decentralized currency that could facilitate transactions without the need for traditional financial intermediaries, thus providing the foundation for the crypto movement we see today. As a matter of fact, the first Bitcoin transaction, commonly known as "The genesis block" took place when Nakamoto mined the first ever block (Block 0) of the Bitcoin blockchain on January 3, 2009. This event marked the birth of Bitcoin as a functional digital currency. In the early days, the general population, financiers, and governments didn't take the power of Bitcoin seriously at all; even to this day, the majority of individuals in 2024 still think Bitcoin is a scam! For the visionaries it was a very different story though, Bitcoin was primarily used by open-minded cryptography enthusiasts and early adopters with a taste for risk. We all remember its first real-world transaction by Laszlo Hanyecz when he (The pepperoni on the first pizza bought with Bitcoin is worth $6.5M today [cointelegraph.com]) famously purchased two pizzas on May 22, 2010, for 10,000 Bitcoins! Today, this historical purchase has become somewhat of a day of celebration for the Web3 community, known as "Bitcoin pizza day."

On top of creating a new way to exchange value as we see with the purchasing of these legendary pizzas, unlike traditional currencies, Bitcoin operates on a completely decentralized network, meaning it's not controlled by governments, banks, or any central authority, making it the world's first borderless and globally accessible currency. With its limited supply of 21 million Bitcoins, it has a capped supply of 21 million coins, a feature designed to mimic the scarcity of precious metals and combat inflation, unlike fiat currencies that can be printed without limit. Not to mention Satoshi Nakamoto remains to this day, unconditionally anonymous, further adding to its decentralized spirit.

From A–Z, Bitcoin respects an incorruptible Modus Operandi, thus operating on a Proof of Work (POW – Glossary 35) consensus mechanism. Bitcoin miners not only secure the network but also distribute new Bitcoins in a decentralized manner. Arguably, we can state that today, this isn't necessarily a fair medium for validation as mining Bitcoin in today's world requires highly sophisticated technology and hash power, which need to constantly be updated, thus requiring major investments, leaving only those with deep pockets the possibility of participating in such activities. Contrary to early Bitcoin miners who were able to mine large quantities using very little equipment, of which many have already sold their coin and have exited the system, creating an even harder market to enter. Think of it like the game Monopoly, at the very beginning, all players are equal and have the same purchasing power. However, after the game becomes serious and a few players go bankrupt, the remaining players have a real Monopoly. Imagine a new player stepping in at this point, due to the dominance of a select few, that player doesn't stand a chance. Bitcoin mining in today's world is the same. Unless you come in with extremely deep pockets and buy out some of the other players and get to their level or above ASAP, you won't stand a chance of mining any Bitcoin as the larger players have somewhat of a Monopoly of the global mining power. This enables them to mine every block faster than you, even if you started mining that block before them, they will come in at the last minute and win. As you will barely mine any Bitcoin at all, you will start to lose money due to the expenses of buying new technology to mine and the cost of electricity. Today, a Bitcoin miner requires a maximum price per KW/h of US$0.02 to stay competitive for the next halving.

The Bitcoin halving is a pivotal event in the world of not only Bitcoin but the entire crypto world. Embedded in the core of the Bitcoin tokenomics, it's instrumental in shaping the Web3 economic health. The majority of VCs and investors in the crypto industry are Bitcoin whales (Glossary 36). Just because the main asset they hold a large quantity of is Bitcoin, it doesn't always mean that they invest directly with Bitcoin.

Much like other financial industries, they're free to leverage their Bitcoin in any ways possible to create liquidity. Imagine a traditional financier, capable of taking out Loans to Value (LTV – Glossary 37) of any agreed upon asset, including real estate, classic cars, fine art, among other high value asset classes. In short, if you own a house but are in dire need of liquidity, you may take out a mortgage on it with your bank. Like an LTV, a mortgage is when your bank lends you funds against=st the foreclosure of the agreed upon asset, in this case your house; often, even if your house has been estimated at US$500,000, seldom will the bank loan you this full amount. More often than not, the bank will give you maybe 50%–75% of this evaluation, granting you approx. US$350,000 cash. If, for some reason, you can't pay the bank back, they're entitled to sell your house at a price they may decide. Often, it's just under the real high street value of your house they're owed plus a profit. In our case, if they loaned you US$350,000 and your house's real value is estimated at US$500,000, the bank would sell it for around US$450,000, making it a great deal for the buyer and reimbursing the bank having also profited US$100,000 in the process. This doesn't mean that you've sold your house in exchange for maybe 50% of its high street value, it means you took out a loan on your house for a sum of cash according to the mutually agreed upon percentage of its real value, usually dictated by the bank providing you the loan. Well, in crypto the same principle exists, cross-pollination between the crypto realm and some specialized yet traditional financial markets for such LTVs. This allows the Web3 investors not to sell their precious digital assets for stablecoins or other fiat currencies, but to take out an LTV (usually 50% of the high street value of the asset plus the commission taken by the LTV provider generally based upon the federal reserve rate of the United States).

As an example, if I'm an investor and own 20,000 BTC with a high street value of approx. US$847 million (approx. US$42,000 per BTC), I know the price of BTC will likely increase dramatically within the next five to ten years, potentially growing 10 x. From a strategic perspective,

I don't want to sell my Bitcoin, but still want to invest in crypto projects to generate income as I wait for Bitcoin to obtain my pre-determined exit price (let's say US$200,000 per BTC). Here, LTVs come in extremely useful as I can take one out on my 20,000 BTC at an approx. percentage of 50%, providing me with half of my Bitcoin's full value (approx. US$435 million) immediately without selling it. Of course, like a mortgage, I must pay back this money with interest, usually based on the federal reserve rate, which is about 5.5% today, plus the commission my LTV provider is making, which could be anywhere from 0.5% to 1%. In short, I would have to pay back US$435 million plus approx. 6.5% (approx. US$28 million) of this value totaling US$463 million. If I make enough successful investments, I can pay back my LTV while generating tremendous positive cashflow on the side, granting me the best of both worlds: Keeping my Bitcoin and investing in many crypto projects.

As we've now understood the importance of Bitcoin within the actual ecosystem of Web3, we can delve into the actual phenomenon of Bitcoin halving and just how it plays a big part in the market cycles. At its core, the Bitcoin halving is a pre-programmed reduction in the rewards given to Bitcoin miners, designed and integrated by Satoshi Nakamoto. The halving event occurs every 210,000 blocks, which roughly translates to four years, given the average time of 10 minutes it takes to mine a single Bitcoin block. When a halving event occurs, the reward for mining new blocks is halved, hence the term "halving." This directly cuts in two the amount of Bitcoin the miners will make for every block validation on the Blockchain, thus cutting in half their profits. It's a part of Bitcoin's deflationary economic model, designed to mimic the extraction of precious metals as, over time, mining becomes more difficult and less rewarding, thus ensuring scarcity.

The first Bitcoin halving occurred in November 2012, when the reward for mining a block was reduced from 50 Bitcoins to 25. Can you imagine? Early Bitcoin miners would be awarded 50 Bitcoins, then 25, all because of the halving. Today, on average, a Bitcoin miner is awarded only 6.25 BTC per block mined. After April 2024, this will drop to a staggering 3.125

BTC per block mined! It's actually quite incredible when we compare this with traditional fiat currencies and the ongoing inflation. The very nature of Bitcoin is deflation oriented from all angles. Subsequent halvings have further reduced this reward, significantly impacting the rate at which new Bitcoins are created and thus projected into the circulating supply available for purchase. This concept of reducing the rate of new currency creation over time contrasts with traditional fiat currencies, where central banks can print money at their own will, leading to inflation.

The following graph illustrates just how conspicuous the difference of value retention and evolution is between Bitcoin and the world's most dominant fiat currency, the US Dollar:

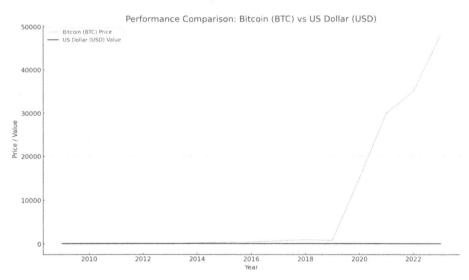

The halving process is one of the driving factors of this substantial value differentiation. Further adding to the decentralized nature of the halving is the full immutable automation of this event, part of Bitcoin's original programming. Each halving event transcends the implications for only Bitcoin miners, as each Bitcoin in circulation now becomes in theory twice as valuable than the price prior to the halving overnight.

This event can also lead to a cleansing in the mining industry, provoking an environment where only the most efficient and cost-effective mining operations remain profitable. Hence why the majority of miners search for very preferential electricity prices, noticeably found through stranded power that often comes from oil extraction sites, remote dams, or other sources far from any major electrical grid. Unfortunately for Bitcoin miners, the Bitcoin's price seldom doubles immediately after the halving, which would cover their original electricity prices, so they have to wait, in many cases, for months or even years, to see such price action, making them immediately less profitable unless they can mine at very preferential prices.

The halving directly impacts Bitcoin's supply by slowing the rate at which new Bitcoins are moved into circulation. This reduced supply growth rate can even lead to bullish sentiments in the market, as seen historically in the periods following halving events. Many in the crypto community speculate that halvings lead to price increases as we witnessed during the third BTC halving on May 11, 2020, when the price per BTC soared from around US$800 to approx. US$60,000 at its peak in April 2021! Actually, if we compare each BTC halving since the first in 2012, where the price of one BTC was at US$12.35, the second halving in 2016 the price of Bitcoin was at US$650.53 BTC, all the way up to the third having in 2020 the price was at US$8821.42 (Bitcoin halving date history, prices & 2024 halving countdown – CryptoAnswers). That's an average price increase of 3200% per halving!

With such price increases after halving events, it's obvious that if the halving is a year or so away, many investors prefer to wait prior to obtaining their LTVs as they will obtain a much bigger LTV as the initial price of the underlying asset will increase dramatically. Using our established example of me being an investor and owning 20,000 BTC at an actual full value of US$847 million, if I know the halving is arriving in seven months, it's wise for me to wait for this very moment, then take out my

LTV. Based on the average price increase per halving, gravitating around 3200%, if I wait a few months, the total value of my assets would be around US$27 billion and US$104 million. If I take out my LTV at this moment, based on 50%, instead of having my initial US$435 million to invest, I will have US$13 billion and 552 million to invest due to the humongous price growth of my underlying asset. Strategic thinking like this provokes broader implications for the entire cryptocurrency ecosystem, impacting investors capacity and amounts they're willing to invest in projects, hence the quality of marketing and other important elements necessary for your token launch due to the level of funding you will acquire.

As one prepares to launch their token, it's vital to consider an often overlooked cycle component affiliated with the more conventional investors of the Web3 space. For these investors don't leverage digital assets to invest in crypto projects, oh no, they actually depend on external investments from much larger investment firms providing direct cash injections. In their specific investment landscape, the fiscal year plays a significant role in how their funds are allocated and spent. Such investors operate on fixed annual budgets, hence pre-determining their entire annual investment capacity and strategy. Ordinarily, the start of the fiscal year brings a fresh influx of capital. As these investors depend on external larger investors, they must abide by rules dictated by the larger firms. Here, there's again a form of cross-pollination between the traditional financial world and the realm of crypto. This is where they prefer to delegate such tasks to new investment firms specializing only in Web3 investments. Often these investment firms are spearheaded by younger individuals having profited themselves as traders or small investors from financial growth in the crypto industry. Actually, quite a lot of large traditional financial firms, family offices, and fiduciaries alike are interested in capitalizing on the crypto market but lack the expertise to do so, hence specializing in Web3 investments due to their own personal experience and success. Of course, these types of investment firms tend to have their allocations replenished at the beginning of every fiscal year. February tends to mark the start of the new investment cycle. However there's always a waiting list so if you're looking for funding for the beginning of a fiscal year, it's recommended to make contact with the investors around the beginning of December before the end of the initial fiscal year so you may be placed at the top of their list for investments once they have fresh funds a couple of months later.

As the fiscal year progresses, the availability of funds for new investments does of course decrease. This isn't to say there's no funds left to be allocated, it simply means that as the year goes on, these investors become less and less liquid. Their goal is to spend their entire allocation wisely before the end of the fiscal year and show positive returns on the investments to their allocation providers. When this is done correctly, they can ask their liquidity providers for larger allocations and grow their company accordingly. This pattern of course impacts how investors approach opportunities toward the year's end, often becoming more selective and conservative in their choices, if they have some funds left over. Keep in mind, if they make poor investment choices, their future allocations may be much smaller, or even annulled altogether. They use other people's money to invest and are obliged to provide positive results.

Understanding the fiscal cycle is crucial if you're seeking funding for your project. A successful token launch requires a successful fundraising campaign so you may lavish on sumptuous marketing and PR campaigns. Be sure to prepare your investment searching activities before the beginning of the fiscal year so when it comes, you're ready to pounce on every liquid investor. It's much better than wasting valuable time, energy, and hype trying to raise funds from October/November to December; use these months to your advantage and prepare yourself strategically for the beginning of the next fiscal year so your chances of obtaining investments will be significantly higher, can be advantageous due to the higher availability of funds. If you do start seeking funds late in the fiscal year, you will without a doubt face many challenges due to the reduced availability of capital.

From your roadmap to your launch, you need to plan your financial needs with an understanding of this funding cycle. This involves considering for both immediate funding needs, but more importantly, your long-term capital requirements and runway. It's always good to build strong relationships with advisors and KOLs who have close ties with investors so they may speak of you from time to time to their investor friends before you engage. This is called "planting the seed." From experience, if nobody in your close circle has good relations with specific investors, it's even harder to raise the necessary funds required for launching your token. Be sure to take some time to build and develop such relations as they will be capital for the advancement of your project. Beyond the fiscal cycle, Web3 investors must sometimes adapt to market trends, potentially structuring budgets for different types of areas of interest within their initial budget. As an example, if Artificial Intelligence (AI) is a hot market trend and GameFi isn't, they may allocate 50% of their total budget to AI and only 5% for GameFi projects. Market trends heavily impact your potential to raise funds so you have to stay informed about these, potentially leaving room in your project to pivot and adapt to such trends.

CHAPTER 5

Go-to-Market Strategy

Segment 1 – Target Audience

As with any business, the go-to-market strategy is a non-negotiable component to ensure a healthy launch and bright future. In regard to your token launch, this is of even higher importance. Your token is more than just a business, often it's built from your very own dreams, after years of pondering on that very idea. Now, imagine yourself for one second, after spending years bringing this dream to life, all of the sleepless nights and fundraising efforts with your team, all of the sweat, blood, and tears gone into your dream to make it into a reality. Imagine you've accomplished all of the above and are about to relish the fruits of your labor, but only to witness the total crash of your token the day you list it on a public exchange... All of that hard work over the years, all for nothing, because your go-to-market strategy failed. Just imagine for one second how you'd feel if that happened to you. Seriously, take a few seconds here, close your eyes, and literally imagine being in that very position after losing millions of dollars from investors, thousands of people calling your project a scam, and the formidable bitter taste of guilt, lingering in your mouth.

Now wipe that image from your mind and that bitter taste from your mouth; we're going to learn everything you need to make your go-to-market strategy a success! First in line, you need to discover and then cater to your target audience. You need to be aware of who you need to target,

© Alexander Rees-Evans 2024
A. Rees-Evans, *How to Launch a Token*, https://doi.org/10.1007/979-8-8688-0533-2_5

then how to onboard them. For example, if you're building a GameFi project, you must understand who will be using your product. Often, GameFi projects also take into consideration the actual scalability of their project by integrating the traditional gaming market value and number of users too. The problem with basing not only your business scalability but also target audience this way is that the majority of the traditional gamers are much more interested in simply playing a great game. The majority of this community are more than happy to use their hard earned money to buy such a game, knowing full well that financially they'll forever be at a loss. However, to their eyes, the pleasure of playing such a game far exceeds the fiscal expenses involved. To top it off, seldom do traditional gamers know how to even use crypto wallets such as the Cyber Wallet or even MetaMask, thus further disheartening them from even trying to engage in Web3 games. On the other hand, normal Web3 degens and traders won't necessarily bother too much about your actual product, the game itself, as they'll be much more interested in the speculative aspect of the token. Here, we can understand the nuances of targeting your appropriate audience as we have one side of the room solely interested in the game but can't use crypto tools easily, and on the other side we have a crypto enthusiastic community, solely interested in a high performing token. GameFi projects often fail as they miss these key points and hence miss their target audience. It's one thing to have a market audience, it's another to be able to tap into it. As a founder, you must understand such complexities and learn to appropriately navigate them, as does a seasoned captain sailing the Atlantic ocean.

One must master how to implement your business ideas in such a way that makes them available and accessible to your target customers. Prior to exploring methods or channels to reach such a community, or even determining who our community is, we must learn how to determine what type of project we're building. Here's a short, non-exhaustive list enumerating the main project types noting that there will always be a large portion of the audience from the crypto speculation side:

1) Metaverse

   A world where the boundaries between the physical and digital blur, appealing to dreamers and digital nomads alike. Here, the typical engaged audience is a blend of crypto degens, project founders, music fans. and some gamers converging in a shared space that transcends reality.

2) GameFi

   In the misunderstood world of crypto gaming, there's a large gap between the classical gamers and the trader community. With the involvement of some large brands such as Ubisoft and EASports, we are seeing some competitive traditional gamers getting involved, but this market is very small. It's best to focus on a great game and easy onboarding backed by simplistic tokenomics to enjoy the best of both audiences.

3) Play2Earn/Do2Earn

   This reward-based landscape, where every challenge and achievement translates into tangible rewards, is quite an interesting one. As a matter of fact, in some developing countries, individuals have quit their day jobs and make an actual living by participating almost 24/7 in such endeavors. It is an especially big market in the Philippines. Of course the rest of the audience is composed majorly of other Web3 degens and, in some cases, young Web2 individuals and sports enthusiasts depending on the concept. For the Lean2Earn side, a lot has yet to be done as people in general stop using it once they've acquired the information they came to learn. Here you need to focus on easy onboarding and continuous incentives for your target audience.

4) Web3

Much like the beginning of the Internet, visionaries and disruptors alike are drawn to the promise of a new Internet bubble they may capture, one where autonomy and decentralization reign supreme. This space is a beacon for crypto enthusiasts who seek to redefine the fabric of online interaction out of pure conviction and values.

5) Protocol

Crypto protocols are basic sets of rules to be shared between computers on the blockchain basis. They're often related to major advancements in the crypto industry such as the Blockchain protocol behind Ethereum, known as Proof Of Stake (POS), or Proof Of Work by the Bitcoin Blockchain. The bulk audience interested in such types of projects is heavily composed of Tech savvy traders and the general Web3 community.

6) Virtual Reality (VR)

This newly dominating technology is not only promoted by some of the most infamous companies in the world such as Meta or Oculus, it's being increasingly leveraged into Web3. Even if small, some crypto communities are highly active in following the bold projects looking to take this path. There is a preponderance, however, of gamers and Web3 degens alike who share a passion for such projects.

7) Artificial Intelligence (AI)

The hot topic of 2023 thanks to OpenAI, AI is not just a trend, but a whole new trailblazing industry. When combined correctly with Blockchain technology, such a project may tackle the audience of AI enthusiasts and the Web3 degen community.

8) SocialFi

One of the most prominent bridges enabling Web2 users to access Web3, SocialFi projects is intrinsically equipped to be the crossroads between both worlds. Meta is carefully aiming to pioneer this very concept with its own cryptocurrency "Libra." If you have a great product combined with easy onboarding and simple tokenomics, you may target Web2 users (prioritize 16-year-olds to 50-year-olds), and the same for the entire Web3 community.

9) DeFi

These projects are financial paradigms, creating new and exciting financial opportunities while challenging the traditional financial, banking, and investment sectors alike. To this day, these projects may attract all the children whose parents' lives were affected by the 2008 financial crisis. Now that they're all grown up, they like to seize every chance possible that pushes against the traditional finance system such as the project "Celcius." Although it turned out to be a pyramid scheme, the demand was definitely there as it was one of the most popular projects in the world at its peak.

10) NFT

The global total market cap for NFTs is approximately $17.3 Billion as of Q1 2024. (Top NFT Collection Prices, Charts & Tracker | Forbes Digital Assets.) However, an often overlooked component as one launches their NFT project is that the actual number of global NFT owners is rather quite niche. In this regard, only approx. 360,000 individuals own NFTs. (How Many People Own NFTs in 2024? (New Data) – EarthWeb.) This means that the majority of NFT wealth is captured and distributed by a small selective few. Of course, if you have a stellar launch, the pond is small enough to make a big splash, hence positioning your NFTs very quickly at the top. Audience wise, there's no way around it, You must target the known NFT community.

11) Blockchain

At the very core of the entire industry, Blockchain is the beating heart. As time goes along, more and more Blockchains emerge, striving to be better than the last. Due to the inherent connection Blockchains have with each and every user of this space, you may target the Web3 degens, traders, and seasoned crypto users in general. It's, however, important to clearly voice the unique selling proposition of your Blockchain from day one in order to stand out among the crowd.

12) Marketing

Today, many crypto platforms are designed to facilitate the user's needs. It's not uncommon for them to centralize service providers on a B2B level and other entities who need them, hence creating an easy-to-navigate environment for those looking for specific services or products within the industry. The appropriate community for such projects are typically other companies in Web2 and Web3.

13) Infrastructure

The ever expanding pipes of the Web3 industry, graciously laying out stepping stones for other projects to leverage and build upon. Moreover, infrastructure projects are greatly valued by investors regardless of the weather as there is and always will be a constant need to further develop the infrastructure of this sector. In regard to targeting an audience, Web2 users are out of the picture, you need to focus on the full Web3 community.

Once you've made clear what type of project you'll be and the global audience you must target, there's a mathematical calculation you may use to help fine-tune and determine your specific target audience:

$$TCS = ((O/T) \times A \times I \times R) \div (C \times (1 - M))$$

TCS = Target Client Score (this rating is on a non-fixed scale, usually obtaining a score of 1 is considered good. If your score exceeds 1, the more prone to targeting a compatible audience you will be).

T = Total addressable market (this is the total market demand for your cryptocurrency, as you do your own market research in order to determine this market size, be sure to read up on how many wallet holders hold which type of tokens.)

S = Serviceable available market (the segment of the total available market targeted by your products or services which is within the possible geographical reach, for example, if you're not regulated to sell your token to investors from the United States, even if you have a great product fit, you must subtract them from the total available market).

O = Serviceable obtainable market (in short, it's the portion of the Serviceable available market audience that your token can actually capture. How many individuals will be interested in buying your token).

A = Affinity to technology (this is the number scaling between 0–1 of individuals from your target audience who will be able to navigate the technicalities of Web3 to actually buy your token).

I = Investment potential (quantified as a score ranging from 0–1 representing the potential investment power of the target audience, which differs heavily depending on the countries where your community resides whether it be developing or developed countries, as the average investment size will differ dramatically, the same may be said for the age of the community you're targeting too).

R = Risk tolerance (on a scope from 0–1, this is a score representing the target audience's willingness to engage with new and potentially risky investments, just how sure are you that your audience will invest?)

C = Competition (here you must stipulate a number from 0–1, representing the level of competition in the market as this may heavily impact the success of your token upon launch and further on down the line.)

M = Market readiness (also based on a score from
0–1, this dictates how prepared the market is for your
crypto token, for example, the market audience will be
less receptive of your token in a Bear market or if the
current trend is AI but you're launching a MemeCoin.
It's also important to read the room, if there has been
a big negative event in the market such as a major
exchange default or even a big regulatory crackdown,
you must hence reciprocate to them in this metric).

To provide you with more depth, let's create a concrete example with some numbers. For context, we're going to find the TCS for a Meme Coin named Smiley. The total market size is 332,000,000 people, our serviceable obtainable market is 89,600,000 people, the market conditions are good as we're just exiting a Bear market, the price of BTC is US$51,000, the current market trend is AI and GameFi, we have created an easy onboarding mechanism to enable all levels of users to purchase our token so we have an A of 0.8, we have a heavy focus on targeting the Turkish and European markets so our I is 0.65, there has been no major launches of any successful Meme Coins in the last six months bringing our C at a 0.2, the risk tolerance should be quite decreased due to the lack of such tokens on the market, making our R a 0.4 as Meme Coins are generally high risk and the BTC ETF has just been validated by the SEC so our M is 0.8.

With these above parameters, we will perform the following calculation in order to determine if we have a good TCS, noting that the highest possible obtainable score is 1, and the worst is 0:

$$TCS = ((O/T) \times A \times I \times R) \div (C \times (1-M))$$

$$TCS = ((89,600,000/332,000,000) \times 0.8 \times 0.65 \times 0.4) \div (0.2 \times (1-0.8))$$

$$TCS = 1.4$$

In this case we can see that our score is 1.4, hence exceeding the "good score" of 1. Thanks to these metrics, you may now be confident that your token is highly compatible with the audience you're targeting and pursue the next steps to creating a perfect go-to-market strategy for your token.

Organic vs. paid following

Once you have a reasonable TCS, you must also create a welcoming environment for your potential investors and community members. By this, you can't expect real, living breathing people, commonly known as the organic audience to take your project seriously if you have zero following on your social media channels. For example, a potential community member will have many doubts on the quality of your project if you have a very small social following. This double-edged sword means that even if you have a great product and a high TCS, if you're starting from scratch you may not have a high conversion rate for your client acquisition. On the other hand, if you have high numbers on your social following to start with, all of the other potential investors and community members will feel much more reassured about participating in your ecosystem, plus following your social media channels.

You must decide which to prioritize depending on your initial budget as even investor VCs will scrutinize your social media following heavily prior to making any investment. The reason being is that in Web3, the more people in your socials, often translates as the more clients you have for buying your token. It's a very strange yet unique model, but interestingly enough, it's often a good indicator of the success of your token launch and longevity. To extend upon this, you must lay out your marketing plan and strategy. Of course, it's important to be aware of the marketing agency you chose as this can define the success or demise of your project. However, one must be very careful, as some marketing agencies will try to sell you very expensive marketing packages but actually provide very little results. Bizarrely enough, the larger marketing firms tend to charge very large fees for minimal results, it's quite a pain point of the industry. The majority of them were able to build up their own brand awareness very well indeed, but use this solely to draw in and then bilk candid new projects looking to have a successful launch. For this is one of the many complexities and pitfalls you must anticipate to avoid wasting strategic funds. To name some honest marketing firms, Rocket Now, Dverse, Luna Strategy, or even Slime marketing provide very good services and value for money.

The best way to determine if your marketing agency is good, is to learn a few tricks about crypto marketing yourself, to monitor what they plan to do and how they plan to do it! All successful marketing campaigns, may they be in Web2 or Web3, start with a marvelous story. Your story is the backbone, the inspiration, and emotional vehicle touching the playful souls of all that encounter your brand. Take Nike, for example, whenever you think of it, the first words that come to mind are along the lines of "Just do it." Dan Wieden, founder of Wieden + Kennedy marketing agency, created this infamous slogan for Nike in 1988. Three simple words, perfectly placed, in perfect harmony. That's all it takes to transform your token's brand into a legend.

Segment 2 – Marketing

This particular segment is aimed at founders and entrepreneurs who want to make this happen, that is, execute a stellar token launch thanks to stellar marketing. You may be a seasoned entrepreneur, a serial token launcher, or just a passionate individual looking to leave your mark in the fertile soil of Web3, but you must take the bull by the horns and relay a clear marketing campaign from day one. In order to promote such a clear and well-executed marketing campaign, your strategy must be first class and well-structured from day one.

Prior to engaging with any form of paid marketing, community builders, or PR agencies, you must start building traction by yourself. There's of course sundry ways you may approach such an endeavor, keeping in mind once you have your story, narrative, and project identity, it's necessary to start building your community. Getting the ball rolling on this is key for building the foundation of your followers, hence future investors. This is one of the reasons why it's recommended to have a marketing whizz onboard as a team member. If that's not the case, all is well, it will just require some more elbow grease and networking if you don't have a portfolio of Key Opinion Leaders (KOL, Glossary 38). If so, it's good to do some searching on LinkedIn.

When using this professional social platform to get in contact with a specific type of entity or person, it's recommended you pay for the premium version as you'll need great outreach capacity. The basic version has limitations for the number of outreaches and you only have a handful of messages you may send to individuals with whom you're not yet connected. As you'll be sending hundreds of messages and connection requests, the limitations will be hit very soon. The great thing here is that you can also cancel your subscription to the premium version once you've achieved your goal of obtaining a few KOLs and don't need it anymore. Now, as you're searching for KOLs on LinkedIn, make sure to use the "Key words" you may tap in the LinkedIn search bar to help curate your search. Some good key words relevant to Web3 KOLs are: "Crypto advisor" "Web3 advisor" "Crypto serial entrepreneur" "Web3 angel investor" etc. It may seem odd to search for advisors and angel investors, yet these are often individuals with a big following within the Web3 industry. Be sure to check how many people are following them prior to shooting out a message. when someone's following is over 5000 on LinkedIn, it is a positive sign.

X, formerly known as Twitter, is also a great place to find some KOLs! X does, however, have a very different engagement structure than LinkedIn, making the actual connection with an individual rather challenging. The easiest way to navigate such an undertaking is to search for the individual on LinkedIn after finding them in X. Not only will this dramatically increase your chances of onboarding that particular KOL, but it will also give you the possibility to cross-reference the veracity of their following. The number of followers on X is often subject to bots, meaning that an entity with 15,000 followers could all be a hoax. However, if you cross-reference this information with their other socials, it should give you an idea of how many people your targeted KOL could actually engage with. Keep in mind that it's not uncommon for communities on X to easily exceed the 40,000-follower mark while their LinkedIn may only have a few thousand followers. All depend on what the focus of the social media is for that particular KOL.

Of course, Facebook is an old classic for connecting with people around the world. Although, trying to engage with a high quality KOL over Facebook may not be the best of ideas to start with as Facebook doesn't have that embedded professional tone, such as LinkedIn. However, if all of the other engagement channels haven't worked, this is your last resort and definitely worth trying as a last resort. Such a method has proven to be very fruitful in the past, and as the old adage goes, you never know until you try.

As your inbox starts to receive some positive replies from KOLs, you will also stumble on some major ego-maniacs too. These KOLs are to be avoided at all costs, even if they have a big following. They may also be quite rude and even send you links to have preliminary discussions with them of which you must pay per minute! These types of KOLs may even boast being advisors for some very large crypto projects but at the end of the day, apart from charging you thousands of dollars for a few tweets and a large percentage of your total token supply to have them onboard as advisors, they will bring very little value. Another trap of the KOL/advisor industry is the hype of the "Forbes 30 under 30" clan. At first glance, it seems very impressive and gives the image of someone extremely wealthy with tremendous business expertise. As a matter of fact, far more often than not, it's an illusion. An interesting fact of which not many founders are familiar with is that you can actually pay Forbes to be on the 30 under 30 list, and it's not as expensive as you'd think!

Some important factors to cross-reference when choosing a KOL may be recent success cases, taking into consideration when they got involved, how the community evolved when that happened, plus how the community evolved one month after the last communication with them for the bespoken project. Don't be afraid to dive into the details behind the shimmer and glimmer they may present, no matter how offended they may get. If a KOL is genuine, they'll be more than happy to demonstrate the above cases, and not just cases from a year or so ago or at the hype of a Bull run. It's important to note that if you have some funds, it is worth spending four or five thousand dollars to get a really good one for optimum results, or better yet, even outsourcing this to a dedicated firm as they have a plethora of KOLs with preferential terms and pricing.

If this isn't the case, it's recommended to go with some smaller KOLs as they can often accept tokens for this. Just be sure to include the cliff and vesting terms in the contract when you negotiate with them. The last thing you want is tremendous selling pressure from your KOLs the day of your token launch. A last little tip is to make sure that your KOLs have access to your target community. For example, if you're aiming for your token to be bought and traded in the Asian market, an American KOL with a matching American community will not be of much help, even if they have one million followers. Make sure your target community will be reached through your chosen KOL.

Once your KOLs are secured and start spreading the word of your project among their communities, it's time to inform and educate. There will be a trickle effect from the massive outreach of your KOLs, and your social media accounts will capture this. Slowly, your social media following will start growing. This is a major turning point of your crypto project and must be handled with great care and precision. You must now transform the individuals from your community into your brand advocates. The goal is to get every single person in your social following to understand what you're doing, and more importantly, for them to understand that your project is serious enough for the tokens you will be issuing to increase exponentially in value once launched. This last part is often misunderstood by the majority of project founders. Nevertheless, you must understand that this small initial group in your social media channels will speak to all of their friends about your project, hence creating a snowball effect and further increasing your social media following. To educate your initial community about what your project is, why they should stay with you and not the other thousands of crypto projects out there all trying to persuade them to join their social media, you need to participate in podcasts and Ask Me Anything (AMAs). Not only will you be able to promote your project to new communities but you will be able to provide important information necessary to educate your community on the perks of your project. However, by and large, if you're making your first foray into the startup world, you may be tempted and preoccupied with perfecting and protecting your idea, of which you may even view as a model of perfection. Far more often than not, after obtaining sufficient market feedback, your model will change, to move toward a successful launch. For example, proceeding with initial assumptions can result in a failure to properly identify the target market of the business, as well as the proper channels to reach this market audience. Moreover, any unwillingness to move beyond your initial idea will also, in most cases, limit the sustained growth and potential of your business. Be sure to keep an open mind as your marketing campaigns may vary in tandem.

As you're further developing your marketing strategy, online platforms will be your primary battleground. Effective use of social media, content marketing, search engine optimization (SEO Glossary 39), and email marketing can drive significant engagement and interest in your project. To further expand upon this, here are some essential marketing tools you'll need to leverage in order to maximize the marketing efforts:

> Social Media Marketing: Platforms like Twitter, Reddit, and LinkedIn are potential hotspots for crypto enthusiasts. Tailoring content that resonates with

your target community, including updates, thought leadership pieces, and interactive engagements, can boost your project's visibility massively while helping onboard relative individuals to your social media accounts.

Content Marketing and SEO: Educational and informative content that addresses your audience's needs and questions can establish your project as a thought leader in the space. Optimizing this content for search engines will enhance your visibility and drive organic traffic to your project's website. Of course, you may enhance your SEOs by paying specific agencies, or you can attempt to do this with your team. If you don't have any experience in this but wish to try without paying an agency, you can find some great tips and hacks by simply watching some videos on YouTube relevant to this subject.

Email Marketing: Despite being one of the oldest digital marketing tools, email remains incredibly effective. Regular updates, newsletters, and exclusive insights can keep your audience engaged over time and provide valuable feedback such as the opening rates of the emails. By tracking this vital information, statistics correlating both your community growth and the opening rates of the emails will reveal the engagement levels and changes of the community at the receiving end.

Paid Advertising: While the crypto space sometimes presents challenges for paid advertising due to platform restrictions, budget restrictions, or even market conditions, carefully targeted campaigns on

crypto-friendly platforms can yield significant returns.
Understanding the nuances of each platform's policies
and tailoring your approach accordingly is key. For
example, the search engine Brave is often used by the
crypto communities due to its preferred privacy and
ad blockers (Brave vs. Chrome: Should You Switch to
Crypto-Friendly Browser? I CoinCodex). This makes
it a wise investment for paid marketing campaigns
as the chance of hitting your desired community is
dramatically increased.

Another important aspect of your marketing campaign is to constantly
evaluate and adjust your strategy by collecting important data from your
current efforts. Monitoring the performance of your marketing activities
through analytics is crucial. Engagement rates, website traffic, conversion
rates, and social media growth are just a few metrics that can provide you
valuable insights into the effectiveness of your strategy. Alongside, due to the
fast-moving nature of the crypto market, for your marketing to be efficient,
it requires a resilient approach. Be prepared to pivot your strategy based on
performance data and changing market dynamics. Continuous learning from
successes and failures will refine your approach over time. One must also
stay ahead of the curve, making sure to keep on top of new market trends as
soon as they appear, as the crypto industry is defined by rapid innovation
and change. Staying informed about the latest trends, technologies, and
regulatory developments can help you anticipate shifts in the market so you
may onboard more users, hence further increasing your community.

In an industry sometimes marred by hype and speculation,
maintaining high ethical standards in your marketing efforts can set your
project apart. Every other project trying to have a successful token launch
is also fighting to attract a large community too. Transparency, honesty,
and respect for your audience's intelligence will build long-term trust and
loyalty, this must be showcased in all of your messaging throughout the
entire duration of your marketing campaign.

Segment 3 – Growth Hacking

Growth hacking is not merely a set of tactics but a mindset. It involves a relentless focus on growth, driven by experimentation, data analysis, and clever iteration. The goal is to identify the most efficient ways to grow your community by leveraging creative, low-cost strategies. In our case, this means finding innovative ways to increase token adoption, user base, and community engagement while optimizing resources. Much like a cheat code for a game, all of the social media channels and crypto platforms have their own weaknesses which, when studied, may be exploited to enhance your marketing efficiency tremendously. At the heart of growth hacking is the intelligent use of data. Crypto projects can harness blockchain analytics, social media metrics, and user engagement data to identify patterns, preferences, and opportunities for growth. This data-driven approach allows for targeted strategies that can adapt in real-time to the market's dynamics.

Community Building and Engagement: The crypto world thrives on community. A strong, engaged community not only supports a project but also evangelizes it. Growth hacking strategies here might involve creating valuable content such as a big problem in the market that you're trying to solve. Fostering open discussions with your community on platforms like Discord and Telegram are also very useful as they help build community engagement and make each individual participating feel like they're actually part of helping make decisions within your project. You may even promote votes in these channels such as what Blockchains would your community like to see your token on and why, what exchanges (CEX/DEX) they would also etc... Of course incentivizing community contributions through contests, Hackathons, airdrops, or token rewards are vital for creating real engagement within your community. Just be sure that if you do airdrop your own native future tokens or SAFTs, for example, do include an automatic vesting schedule. If not, the US$10,000 worth of tokens you gave away can quickly turn into US$70,000 selling pressure when you list your token due to the organic price growth. It's always best to give away stablecoins as prizes, first of all individuals will be more interested to participate, plus they will not impact your token price when you launch.

Viral Marketing Techniques: All crypto projects are uniquely positioned to leverage the vast potential of viral marketing, given the digital and networked nature of their audience. You may want to put a heavy focus of your campaign on easy to access and shareable content, launching referral programs, and utilizing social media platforms can trigger a viral spread. It's possible to also leverage the power of meme culture by creating a viral mascot or slogan, just because you're not creating a MemeCoin, it doesn't mean that you can't harness the viral marketing power of such a culture. Strategic partnerships with other projects, influencers, and platforms can significantly amplify this culture. These collaborations can offer mutual benefits, such as cross-promotion, shared resources, and increased credibility. However, one must be cautious of which entities to strike partnerships with, for if the partner defaults or has Public Relations (PR) problems, you may find yourself quickly tangled into bad publicity. Be sure to fully vet the entity prior to linking your brand and support with them. This may be done by checking the background and experiences of the team members, cross-referencing their white paper, pitch decks, and Litepaper with their current status in accordance with their roadmap.

Growth Hacking Tactics: The essence of growth hacking is experimentation. You should constantly test different approaches, from marketing messages and channels to user interface changes and new features. Keep notes of user engagement as you change and tweak your product until you reach an interesting level of growth and user retention. Do visit industry-leading competitor's platforms, websites, and interfaces to further adapt your own. This way, not only can you obtain some new ideas, but it can also allow you to see downsides of your competition such as complex user onboarding. Armed with such information, you may create your platform or website with a more optimized onboarding system, for example, giving you the edge over your competition.

All successful growth hacking tactics will increase the number of individuals joining your project's social media while enhancing your brand awareness. Another trick within growth hacking is how to convert the social following into real users willing to buy your token. Conversion rate optimization (CRO), is hence crucial for turning interest into action. For crypto projects, this means ensuring that the journey from discovering the project to becoming a user or investor is as frictionless as possible. For example, it's not because you did an email blast to 10,000 email addresses that you will receive 10,000 users. If you're structuring very analytical and strategic growth hacking, but the opening rate of these emails is usually around 15%. Furthermore, the actual conversion rate for the world of Web3 isn't yet explored due to the lack of data and transparency between companies. With this in mind, we can look at Web3's distant cousin, Finance, which this industry has on average a conversion rate of 3.1% for emails. (Updated 2023: Average Conversion Rate by Industry and Marketing Source – Ruler Analytics.) Noting the importance of such information during your campaign, you must learn how to calculate your conversion rate for optimal results. Without calculating this, your growth hacking will suffer as in appearance you may be onboarding many individuals into your social media channels, but in reality you may only transfer a fraction of them into clients willing to buy your token. To be sure you're on the right path, you may also cross-reference your Target Client Score (TCS) with your ongoing Conversion Rate (CR). If, for some reason, you have a high TCS but a low CR, this generally means that the community you've been onboarding to your social media channels is not the right community. Hence your marketing and growth hacking strategies have been targeting the wrong individuals. On the other hand, if your TCS and CR are both high, it means that your marketing and growth hacking have been well executed and you've targeted the right community. Your CR will help confirm if your marketing and growth strategy are being well executed. To determine your CR, you will need to consider the following calculation:

CR = (Number of goal achievements/Total number of visitors) x 100

> Number of Goal Achievements: How many times the desired action was taken by your community. For example, a goal achievement might be defined as the number of new wallet sign-ups, token purchases, or re-tweets on X (Twitter). As every project is different, your goal achievements will be unique to your project.

> Total Number of Visitors: This is the total count of individuals who visited the site or landing page where the desired action can be taken. In short, the number of individuals who didn't follow through with your

proposed action after seeing it. This could be that
they opened your email, but never replied or reacted
positively to what you wished.

As a live case, we'll continue using our Meme Coin project which we
calculated the TCS of earlier in this chapter.

Following suit, our context will be that we did an email blast to
20,000 individuals. We chose to target these individuals as they're part
of multiple DAOs in the crypto space so they should be prone to new
trading opportunities. Our goal from this email blast was to direct them
and subscribe to our X (Twitter) account. As we don't have access to the
number of individuals visiting our X account, the closest action to the total
number of visitors will be the number of emails opened. In our case, let's
imagine that 1438 emails were opened:

$$CR = (1438/20000) \times 100$$

$$CR = 7.9\%$$

This means that our conversion rate of our community is at 7.9%,
which is very high as the usual conversion rate across sales in the
finance sector borderlines 3%. (Updated 2023: Average Conversion Rate
by Industry and Marketing Source – Ruler Analytics.) This exceptional
CR reveals that we've been targeting the right individuals to join our
community, our marketing is on par and our growth hacking may now be
accentuated as we are on the right track.

If, however, our CR would have been below 3%, this would mean that
we've been targeting the wrong community. If we start growth hacking
under such unfavorable conditions, it will further accentuate the disparity
between your number of visitors and your goal achievements.

A successful go-to-market strategy must combine a high TCS, targeted
marketing, strategic growth hacking, KOLs, and a strong social following.
Combining all of the above is capital to creating a large and engaged
community, which will stick with you through thick and thin, promote

your ideas and become your brand advocates, creating a snowball effect until your community rivals those of the larger projects such as Ethereum or Dogecoin. On this journey, constantly checking the temperature as you innovate your strategies will help guide your campaigns and keep you on track. For these reasons, calculating your conversion rate as often as possible will be key to maintaining positive growth of your community before, during, and after your token launch.

CHAPTER 6

Mandatory Stages of Your Project

Segment 1 – What Is a Whitepaper and How to Develop It

As the nuts and bolts of your project slowly start coming together, you'll become accustomed to feedback on your product and market fit. While crafting away in this permuting process, you will eventually find the right vertical for your project and token. Once this path is discovered, investors, VCs, community members, and every single person with whom you interact will want to see tangible evidence of your project. It's one thing to have a vision, it's another to bring it to life.

Let's take a step back here and think for a second, just why is it that everybody wants to see something tangible from you side before getting involved with your project? One of the biggest myths in this industry is that you can raise millions of dollars with a Pitch deck. Sure, it may have happened a few times in the old bull runs (Brief History of Bitcoin Bull & Bear Markets (2008–2024) (altcoininvestor.com)), but many of the more risk-tolerant VCs have been wiped out due to poor investment decisions and the average trader is more skeptical of projects due to past scams. Since the bull run in 2017, the remaining investors have placed risk

© Alexander Rees-Evans 2024
A. Rees-Evans, *How to Launch a Token*, https://doi.org/10.1007/979-8-8688-0533-2_6

litigation at the top of their lists when considering investment, making them much harder to impress, regardless of how revolutionary your idea may be. Many community members also require much more proof of your project's viability prior to letting their guard down. In order to satisfy both parties simultaneously, you must be fully capable of conveying your idea in graphic detail. In the world of Web3, the document which does just that is commonly known as the Whitepaper. Every single project must have one to be taken seriously, regardless of your status. Even the Godfather of the industry himself, Satoshi illustrated the innings of Bitcoin on such a public document for all to see. Yes, it's a public document that any person at any given time, anywhere across the globe may view and scrutinize at their will. The Whitepaper is a kaleidoscope into not just your project but the vision and mechanics of how it will work. Much like a blueprint, all of the necessary steps to complete your project will be there apart from one difference, the depth of details. Exactly, a Whitepaper isn't just an instruction book on how to build something, it's filled with the storyline, the why, the how, and the value propositions as well. Without a doubt it's one of the most important documents with which you will need to reassure investors and community members alike.

On top of bringing powerful credibility and weight to your fundraising efforts, this document will also be the technical instructions for your project, possibly leading the way for new ideas and protocols in the industry. Yes, your Whitepaper could literally go down in the history books as the norm for a specific vertical within the crypto industry. Finally, your vision, ideas, and strategy will be locked within these pages, further differentiating your project and token from the competition. For these reasons, it's noteworthy to craft your Whitepaper with the utmost care and clarity. As you dive into technical, strategic, and intense details, you'll soon find yourself filling page after page, after page. If gone into enough details, your Whitepaper can easily reach over 50 pages in length, with each page specifically providing unique value and content. It is de rigueur for such documents to be carefully crafted with a pre-designed structure in mind. Abiding by the following table of content will provide your readers with a clear understanding of the seriousness and uniqueness of your project and token (How to Write a Crypto Whitepaper? Complete Guide (coinbound.io)):

1) Synopsis:

> The first piece your readers will engage with is the synopsis of your project. As soon as they open your Whitepaper and flick past the cover, a simplistic overview of your work should await them. Without going into too much detail, use this part to give a bird's-eye view of what you're building and why it's relevant. Just by reading this, one must comprehend the underlying concept of what you're aiming to achieve through your project. Try to keep the synopsis to around 350 words length. It shouldn't be a long forceful read, but rather an illuminating piece someone may read while waiting for their coffee to brew early in the morning.

> Example from Hypersphere (HyperSphere technical whitepaper v1.8.0.pdf):

he HyperSphere – a Real-time Cybersecure Privacy Network with Embedded DyDAG Blockchain for Global e-Commerce

Evgen Verzun & Richard K. Williams

www.hypersphere.ai

synopsis

A fully decentralized autonomous real-time cybersecure privacy network with enterprise-grade certificate authority (user identity), privacy protections (including pseudonymity), and energy-efficient network-native embedded blockchain for global e-commerce is described. Unlike the cyberattack vulnerability of financial and blockchain transactions executed over the Internet using TCP/IP, the HyperSphere employs a new communication protocol with military-grade hypersecurity– the Secure Dynamic Network & Protocol (SDNP). The SDNP protocol combines autonomous dispatcher-based packet routing and fragmented data transport of anonymous data packets over a meshed network with hop-by-hop dynamic encryption and state-based concealment techniques to repel packet hijacking, man-in-the-middle attacks, and metadata surveillance of network traffic. The HyperSphere cloud comprises an *ad hoc* dynamic array of cloud portals called 'HyperNodes', downloaded software hosted on global server clouds, local ISPs, and personal devices, representing a heterogeneous hybrid network of its users, i.e. the 'people's network', whereby HyperNode users participate as *resource providers* to execute transactions, perform computing, and transport data for HyperSphere merchants and service providers.

As compensation, HyperNodes participating in the successful completion of HyperContracts mint network-native eco-friendly digital utility token useful in purchasing HyperSphere services and tradable in digital currency exchanges. The process of minting is network-native, using (OSI Layer-3, Layer-4) data transport in the cloud to generate cryptographically unique HyperNode hop codes (HHCs)– hashed data required as Proof-of-Performance to adjunctively generate new digital currency using one-trillionth (10^{-12}) the energy required by Bitcoin mining.

All token transactions are recorded on multi-tree (non-communal) perpetual blockchains called *dynamic* directed acyclic graphs (DyDAGs) with ownership established through a private identity-trust-chain linked to a user's identity and root CA-certificates. Transactional integrity, privacy, and blockchain security are protected by numerous innovative mechanisms limiting access to a blockchain on a need-to-know basis, including blockchain replicant blockchain observer segments (RBOS), one-time transaction token (OT^3) proxies, blockchain defragmentation, pseudonymous transactions, auxiliary sidechains (for documentation), and more...

In the HyperSphere, merchants and service providers are able to access vast global resources at superior cost efficiencies to securely and privately conduct e-commerce including cloud communication, cloud computing, disaggregated cloud storage, cloud connected (IoT, V2X) devices, and e-services including financial transactions and blockchain-as-a-service (BaaS). The HyperSphere and SDNP protocol stack, licensed to the non-profit HyperSphere Foundation, represents an extensive portfolio of inventive matter including US and international patents, issued and pending.

2) Abstract:

Specifically designed to provide the reader with a high-level overview of your Whitepaper's content, the Abstract must elaborate from a researcher's perspective on what your project's goals are. You may even use this piece to add more examples of existing problems while examining them from a technical point of view. In short, think of the abstract as a very technical in-depth version of your synopsis. Relative images, graphics, or any other form of technical charts may also be integrated if they help provide greater depth to the reader.

Example from Hypersphere:

The HyperSphere – a Real-time Cybersecure Privacy Network with Embedded DyDAG Blockchain for Global e-Commerce

Evgen Verzun & Richard K. Williams

Abstract– An innovative and highly advanced cybersecure 'privacy' network for global e-commerce, realtime communication, and cloud computing– the HyperSphere, is introduced. Featuring military-grade 'hypersecure' data transport, enterprise-grade certificate authority (identity verification), and network-generated eco-friendly cryptocurrency, the HyperSphere mitigates security, transactional, and privacy risks of the Internet while enabling a self-contained economic environment for commercial and private transactions and e-services using its own network-generated cryptocurrency. The HyperSphere comprises a global dynamic *ad hoc* heterogeneous network of 'HyperNodes', software downloaded onto servers, PCs, and smartphones delivering resources to merchants and businesses while earning HyperNode owners (resource providers) payment in network utility tokens. HyperNodes operate metamorphically, changing adaptively into authority nodes, task (process) nodes, or name-server nodes as required to execute HyperContract tasks and services, and to apportion HyperNode payments ratably in accordance with its contributions. Unlike conventional PoW, HyperSphere employ lightweight multi-tree blockchains comprising *dynamic directed-acyclic-graphs* (DyDAGs), introduced herein for the first time, uniquely designed for rapid execution, robust dynamic security, cloaked distributed consensus, attack resilience, and inherent privacy protection. Using replicant blockchain observer segments (RBOS) and a cloaked jury-of-peers with limited access to blockchain provenance, the HyperSphere is able to mitigate double spending, prevent fraud, and repel attacks while prohibiting backtracing and privacy leakage. In the HyperSphere, network security is wholly unique: Using hypersecure technology originally developed and deployed in professional communication, the patented "secure dynamic network and protocol" (SDNP) offers anonymous packets of fragmented data dynamically routed over an ever-changing 'meshed' network, minimizing propagation delays while confounding surveillance, thereby rendering packet sniffing, hijacking, network surveillance, and man-in-middle attacks meaningless.

3)   Index Terms:

Regrouping all of the main words and vocabulary used in your Whitepaper, the Index terms serve as an easy to navigate word database. Linking key words representing topics or important information with the page numbers where they're used, it enables the reader to reverse search information. Simply by looking at a word they feel the surrounding topic will be of interest to them, they can find all of the page numbers where that word/topic will be found and go straight to reading those segments. In short, it will point your readers to relevant pages for them.

4) Introduction:

This is the opening segment placing the spotlight upon the problem your project aims to resolve. You must make evident that the problem exists with a heavy emphasis on its presence. Also, you need to explain what it affects within the industry and why it's relevant. Be sure to use this portion to leave the readers in awe as you set the stage where your project and token resolve this very problem by enumerating as many problems or entities enduring these problems as possible. Do go into very dense details about each and every one without holding back.

5) Project Helicopter View:

This is where you introduce your project as the hero of the day, but first, by presenting exactly what it is that you're building. An overview, the technical architecture and different layers are to be exposed in full transparency here. Touching upon the token's utility within the ecosystem is also useful content to add. Keep this part simple but try to break down your project into as many layers as possible, be they 10, 15, or even 50 for that matter! The goal is to show the structure of your project and why every element is necessary.

6) Project Technical View:

Much like the helicopter view of your project, the technical view requires the same structure but solely for the technicality of your project. If you have a developer on board, it's probably best to leave this part to them as you must explain what new technology you're bringing to the table, what technology is being used, how that technology will be interoperable and why your technical solution is the best. To the untrained eye, it will appear as gibberish, but to a keen and experienced one, they will understand and judge you heavily on this topic so it needs to be stellar.

7)   Markets and Applications:

Within this segment, start off with a general overview of the market, size, and geolocations your project aims to reach. Secondly, show how your project and token are a perfect fit in that specific market you're targeting by enumerating some examples. Show how integrating your project in that realm would provide value and alleviate certain pain points. Feel free to do some market research and provide data to back up your examples.

8)   Token Utility and Tokenomics:

As one of the most important intricacies of your Whitepaper and project, you must explain the use case of your token. One must be able to browse through this section and fully understand that there's without a doubt a need for a token in your project. Providing the dense details on your token's ecosystem will help others understand why you have a token and what role it will play in the greater scheme of your project. Tokenomics must also be included in this section in order to provide the necessary metrics required for the sustainability of your ecosystem and token ecosystem.

9) Business Strategy:

Exhibiting your global business strategy is key for sporting the seriousness of your endeavor, for many projects fail due to bad execution even if their product or service is great. Here, you must not only show your go-to-market strategy but also how you will monetize, sustain, and scale the project financially. You don't need to go into details about your burn rate, etc... but more so about the direct correlation of positive cashflow and your token. Not to forget about where the buying pressure from your token will come from and why, plus how you will mitigate potential selling pressure throughout the longevity of your token's lifespan.

10) Regulatory Structure:

Another important component you must elaborate upon is how you plan to structure the company while being compliant. Complying with regulations and fiscal ramifications play a big part in your project and token launch, so depending on which jurisdictions you'll be obliged to comply with, having a structural plan for this is imperative. Stating legal advice and even providing your legal opinion in full, both enhance your brand and image positively while laying out the Blueprint of just how everything will be set up in a legal friendly manner.

11) Team:

Of course, your lecturers will be impatient to see who's going to be executing on everything related to bringing your project to life. Now's the time to show them just that! Unlike your pitch deck, containing a brief bio of each member, here, you can unleash the horses and go all out on really explaining in prodigious depth the background, achievements and exceptional endeavors of each team member without holding back. The goal is to bring supreme confidence in your project through the supreme quality of your team. Be sure to input some nice, professional headshots of them attached to their detailed bios.

12) Acknowledgement:

Just like a book, there's always time and space for citing important individuals who helped and are helping you along your journey of launching your token. Quoting such individuals in your Whitepaper isn't only a sign of respect, but depending on their credibility, it can also bring further credibility to your entire project. As you've previously cited your team members, you need to put the spotlight on the individuals behind the scenes supplying you with technical or strategic advice, propelling your general concept to higher grounds. Be sure to mention them and their executive backgrounds.

13) References:

As one develops their Whitepaper, leveraging resources from valid sources, may they be from esteemed literature or the Internet, is preordained. Indulging in these assets can provide depth and further credibility to your document; however, plagiarism is never an option. As you pluck relevant information, it's your duty to cite the source not only for accuracy but also for integrity. Even if it requires filling up five pages just with names and hyperlinks, it's perfectly fine and will actually show the readers just how much research has gone into your work.

14) Authors Biographies:

Just because you're a founder or valuable member of the team doesn't necessarily translate into great writing skills, and that's fine. Outsourcing the crafting of such a document to a specialized entity (this can however prove costly), talented family member, or even professional copywriters is not uncommon. For it doesn't even have to be just one person or entity, it may be a consortium of them. Just be sure that the individual, entity, or group of individuals tasked with this mission have a refined background, as this segment is reserved for just that. It can either bring weight and confidence, or make the whole thing look amateurish.

15) Appendix:

Utilize this section to add deep materials supporting your general idea and concept. In short, your reference section is simply filled with names and hyperlinks, here you may add charts, graphics, entire research papers, theses, or books to back up your project. Generally speaking, it's preferred to inject some self-made charts and graphics through combining important data and analytics included in your paper. Also, take this opportunity to visually compare your project's value propositions with your competitor's, making your project's value propositions and market edge obvious to all, such as the chart below from AIWorlds (AI Worlds: No rules, no objective. Only adventure):

Comparison

	AI Worlds	AI Hero	AI Dungeon	The Sandbox
Scenarios driven by AI	✓	✓	✓	✗
Open World	✓	✗	✓	✓
Endless Scenarios	✓	✓	✓	✓
Voice Recognition	✓	✗	✗	✗
Available in messengers	✓	✗	✗	✗
Able to generate graphics	✓	✗	✗	✗

16) Glossary:

The final touch to your Whitepaper is the link between complex or not-so-often-used words you've included, and their definitions. As you're crafting away, be sure to keep a separate document close by at all times, so as soon as you write one glossary-worthy word down, you're able to enumerate it and jot it down alongside the definition and relative number on your separate document. Proceeding in this manner enables you to keep track of the words as you go along, making it hard to miss one while optimizing your time.

With the above order of segments, you have a versatile layout that should cover the content for the majority of Whitepaper creations. Another quick tip is to ask around from close friends and industry experts for constant feedback. Nevertheless, your Whitepaper literally is the blueprint of your project, so be careful with who you decide to share it with as it has happened in the past that the entire concept gets hijacked and peculated.

In the current world of crypto, it can be hard to prevent such malicious actions, especially due to the lack of policing. Furthermore, it can be even harder to prove you are actually the owner of such a document so it's always best to take a few precautions prior to sharing it, even with close friends. There's always a chance that they themselves may be the victims of a hack and your documents being leaked this way too. Although it may not prevent you from becoming the victim of your Whitepaper being stolen, it's best to keep a paper and digital trace starting from emailing the Whitepaper to yourself upon completion. This will at least provide you with an immutable digital timestamp that may undercut any claims from the pirates in a legal case as to who created it and when it was created. Secondly, sign Non-Disclosure Agreements (NDAs – Glossary 40) with any counterpart that will interact with your document during and after completion. Yes, even the individuals who will be assisting you to create it; you can never be too careful. Note that this will formally establish your collaboration on this piece together.

Of course, once your website is up and you're making your idea public, your Whitepaper will need to be made public too, and accessible to anybody who wishes to view it. Executing upon the two above steps will just provide you with some ammunition to defend yourself if ever the need occurs. Once you're ready to make your Whitepaper public, it's common practice to have a direct link to it on your website page. This will help centralize all information and generate organic traffic to your website as those who wish to review your document will be required to visit your website. You may also feature it in your GitHub if you're creating one.

Finally, prior to crafting your Whitepaper, I strongly encourage you to read at least once the most infamous Whitepaper of all. The paper at the origin of this incredible new technology we know as crypto: "Bitcoin : A Peer-to-Peer electronic cash system" by the legendary Satoshi Nakamoto, available for free on the web.

Segment 2 – What Is a Proof of Concept (POC – Glossary 41) and How to Develop One

At its core, a PoC is akin to the first spark of fire in the hands of our early ancestors. A Minimum Viable Product, on the other hand (MVP – Glossary 42), is the first fire created from that initial spark. The POC is the first of the two, demonstrating tangible potential, and a promise of warmth and light. In our case, it is the initial implementation of your cryptocurrency project, designed to demonstrate its feasibility and the viability of its underlying technology. Much like an embryo, it's a crucial stage of development, serving simultaneously as a litmus test for your project's foundational principles and the scaffolding against which your full-scale development can be erected.

To avoid ending up like Icarus in Greek mythology, you must validate your theory on all levels prior to leaping out of the window and spreading your wings. It's one thing for your wings to open and do the job in gentle flight conditions, it's another to stress test them against the violent winds and heat of a real token launch in the industry. A strong POC will help you build the solid foundations necessary to support future development without crashing later on down the line. Regardless of the nature, all projects will face scalability, security, and speed issues at a certain point down the line. By transforming research into evidence, you will validate your idea while creating the correct foundations to build upon, making your project a strong candidate for investment opportunities and a healthy future, further validating your vision.

During this trial-and-error period necessary to obtain the correct trajectory, your developers will be able to run simulations on the best formulas that will shape and mold your base technology from a consensus into a curated form, ready to handle scalability, cyberattacks, and swift data transfers. One may classify this time as an iterative process of creation which the constant testing and refinement will transform your initial concept and idea into a more tangible version. This is key to obtain traction with your community, also everything from this stage on will be built and designed based on these exact results. If your POC isn't curated in a serious manner, you may end up with a frail house of cards, ready to tumble at the slightest countercurrent after your launch. One must not forget that a large part of the crypto community has some knowledge in the basics of how the underlying technology works. Another reason to pay extra attention to the correct development of your POC is that some of your future investors and traders will know in an instant if your project is viable after they test it out themselves once it's in the MVP stage.

It's important to foster an early sense of culture through your POC also. It may be through the user onboarding, colors, graphics, rewards, or even the storyline. A sense of belonging through user engagement is a complexity that must start at the POC stage, allowing you to further expand and develop upon the engagement verticals already embedded within. Quality will also play a large part among your community. Within the first thirty seconds of exploring your product or services, they must get a sense of confidence and a clear vision as to what your project may become once fully developed. Keep in mind that a solid POC leads to a solid MVP and user adoption, hence, a solid and successful token launch.

Laying out a consensus of your fiscal and legal structures will also play a big part in your POC. You could have the best product in the world but if your company isn't compliant, it can be shut down faster than you can say "Please don't." Now you don't have to pay an expensive team of lawyers to create an ostentatious company structure. Seeking a legal opinion from one lawyer who is well-versed in the Web3 industry is more than enough to establish that your regulatory framework is viable. Not nailing this down during your POC stage can also infringe upon your chances of raising funds, so best to sort this out as soon as possible as it will also impact your TCS, exchanges to list on, Tokenomics, investors, and pretty much every single aspect moving forward.

As the proficiency of one's workmanship begins to devise a POC, naturally there are some mandatory steps which need to be followed to enhance the entire process. Ensuring your POC is designed correctly can play a big difference in the long run, with the effects trickling all the way down to your token launch and end product. Below you will find all of the mandatory steps required to make your POC a great foundation for just that (A Step-By-Step Guide To Writing A Proof of Concept (ccn.com)):

1) Goal:

>One of the best things you can do to kick start your POC development is to write down what you wish to exemplify. To cut a long story short, a great way of doing this is by getting straight to the point and summing up what you want it to do. For example, let's say that your project is a new concept to tokenize fidelity programs of hotels, you need to illustrate just how your use of the Blockchain, technical components, and token will do just that. Writing your goal down will help keep you on track. Every time you accomplish a new stage of your POC, a quick glance at your goal will indicate if the segment you've just developed is on target or misaligned. In the POC stage, developers can sometimes get carried away and create unnecessary parts. No matter how much they may adorn your project, the goal is to keep it simple and show that your POC does what it says on the tin.

2) Problem:

>By nature, businesses are designed to resolve a problem, the same goes for your project and token. Putting pen to paper here will bring further clarity to the developers as they are engineering your

product. Developers need to fully understand what problems you're trying to solve so they may create the exact technology that resolves that exact problem. Sometimes scopes of work just give a brief overview of what tech needs to be created, your developers will blindly create it. By giving them exceptional depth and a full understanding of not what but why you want to build this, they will find many different ways that could resolve the problem then pick the best one. Providing these details will ensure that your POC will solve the problem you're aiming to solve.

3) At this time, choosing your Blockchain is a must to enable the functionalities of your POC. One may choose their Blockchain by comparing the following criteria:

- Volume

- Number of users

- Hype

- Potential

- Scalability

- Security

- TPS (Transactions Per Second – Glossary 43)

- Interoperability

- Gas fees

- Regulatory serenity

- Decentralization

- Compatibility with your project's nature

- Facility to build

- Grants

- Support provided by the Blockchain to your project

4) Verticals:

   Your POC can't be the polished, final version with all
   the bells and whistles that go with it. This said, you
   need to choose which verticals you will have in your
   end product and plant those seeds. For instance, if
   your end product will have AI generated NFTs, an NFT
   launchpad and an NFT market place with a governance
   token, your POC should include a very small part of
   each. Every one of these needs to simply show it can do
   a very simple version of the end result, but enough of
   it is there to actually show what could be with further
   development. Starting small and simple, yet showing a
   little bit of everything is the best way to go.

5) Smart Contracts:

   Again, this isn't the end result so it doesn't have to
   have everything; however, it's recommended to use
   upgradable technology. Reason being that as you
   build your entire project, time will pass and new
   revolutionary technology will probably be available.
   If you build everything in an immutable fashion, the
   chances are that your entire tech stack may be obsolete
   or you may have simply just come across a more
   efficient version. By keeping your code upgradable,
   further on down the line you will be able to adopt new
   and superior technology instead of scrapping your
   entire tech stack to start afresh. Once your upgradable

smart contracts and code have been developed, make
sure that they will bring your POC to life, and that
everything works without bugs.

Independent of who or what entities are carrying out the development
work, be sure to stipulate in the contract that you own all of the code and
keys, even the parts still under development. The last thing you want
is to spend all of this time and money to find out that the development
company you hired defaulted or a rogue developer is holding the source
code you paid for hostage until you pay extra. It may seem far-fetched,
but you'd be surprised the number of individuals such travesties have
happened to. If possible, request the newly developed code be sent to
you at the end of every work day via email. This way, if something does go
south, you're only missing one page of code instead of thirty. Equipped
with 99% of your code, it will be far easier to ask another development
studio to finalize than for them to start from scratch.

Also, depending on your degree of funding, it can be a good option
to have your POC audited by a couple of reputable audit firms. The
reason why it's good to have audits from multiple firms simultaneously
is because nobody's perfect and more often than not, the audit firms
find different vulnerabilities. It is completely possible that one audit firm
finds completely different vulnerabilities than another, but misses the
ones found by the other auditors. Not using multiple audit firms can lead
to you building out your entire project from the ground up, then finding
out days before your token launch that you've just been hacked, messing
up your launchpad agreements, exchange listing contracts, and the
confidence of your hard-earned community. Simply using one audit firm
can actually crash your entire project before you've even had the time to
launch your token, as goes the old adage, better safe than sorry... When
you do approach auditors, again, don't get lost in the marketing mist as
the majority of tokens that crash have indeed been audited by the likes of
Certik and Hacken. Go for the smaller audit firms with a real background

in cybersecurity prior to them joining the Web3 realm. Not only will going with experienced, smaller size audit firms be more bespoke, they will pay more attention to your code during the audit, and they're likely to have real engineers actually going through your code line by line instead of some automated protocols. Just be sure to ask what they did before Web3 and don't be afraid to push them on this. Any serious auditing firm will be very proud to tell you their prior success cases with top banks or governments, for example. If they shy away from this question, it's probably because they have nothing relevant and more than likely were in the right place at the right time and raised a lot of money from this industry that they put into marketing, hence becoming "experts."

Finally, don't take shortcuts. As we've learnt, your POC is the rock for everything else you'll build from this stage onwards. Take the necessary time to make sure it works without bugs and that every main vertical is visible. Remember, the goal is to show investors that it's technically possible to transform your idea into a reality!

Segment 3 – What Is an MVP and How to Develop It

Following suit, the next logical step you'll need to take after successfully creating your POC is creating your MVP. Akin to your final product, this fundamental component will be the housing structure (MVP) placed upon your rock (POC). In short, it's a compromise between your POC and final product that may be open to your community to try and test. To elucidate, if you're building a GameFi project, your MVP could be an almost fully functioning game without the token, some players, maps, skins, or rewards; however, you can fully play it. Not only is an MVP a demonstration of your hard work and dedication, it gives every single person with an Internet connection the possibility to try out your base product or service. This will provide you with direct feedback, enabling you to tweak your product or service as you go along, rather than polishing an element that may not be to the liking of your community. It's also a physical portrait of your goals and vision, helping further align interests with your community and needs.

The importance of having a perfect MVP is capital to really engage your community, transform future flippers into users and holders of your token, while reassuring investors. Yes, one of the main objectives of your MVP is to optimize your chances of raising funds. Seldom will investors allocate funds to a very early-stage project. A great MVP will not only show investors and VCs that you have more than just a pitch deck, it will also enable them to immerse themselves in your project, helping them understand what you're building. It's far easier for them to comprehend the full spectrum of your project by experiencing it themselves first hand, rather than through reading a document.

Of course, prior to having a fine-tuned MVP ready to be shown to the world, you must start with the foundation of your POC and work your way up from there. The goal is to make your MVP available for public use so they can see, experience, and witness what you've been building. The community you've nurtured since day one needs to feel reassured and confident enough to stick with you and become investors themselves. If your MVP isn't up to their expectations, the result could be devastating, leading to the demise of your project as your community will stop engaging and create negative press, not all publicity is good publicity. Far too often MVPs don't provide the expected value and often are a very low-quality version with far too many features not necessarily of a high standing, coupled with poor UI/UX. All of which leaves a sour taste in the mouths of users besides a lackluster impression.

One of the main wrongdoings during the development of the MVP is trying to create the final product. Again, this is the Minimum Viable Product, which means that it should bring your project to life only relying on the minimum technology stack and features. Like with anything in life, the perfect end result is never achieved without going through stages of change, including trial and error. Your MVP is just that, it will enable you to gather feedback from users, investors, and community members, helping you tweak until you've found the perfect market fit. This is also an occasion to interact with your community and let them take part in shaping the product through voting, tasks, or other activities.

As your MVP will be the first segment of your project available to the public, it's wise to explore some of the main mistakes made, prior to engaging on how to structure the MVP itself. (5 Common Mistakes to Avoid When Designing an MVP for Crypto Projects | HackerNoon, 7 Dangerous Mistakes to Avoid When Building an MVP : r/Vechain (reddit.com), 5 Common Mistakes To Avoid When Building Your MVP (f22labs.com)). Below you'll find some of the most common mistakes to avoid at all costs as you undertake this task:

Mistake 1) Features:

More often than not, MVPs are overloaded with features that aren't yet relevant. On top of confusing users, seldom are they of great quality. Your MVP isn't supposed to have all of the amazing features of a polished end product, hence the acronym MVP. Another problem with adding more features than necessary is that it takes valuable development time away from your engineers that they could use to enhance the main features. This can lead to confusion instead of making your main requirements of far greater quality and efficiency.

Mistake 2) Speed:

Here we have somewhat of a double-edged sword as your community will want the release of your MVP as soon as possible; however, the speed of the release must not be prioritized over quality. Much like waiting in a restaurant for your order to arrive, you don't want

121

to wait one hour. However, if it comes out of the kitchen five minutes after you placed your order, the quality probably won't be great as anything of value takes time to create. You must be able to juggle not just with these two components for your MVP but also the security. Leaving the cybersecurity aspect to be implemented just before the launch of your product and token can lead to fatal repercussions as your MVP will indeed be available to the public. Once your MVP is live, it can also be a target of cyberattacks.

Mistake 3) Technology:

Even if your POC was crafted with great care, the new code and technology you will be integrating can still lead to big problems. Often, you will be integrating some third-party solutions or building everything in-house, regardless of which road you'll be taking; make sure that the entire technology stack is interoperable and works. Go for the best quality and try to make sure that every new integration is upgradable and can be modified further on down the line. You may find that after constant tweaking prior to the final MVP, some of the tech either isn't up to scratch, or simply just not needed. If you've developed everything in-house, the price to pay will be time you could have allocated elsewhere; if you've used a third party, the price to pay may be being locked in a contract that you can't get out of.

Mistake 4) UI/UX:

One of the worst omnipresent mistakes in the development of MVPs is the neglect of the UI/UX. This may not seem very important if all of your tech stack works, nonetheless it is in fact just as important. If you've been able to create fantastic tech but the design and feel isn't up to scratch, the overall user experience can be excruciating. Depending on the nature of your project and target clientele, you will have to create the matching environment. If you're going to be a Real-World Asset (RWA – Glossary 44) marketplace, supposedly you will need to focus on easy onboarding and usage for non-crypto native individuals plus a chic high-end design. Without this your target community will struggle using it while not adhering to your proposed culture.

Mistake 5) Team:

You may have a fantastic CTO who used to work at Google as an engineer; this doesn't mean that he's the right person to help design the UI/UX of the MVP. You may have a fantastic CMO who used to work at Nike in the marketing division; it doesn't mean she's the right person to give a hand on the cybersecurity component. The same goes for your developers or outsourced development firm. Just because they're very good at one thing, they shouldn't be helping outside of their respective jurisdictions. A poor end result easily results from this free-for-all approach. There's nothing more expensive than trying to save some money in the wrong place at the wrong time.

Now we've acknowledged the main mistakes to avoid during the creation of your MVP, it's time to explore the necessary ingredients to build it correctly. Of course, the goal is to create a slick and functional MVP, sexy enough for users to enjoy, and functional enough for investors to comprehend the full ambit of your project's potential. Subsequently, it's only right that we now explore these noteworthy sections one should include in their MVP, to help obtain those exact results. (Guide to Building a Crypto Project MVP | by Rock'n'Block | Medium):

1) Services:

The value proposition of your business must be underlined and obvious to anyone using your MVP. Be that resolving a problem you're aiming to solve, creating the next best shooter game or bringing traceability to a supply chain. The user must be able to experience and understand that your product does exactly what it says on the tin. Firstly, focus on enhancing your POC by scaling the components directly linked with your end goal. For example, if your project is designed to bring traceability to the supply chain of coffee beans around the world, do the business development and partner with some coffee bean suppliers in different places around the world and start onboarding their data. Secondly, partner up with a handful of entities from each of the other segments of that supply chain, including middle men, traders, distributors, and resellers and obtain relative data too.

2) Features:

Following the above example, be sure to create the mechanisms that will allow you to transform the collected data into real analytics and facts you wish to communicate in your end product. In short, it's important to show that your core product actually works. Again, it doesn't need to do anything fancy at this stage, you just need to have some tangible and functional use cases that anyone can try at any time of the day and have no issues. Scalability and upgradability are a core focus here as they can cause quite some pain later on if some thought hasn't already gone into it. Technical preparation and some technical integrations are necessary at this stage to prepare your project for hundreds of thousands of users once your final project is launched. You must demonstrate that your project is ready for serious scalability.

3) Security:

In the realm of cryptocurrency, there aren't police officers waiting around corners to help projects in distress. The same may be said for lawyers and insurance companies. In this industry, the only protection you have is your code. State the importance of this every single morning to your developers or outsourced development house. If you have a CTO, make this their top priority. Once your MVP is ready to go live, have it audited by multiple audit firms, as you did with the POC. You will have modified, added, and removed some parts of code, creating new vulnerabilities. Any company seeking millions of dollars in market cap should be able to allocate appropriate funding to this as like we said in the beginning of this segment, if something goes wrong, you can't go to the local police station. When you get hacked in this industry during your early days, it usually means game over.

4) UI/UX:

Making sure that your website has a lush look and a seamless user interface are key components to your users' experience, no matter how great your product is. We've all been there before, trying to connect to something on the Internet and it not working properly, or simply landing on a cheap looking website and thinking it may be a scam. These are just some of the many reasons why your UI/UX need to be impeccable. The nicer it will look, the more reassured your community will be in the quality; the easier it will be to navigate throughout your website and/or platform, the more comfortable your community will be exploring the features. If all of the above are optimized, it will translate into a longer stay time by users on your website and/or platform. At the end of the day, the more time someone spends on something, the more susceptible they are to buy the product.

5) Onboarding:

It's one thing having a great tech stack, service, product, and even UI/UX, but if nobody can access it, all will be in vain. The onboarding mechanisms can range from targeted social log-ins such as enabling users to connect using a social login they're familiar with like Kakao for the Asian market, Steam for the gaming community, TikTok for the new generation, or even the classic old email address for the more mature community members, to wallet integrations, KYC, and digital identity management. You must simplify and tailor the entire onboarding process in order to obtain the highest conversion rate and numbers of users. If it becomes even remotely challenging, that individual is only a click away from exiting your website. It's actually easy to get an idea of your conversion rate. Simply by knowing how many people are in your socials and how many visits to your website you have per day, it gives you a delta of which the goal is to get to zero. For example, if you have 100,000 people in your social following, and you have around 60,000 users per day, you have a delta of 40,000. What many founders don't know is that individuals in your socials can easily become dormant. If one of them tried to log in to your project and struggled, they can simply exit your website page and turn off the notifications of your group in his Telegram. In your eyes, that individual is still part of your community, but because something went wrong at one point, they'll never buy your token, product, or service. Make the onboarding so easy and fast that before they know it, they're already signed up and using your product.

CHAPTER 7

Raising Funds

Segment 1 – Types of Investors in This Space

The crypto industry boasts many advantages when it comes to fundraising. Since Bitcoin went mainstream around 2013 (A timeline of bitcoin's history: Bitcoin turns 10 (yahoo.com)) thanks to the media shining a spotlight on companies deciding to accept Bitcoin as a method of payment, the industry has remarkably evolved. As you take a look back at the evolution building up to 2024, you'll notice that even the tokens being launched have dramatically changed too. Take Reddcoin for example, one of the first socialFi tokens that launched in February 2014 (About Reddcoin - Reddcoin Wiki) it was a simple token, on a simple Blockchain destined just to be sent to others as a form of social tipping. The majority of tokens that launched in the early days didn't really have a lot of utility, the goal was just to create a token and align it with a very basic narrative.

One may even reminisce to the simplistic and pragmatic approach of these early days, as tokens have since stepped away from being very simple with no core product. In recent years, tokens went from being just a token with a narrative, to a token with a narrative and some use cases thanks to the boom of ICOs and vesting in 2017 to the development of staking around 2020. For a short period, this was enough for the "use cases" of your token. Anon after this, use cases of tokens started to bloom as staking

© Alexander Rees-Evans 2024
A. Rees-Evans, *How to Launch a Token*, https://doi.org/10.1007/979-8-8688-0533-2_7

and vesting simply weren't enough anymore. Adding a real core business and value proposition to your token became the norm, opening the door for real businesses trying to raise funds through tokenization. These real-world businesses started to take advantage of the token model and simply fractionalized ownership of their company or future profits. Holding these tokens would grant you a piece of a real company and/or their profits. This model soon became omnipresent in the space as more and more entrepreneurs from the analog world started to leverage Blockchain technology, offering a new, diverse investment opportunity with a very different level of risk/reward and scalability potential. Around 2021, yet another wave of utility swept the banks of tokenization. Apart from meme coins, it's no longer possible to have just a token, a narrative, staking, vesting, and a potential to distribute rewards from your company's profits. Nowadays you need to have a core product and value proposition for your token. As an example, your token must have a narrative, staking, vesting (always good to have vesting to reduce selling pressure), profit share, and utility either inside or outside of your project.

Your token utility is one of the most scrutinized components of your entire project. If investors don't understand it or feel the token utility isn't strong enough, they will simply pass up the investment opportunity. It's always best to start small, then work your way up the investment ladder because different investors have different criteria. There are also levels and stages of which different categories of investors are only interested in too. Knowing the types of investors and criteria can not only accelerate your investment rounds but also more or less guarantee you do actually raise funds. Yes, as the parameters of tokens have evolved, so have the investors. Maybe some years ago you could indeed approach any investor with a Pitch deck and a plan in the hope of raising funds, today, the investors probably wouldn't even get on a call with you to discuss. Not only has the criteria to be eligible to raise funds become more stringent but the pool of investors in this space has also matured and structured itself immensely.

If you just approach any investor at any old stage of your project's raise, seldom will it be fruitful. For this reason, the following content will guide you

Due to this hyper-evolution, a myriad of investors have entered this space, all with different goals, profiles, and investment styles, ranging from Angel investors (Glossary – 46), Venture Capitalists (VCs) (Glossary – 47) all the way up to institutional investors such as Fidelity or Blackrock. Much as a seasoned fisherman, you must learn which type of investors you should approach, and when to approach them. If you cast your line with an inappropriate lure in the middle of the ocean, even if there are huge fish, they'll never bite. However, if you start in a small pond with the same lure, you're more than likely to catch a small fish. Once you've caught your first one, you can use it as bait for the bigger fish until you work your way up to trophy fish. In our case, by catching a few angel investors, then a lead investor, the bigger investors will be enticed to follow suit, hence making your entire fundraising process much easier, quicker, and powerful.

Prior to learning what equipment is needed and how to cast your line, let's delve into the specific types of investors and their unique characteristics by order of approach:

1) Friends and Family:

At the beginning of any start-up, you need some money to start transforming your idea into a tangible reality. Often this is an opportunity for you to reach out to close friends and relatives for some early support. These investments are purely based on personal relationships and trust rather than extensive due diligence. Friends and family investors can also offer valuable feedback before reaching out to professional investors and potentially missing opportunities due to lack of readiness. You only get one chance to make a first impression, and when speaking with investors of any type, this couldn't be more true. In short, this particular round of investment can be crucial in your very early stages to help gain initial traction as depending on your friends and family, you can get anywhere from US$2,000 to over US$100,000. It's completely possible to even create a special round in your tokenomics with unique vesting and cliff periods for them.

2)   Angel Investors:

The first professional investors when you start your quest of fundraising are in this category. Angels provide capital for startups in their very early stages before any big money is raised or you're backed by a reputable investor. These investors are usually high net worth individuals and invest their own money rather than funds from others. In the realm of crypto, Angel investors generally made their money through trading, got in early on a successful project, or simply made a great financial exit from a previous endeavor. Due to their backgrounds, they can offer valuable mentorship, connections, and expertise to the startups they invest in. It's important to note that they can invest in multiple startups simultaneously, thus meaning their initial capital is heavily spread among all of them. Angels can invest anywhere from US$10,000 to US$100,000 in a single project, although the average ticket size is around US$30,000. As you're raising funds from this category of investors, it's good to target as many as possible to obtain around 10% of your first initial raise depending on your parameters.

3) Crowdfunders:

This particular type of funding has become very popular over the years, even in the traditional world of finance thanks to platforms such as "GoFundMe," "Patreon," or the infamous "Kickstarter." One of the beauties of the world of crypto is the demonstrative power of community. Previously we learnt that the larger and more engaged your community will be, the more successful your token launch will be. It is completely possible to leverage a portion of your community beforehand so that you may fundraise. For example, if you already have a few thousand followers or are able to build a large community thanks to some strategic marketing or KOLs before you've raised funds from investors, you can host a pre-sale event for them. By providing the opportunity to your early followers to buy your future tokens with preferential terms, not only will they feel special, they will become your brand advocates, spreading the word as their incentives are now aligned with yours, making your token successful. Creating this snowball effect can not only get anywhere from US$1000 to US$1,000,000 in your bank, it can also help further grow and establish your community. The only complexity is that your community must still have an appetite to buy your tokens once they're listed and tradable, not just sell them so there's a delicate balance to put in place between raising funds and maintaining high buying pressure from your community once your token is tradable.

4) Lead Investors:

Finding appropriate lead investors is one of the most prudent and strategic decisions you'll make on your fundraising journey. Depending on their reputation, they can make your entire fundraising process much easier. It is for curating these investors that you must spend the most time. Finding which ones are the most respected in the industry, which ones can help you with introductions to other bigger investors, while not requiring you to modify your tokenomics too much. Oft, they adopt a proactive posture in organizing and leading investment rounds and are the first major investors you can hope for. Compared to friends and family investors, or even an Angel investor, lead investors do conduct due diligence, negotiate terms, and coordinate with other investors. They can also ask to modify your go-to-market strategy, your business model, token utility, and much more. Sometimes it can be for their benefit such as shorter vesting periods, etc. However, if they're advising to modify segments of your business, generally speaking, the major investors above them will require similar modifications. It's important to find a balance with smart trade-offs for both parties but at the end of the day, they're the ones with the money, so be graceful during negotiations.

They can invest anywhere from US$50,000 to US$300,000.

5) Venture Capitalists:

VC firms are the most dominant sources of large investments into individual projects in this space as they invested a whopping US$33 billion into projects in 2021 (Report: VCs Invested $33 billion in Crypto and Blockchain Startups in 2021 – Blockworks!) Leveraging pools of money from various sources, such as pension funds, endowments, and wealthy individuals, they are the structured money flow in this industry. They typically invest in exchange for equity and/or tokens while aiming for significant returns. Prior to investing, they perform a deep due diligence and may want to restructure your tokenomics, among other segments. If you've managed to secure a reputable lead investor, the potential modifications from VCs should be minor. Again, since VCs are investing anywhere from US$200,000 to US$20,000,000, they often take a seat on the board of your company to monitor progress and provide strategic guidance to make sure your project is a success. Finally, they have a portfolio approach, investing in multiple startups with the expectation that some will fail, but others will generate high returns, hence covering their losses and making high profits.

6) Institutional Investors:

As the crypto industry matures, the interests of traditional entities such as hedge funds, pension funds, and banks are becoming more and more involved. Blackrock, Fidelity, and others have not only taken a firm stance on their interest within the blockchain industry but are actively participating! Deutsche Bank has started tokenizing, Société Générale has launched their own stablecoin and Blackrock has not only started tokenizing but they've invested in Web3 projects plus pioneered the BTC ETF. Although the goals of such institutions are far different than the majority of degens, they are important to our ecosystem. These types of investors can place any sum of money they want, easily superseding the power and influence of VCs. If you're from the traditional corporate world and have connections, this may actually be the best place to start your fundraise. Now, although they do invest large sums of money on behalf of their clients or shareholders, their investment criteria and due diligence processes can be far more stringent and longer than VCs. If you do have the connections, involvement from such entities can bring far more than just funds, as credibility and stability will echo from their involvement, resonating through your project into the entire Web3 ecosystem.

7) Launchpads:

Completely unique to the crypto industry, this endemic tool made popular by Binance in 2019 revolutionized the entire concept of fundraising in the Web3 space. Launchpads do exactly what they say they do, they're a pad for launching tokens before your tokens are tradable on an exchange. Today's launchpads are no longer exclusive and some entities have specialized just in doing that one thing, such as Seedify or Enjinstarter. Such launchpads do, however, require investors to buy and stake their native tokens to buy tokens that are using their launchpad. For projects wishing to launch their tokens on their launchpad, they can sometimes charge an up-front fee but always take around 10% of the funds raised. All sounds reasonable from afar, however, they can have some very harsh terms such as refund policies if you're not able to keep your token price above a certain number for several days once your token is tradable. Adding to this complexity is the fact that you don't get your funds straight away, you can't use them until all conditions are met. Finally, the communities of launchpads are only interested in making quick profits so will likely sell the tokens they bought from you as soon as they're able to. Depending on the launchpad you can raise anywhere from US$50,000 to US$500,000, but all will be potential gradual selling pressure; it's better to think of using a launchpad like applying for a loan, you will have to pay the funds back with some interest over time. It's best to use one or two tier-one launchpads for small ticket sizes such as US$100,000 each purely to obtain the hype and attention from them. At the end of the day, you want the buyers of your tokens to hold and keep buying, not to buy low then sell high as will the community of launchpads.

Segment 2 – How to Approach These Investors

After reviewing the many intricacies of the diverse investors and fundraisers in Web3, it's now time to understand how and when to approach them. Using the fisherman analogy, we know what fish exist and which fish we need, but what lures do we use? What ponds, rivers, or oceans do we cast our line in? And equally as important, what season and time of day?

First of all, you need to structure your fundraising process by correlating raise tranches with your tokenomics like we touched upon in Chapter 3 of this book. Now, we will delve into the more complex segment of crafting your fundraising rounds based on the following example of the need to raise US$3,000,000 and your token price on the day of listing will be US$0.05:

1) Pre-seed Round:

   – Percentage of the total fundraise: 7% (US$210,000)

   – Discount per token from initial launch price: 50%(US$0.025)

   – Types of investors: Friends and family, Angel investors, Lead investors

   This is the first fundraising round you must fill. Besides a potential small friends and family round, the earliest real stage of fundraising for your project, typically before the product or service is fully developed is pre-seed. The goal of pre-seed funding is to develop a prototype, conduct market research, and validate the business idea. Usually, the friends and family round is a small reserved portion of this Pre-seed round, even if in some rare cases they may differ slightly. This is the first round you will need to fill by targeting friends, family, and angel investors. They're incentivized to buy in early at this stage by a large discount from the listing price of your tokens. Try not to make the discount more than half of the initial launch price so they don't sell immediately. For example, if you give them a discount of 500%, regardless of your efforts, they will sell at every chance possible to gain 500% on their initial investment. If they only get a 50% discount, they're at a small win, but will most likely not sell all the time in exchange for better price action and more profitable sales in the future.

Steps to Find Friends and Family Investors:

Regardless of your upbringing, everyone is connected somehow. If you're from a wealthy family, you simply need to enquire with the money manager of the family about investments. If you're from any other type of family, don't be afraid to ask your well-known relatives, brothers, sisters, parents, grandparents, cousins, and close friends. If not successful, ask your relatives and friends if they know of anyone with a business or entrepreneurial background in your distant relatives. Keep on doing this until you've found someone who can help.

Steps to Find Angel Investors:

I know I've said this before but having a paid LinkedIn account really can be a great way to connect in a formal fashion with anyone around the world at any given time. By curating your key words in the search bar such as "Crypto investor," "Angel investor," "Early stage investor," among others, you'll open the door to a copious sundry of potential investors.

Secondly, connect with project founders who successfully raised their rounds and simply ask them if they can connect you with any. If you ask one hundred founders who successfully raised funds, you're bound to get some introductions to Angel investors and maybe some valuable feedback along the way!

Steps to Find Lead Investors:

Once you've secured some Angel funding and have a working product, you may join an incubator or accelerator to help secure your lead investor. It's also possible to simply ask your Angel investors or industry relations to help connect you with some. LinkedIn can work but lead investors are typically represented by companies so it's preferable to focus on leveraging your network here.

2) Seed Round:

– Percentage of the total fundraise: 15% (US$450,000)

– Discount per token from initial launch price: 40%(US$0.03)

– Types of investors: Angel investors. lead investors, crowdfunders, VCs, institutional investors

Once your pre-seed round has been filled and you have a good lead investor on board, you can start filling your seed round. However, if your pre-seed round was filled without a lead investor, that's perfectly fine also, but now you need to focus on securing one. Once your lead investor is on board, you may focus on getting some VC and/or institutional backing. If the market conditions aren't great, it may be worth forgetting the above and just focus on building a community then raise your required funds through a community sale. As you can see, the discount of the token price is slightly less than the previous round entitled "Pre-seed." This is designed to promote and incentivize the new investors to start investing now as the token price will continue to rise and they may miss out on a lucrative opportunity. It also reassures your early investors in their investment decision as they're now already making hypothetical profits.

How to Find Crowdfunders:

If you've already built a community of over 50,000 people strong, you have a very good chance of having a successful raise from your community. In order to build up to these numbers, you may need to use some of the funds raised from your Pre-seed round to hire specialized companies to help build up your community. Cross-marketing and co-marketing activities with partners can also help expand your internal community. Leveraging your KOLs, marketing agencies, and team's social media accounts can be a good way to start too. Another trick is simply to tag trending Hashtags on every one of your social media posts to try and attract more organic users. SEOs and other growth hacking areas can be useful to target too. Once you've obtained at least 20,000 organic followers across your social media accounts, you can start promoting your crowd fundraise.

How to Find VCs:

As usual, LinkedIn can be one way, but conferences and crypto events may be good options too. By attending in-person events, you'll be sure to find some VCs you can grab a coffee with. Another way is by asking your industry connections and investors to make some warm introductions as well. Finally, if you are struggling in this segment, it may be worth joining an accelerator, incubator, or even paying a specialized entity to help with this.

How to Find Institutional Investors:

Raising funds through "old money" for your crypto project can reveal itself to be very tricky if you don't already have a background or high-level connections with institutional investors such as Blackrock. If you're really eager to go after funds from this sector and aren't yet connected with them, you need to build a relationship with individuals who are. By your own business development efforts, networking or LinkedIn, find someone who works in a relative department in one of these institutional firms and focus on building a relationship with them. This may take some time, but once they're comfortable enough, you can indirectly pitch your project to them, and if they can help, they will try.

3) Community Round

– Percentage of the total fundraise: 20% (US$600,000)

– Discount per token from initial launch price: 20%(US$0.04)

– Types of investors: Angel investors, crowdfunders

Now you have completed your pre-seed and seed rounds, you need to raise your community round. This is a round designed to obtain funds from your community in exchange for providing preferential token prices to the participants. Even though third parties propose hosting these sales for you, it's preferred to avoid all forms of custodian risk, security risk, technology risk, regulation risk, and scam risk. If you send your community to someone else's shop and they default, your community can easily lose faith in you.

Be sure to host the community round by your own means on your own website with DDOS protection. The last thing you want is for a hacker to take down your website during the sale then blackmail you for money in exchange for putting your website back up. Once your community sale page is up and running, creating an embedded referral link for participants can be a plus too so as to incentivize and enhance community engagement. With regard to the discount of the token compared to the actual listing price, try to keep it around 20%. The goal is to allow early believers in your social following to buy your tokens with a slight discount so they feel like they're getting a good deal, but not too good a deal so they'll sell as soon as possible. It's important to note that depending on the size and engagement of your community, let a maximum of only 30% of them participate in your pre-sale so the remaining 70% will provide buying pressure on the day of your launch. As for ticket sizes, they mustn't be too high either. If they're too high, a few people could buy up the monopoly and create problems when they're able to sell, plus, the majority of your community won't have the budget to participate. It's good to keep a minimum ticket size of around US$200 and a maximum of US$2000 depending on the type of community you have. If the majority of your community is from a developing country like the Philippines, you may even want to drop the lowest ticket size to US$50 or less, so more people can participate. You'll need to decide to go for small tickets from a very large community, or larger tickets from a very small community, or try to find a balance in the middle.

4) KOL Round:

  – Percentage of the total fundraise: 13% (US$390,000)

  – Discount per token from initial launch price: 20%(US$0.04)

  – Types of investors: Angel investors, crowdfunders

The final round of your private fundraising rounds is your KOL round. In short, you provide the opportunity to as many influential and relevant KOLs as possible to purchase your tokens with an approximate 20% discount prior to your launch. The goal is to get as many KOLs as possible to partake in this round, and the smaller the maximum ticket size, the better. As an example, instead of having 10 KOLs buy up all of the round, you could have 130 KOLs buy US$3000 worth of tokens each and the publicity would be far greater! Now of course you can negotiate the ticket sizes and more, but the goal is to have as many KOLs as possible, with the same incentive as yourself, to make the token price grow. It's important to target KOLs who actually engage with your type of client/buyer also, if not, it can just be a big marketing miss. If you have a blockchain European football game project, working with a Japanese KOL specialized in Manga promotions probably won't work very well. Be sure to spend some time curating your KOLs and checking their real past results, not just some hype and buzz words. As you approach KOLs, some of them may have very big egos and even request free tokens or for you to pay them, beware, the majority of KOLs doing this doesn't and won't care about your project. Try to align interests, community, and goals.

Combined, the four above rounds compose what is commonly known as your "Private round." Of course you can add, remove, or modify some rounds under your Private round; however, the above cases build a real and tangible fundraising structure that would work for almost any project once tweaked. In our example case, out of the US$3,000,000 our project is looking to raise, 55% will be raised through the private round. The remaining 45% will be raised through the "Public round" from ICOs using tools like launchpads, etc.

When your fundraising structure is complete, you'll need to abide by the simple rules of "don't run before you can walk." Speaking with big investors and raising millions of dollars quickly may be enticing, yet you must build your project up enough prior to engaging with them. Thousands of projects try to raise funds every day, investment opportunities aren't what's missing. On the other hand, safe and solid investment opportunities have become scarce over the years and this is what will make the difference between a founder with an idea pitching to a saturated investor, and an investor sending you a message in Telegram asking if he can discuss investment opportunities with you. If your project is made as attractive as possible, your pitch perfectioned, tokenomics up with the trends, have built a large community, some fundraising traction and active announcements on all of your social media accounts, word of your project will promulgate. This doesn't mean that you shouldn't reach out to each type of investor at the appropriate stages, but if you build a solid project with traction, they can reach out to you. Put yourself in this most favorable position by maximizing efforts in the early stages of your fundraising venture and partnering up with big names and brands. The more attractive you'll be, the easier it will be.

Segment 3 – How to Manage Your Funds

No token launch can be a success in today's crypto market without sufficient funding. The golden days of being able to launch with little to no funds is virtually impossible as the market beholds so many other tokens aspiring to launch and raise funds. It goes without saying that a well-funded project will always have the upper edge. Acquiring sufficient funds is actually one of the most accurate indicators if your project will be prosperous or not. Building your MVP, hiring a top tier team, liquidity provisions, marketing, infrastructure costs, travel expenses, organizing events, Market Making to listing on exchanges, everything costs money.

Imagine a brand new, top-of-the-line Aston Martin car engineers spent years developing and designers crafting, a marvelous piece of technology, rivalling the most prestigious of cars on all levels. However, it can't leave the showroom without fuel. Even if it's capable of incredible feats, it's completely useless without a full tank of gas. The same may be said about your project. You may have a revolutionary idea, but it can never leave your mind without funding. Sufficient funding can make the difference on many levels, with a general cost of about half a million dollars (not taking into consideration your runway or project development cost), depending on the cost of your MVP. First of all, a good marketing campaign can easily cost anywhere from US$200,000 to over a few million dollars. Community building gravitates around US$50,000, the tokenization and cyber security aspects can cost a few hundred thousand dollars and listings in a good tier 2 to tier 3 centralized exchange goes anywhere from US$50,000 to half a million dollars depending on the market conditions, relationship, and negotiations which we'll explore in chapter 10 of this book. Raising adequate funds can even help with the very survival of your project and token. Yes indeed, you heard me, if a bear market hits and 90% of your clients stop paying for a year or two, your treasury needs to be very strong, we call this your "runway" (Glossary 45).

In short, your runway usually consists of 12–18 months' worth of funds (Runway: What is it, types, calculation and formula, why track it (sturppy. com)) and the following formula will provide you with an accurate version:

Available funds/monthly burn rate = Runway

One of the easiest ways to manage your runway is by creating a simple Excel spreadsheet taking into consideration every month for the next 12–18 months and jotting down the following information in your project management sheet with the months for the columns, and your segment titles in the rows:

1) Available Funds:

It goes without saying that it's not because you initially raised US$5,000,000 that you will always have those funds available to spend. Every time you make a purchase or pay salaries, your funds will slowly start to diminish. You need to note down what your initial raise was, then create a new column for every month for at least two years. In each row, a projection of your new available funds should be calculated by subtracting the monthly costs such as salaries and basic expenses. The remaining funds will be your available funds. However, this doesn't mean that you can spend them as you will need to reserve the majority of these funds for future predetermined expenses. It's useful to fill up as many months as possible in advance so you can see if you're on track with your previsions as you go along. If not, you have the possibility to compare the data and adapt your entire strategy accordingly.

2) Spare Funds:

Much different from your available funds, this row will tell you what funds you actually have to spare. For instance, think of your available funds as a gross, and your spare funds as a net, they're what's left over after you've covered all necessary expenses and obligations. You can actually use them on whatever you want, be that expanding your team, opening a new office, purchasing company cars, buying first-class flight tickets instead of coach etc. To calculate your spare funds, you must simply add your monthly profits to your monthly available funds. You're free to withhold on spending your monthly spare funds and carry them into the next month to create a bigger pool for a larger purchase, or simply transfer them to your available funds to build up more runway and treasury if you feel the market sentiment is changing.

3) Salaries:

As your company will evolve and adapt to different market conditions, your salary expenses will follow suit. In a Bull run, you may wish to triple your sales team, but in a Bear market, reduce it by half to save expenses. Regardless of the direction you take, your salary row content will fluctuate over time. It's necessary to keep track of such expenses so you may correlate your salaries with profits also. If you just hired another ten individuals, are you making more money, or are they costing you more? Are they streamlining your business process, or are they complicating it? Of course, keeping an eye on your salaries is necessary to calculate your available funds, hence impacting all of your other rows and columns.

4) Basic Expenses:

Whether you're hiring a team of digital nomads or going big with a luxury office in Dubai, you will have some inevitable related costs. Your basic expenses cover everything from your professional phone bill to Wi-Fi, even the communication tools and every other necessity to make your business operational. You could classify your basic expenses as all of the primary monthly expenses that are tax deductible, or, if worse came to worst, your company would be functional on this bare minimum. When calculating your basic expenses, be sure to add the cost of every single essential monthly component you need to make your business run, from electricity to your office rent.

5) Extra Expenses:

Behind all crypto projects is a business. Behind all businesses are unexpected expenses, ranging anywhere from purchasing a replacement laptop, employee leave or sickness all the way to extra nights in a hotel due to a cancelled flight from a conference. Often, you'll have to use funds to cover an unanticipated event of which you need to account for in your project management sheet. For this row, simply add all of your business-related unexpected expenses together. It may not be as pen-worthy a row as the others, nonetheless, it's better to have it and not need it, than need it and not have it. Implementing this column from day one will provide further clarity to your project management sheet further on down the line. As these expenses can't be anticipated, this column's usually filled as you go along.

6) Technical Development:

Seldom will your core product be scaled to its fullest extent once your token is launched. Nor will your token be an autarkic marvel, set free to never be touched again. Once your token is launched, it's only the start of your venture and this of course requires a carefully crafted roadmap of future development for both your core product, and your token. Perhaps you've announced the creation of a marketplace five months after your token is live, maybe you've promised your community to list your token on Binance one year after your initial launch, or maybe, you need to fork your token as the Blockchain you launched on will be shut down by the SEC next quarter. Some of these later stage technical developments may be anticipated, however, nine months down the line, their costs may have changed due to a better market sentiment, hence all developers are now charging more per hour. It's important to keep bandwidth facing such changes, as they're simply beyond your power and inevitable. For the non-expected technical developments, they don't quite fit into the "Extra expenses" category as they may not be an immediate expense and do provide you with some time to anticipate the change. This column must take into consideration all of the anticipated developments that you may have from day one, or may pop up out of the blue half a year down the line. Once you're sure of the date the technical development must occur, feel free to note it down in advance for that particular month. Doing this will provide you with a helicopter view of all technical development and a timeline of cost, so you may calculate a saving plan to cover the development cost.

7) Event Costs:

One of the main places to connect with prospects and partners is at crypto events around the globe. From Token 2049 to BTC Miami, all of the major "need to know" industry leaders will be there and potential clients besides. All serious projects must attend at a minimum the main ones. You can simply attend with a basic ticket, rent a booth to promote your project and token, or even organize a lavish side event to entertain clients and partners! Be that as it may, every single option has a cost starting from your travel, stay, all the way up to food expenses. Within this column, all of the anticipated expenses need to be injected prior to departing so you may prevision a budget. If you know for sure which conferences you wish to attend in a year, it is indeed possible to integrate the anticipated expenses for each and every one of them in the appropriate month columns. Once you've returned home, replacing the initial jotted down expenses with the actual expenses is a must. This way you can keep track accurately of your spending and remaining funds, enabling you to tweak your budgets for future conferences and events.

8) Liquidity Provisions:

Liquidity provisions can have many definitions depending on the context; in our case, we're talking about liquidity provisions for your market-making activities. Some market makers often do an enticing model where they provide liquidity for you in exchange for certain things, but we'll delve into those details in Chapter 9. For now, just know that in order for your token to be bought and sold with ease, you need liquidity provisions. Depending on the size of your project, they can range anywhere from US$20,000T paired with US$20,000 worth of your native token, all the way up to a few million dollars for each one. From the day of your launch to ten years after, you will need liquidity provisions. In this row, it's best to split it in two, one for your USDT, and another for your native tokens. Of course, add an extra row for every other trading pair, be that ETH, SOL, or even BRC20. Keeping a backlog of your liquidity provisions will help show you which pairs are the most efficient and which ones may need replenishing from your own funds. Liquidity provisions can even be kept separately on a weekly or even daily basis as they fluctuate much more than any other category and if not sufficient, can lead to the demise of your token.

9) Marketing:

Marketing, KOLs, merchandise, PR, community building and Guilds, all fit into this one category. Marketing is something you will need prior to launch, during launch, and after launch, helping you build trust, and enhance user engagement with your token and product. As touched upon previously, a decent marketing campaign from before launch to during launch can easily cost anywhere from US$200,000 to a few million dollars depending on the size of your project and levels of funding. Once your token is launched, you will need to use marketing on a regular basis to help keep users engaged while attracting new ones. Stopping marketing after you've launched will entail a downfall of user engagement and generally speaking, people will simply forget about your product. Coca Cola doesn't do constant advertisements of Coke to let people know they exist, but rather to keep it in the minds of people already aware of their brand and product so they don't forget about them, the same applies for your project. For this, you need a constant supply of available funding, plus some extra to inject immediately to counter any bad press that may occur. For your general marketing plan and strategy that's predetermined, be sure to budget this in advance and inscribe each one in the appropriate monthly column. For the remaining marketing activities, it's best to jot them down at first notice.

10) Cost to Produce:

This one is somewhat overlooked at a large scale, but is just as important as all of the other categories. In short, it's the occurring cost you may have related to providing your core service or product. For example, if you're using some unreleased forms of AI in your core product, this may have a specific cost per action. The use frequency per user may vary heavily, either decreasing or increasing your bill for the AI usage. Such a cost may of course be integrated into the end users' fee; however, depending on your go-to-market strategy, you may wish to absorb these initial costs yourself to enhance user engagement with a freemium model. You may plan to start charging these users at some stage for this cost, having said that, you will need to budget this initially, and depending on user engagement, it can leave a big check on the table. If you have such an additional cost, do create an adequate row and column tracking the total expenses of this per month.

11) Revenue:

Your project management sheet can't be complete without including something positive for your business, this of course is your revenue. This may be split into two separate rows and columns depending on your revenue models. Firstly, the revenue generated from the liquidation of your tokens on exchanges is a primary source of income. The higher the trading volume on the exchanges generally translates into the more of your tokens you can sell. You may even count this on a weekly basis depending on your liquidation program, but must at least keep a monthly track of it. Secondly, is the sale of your core product or derivatives? Even if you've launched a meme coin and you don't have a service per say, you may start a line of merchandise to leverage the brand awareness and generate extra income. If you do have a core product on top of your token like a launchpad where individuals must buy then stake your native token to participate in investing, you may take 10% of the raise of each project using your launchpad. This is an extra stream of revenue on top of your token sales. A separate column is mandatory for this stream of revenue as it's of inherently different origin and frequency than your other source/s of revenue. A derivative form of revenue could even be a quick sale of a new line of NFTs or limited-edition access to an ephemeral product. For the

derivative forms of revenue, you may create a separate
row and column also, so you may carefully monitor the
success of this one event.

In order to provide you with a concrete example, the below project
management sheet is based on a fictive token named "Sunny coin" and all
of Sunny coin's information relative to the business aspect.

Another important factor, if you don't hit your projected monthly
revenue after the first six months, it's best to cut expenses immediately.
Keeping high salaries without adequate funding can be dangerous as your
burn rate exceeds your positive cash flow. The goal is to have more funds
coming in than going out. If you're not able to achieve a positive cashflow,
cutting salaries temporarily is often a smart decision, this means that you
often start with the largest salaries, including yourself and other C-levels.
Once you've fixed the cash flow problem, you can easily ramp the salaries
back up. This maneuver is designed to increase your runway, giving
you more time to adjust your sales strategy and sort out your cash flow
problem. The worst scenario is waiting too long to make such cuts, often
leading to a very small runway, hence the time frame to resolve your sales
issues. If you're not able to fix that issue with your remaining runway, it's
game over unless you're able to raise more funds. Best to cut unnecessary
expenses and lavish lifestyles early on, making sure you have the best
possible chance to fix the cash flow problem, there's never any shame in
making such strategic decisions as even large companies in the industry
do this during Bear markets.

CHAPTER 8

Storage and Custody of Funds

Segment 1 – Custodians

During my early days in this industry, I worked in the centralized exchange LAtoken, that was one of the largest centralized exchanges in the world per number of listed tokens and available trading pairs (LATOKEN CEO: In 2021 Crypto Went Mainstream and Token Market Started to Absorb Traditional Capital Markets (yahoo.com)). What really astonished me was the amount of projects we would speak with of those who wanted to list their tokens but couldn't afford the initial fee to move forward, even more shocking were the reasons behind this. The majority of them would be listed on DEXs already or had raised some funds and were planning on listing straight away on a CEX. Very often, prior to them listing on a CEX, they would have a streak of misfortune leading to major setbacks. For example, those who had already raised some funds would engage with a shady investor who would simply receive tokens then never pay. Others would have their wallets scraped then tokens dumped on DEXs, while even more tragic are those whose trusted team members would modify the code of the project's native tokens to modify the vesting periods then steal this portion upon the day of the launch, dump them, then disappear with US$500,000T.

© Alexander Rees-Evans 2024
A. Rees-Evans, *How to Launch a Token*, https://doi.org/10.1007/979-8-8688-0533-2_8

The goal of this segment is to bring forth awareness of the intricacies, dangers, and characteristics of both custodians and non-custodians for holding your raised funds and/or your native tokens.

As you start to raise funds or generate your tokens, you will need a safe place to store them. The beauty and primary goal of cryptocurrency is to provide full ownership of the digital assets without any third party being able to take them away from you. Since some years now, the narrative has appeared to somewhat change. Many digital asset custodians have emerged and all of a sudden specialize in digital asset custody. The strange thing is that you don't need a custodian to hold your assets, this is the main point of cryptocurrency, owning and controlling your own digital assets, period.

A crypto custodian does the exact opposite and heavily restrains your rights on your own digital assets, the same as a bank with your fiat funds. Many of them spend millions in marketing and do indeed possess very large brand awareness; however, they never really talk about the underlying security behind them. Often, the people you will speak with are purely there to sell you the product, they may even come across as experts and use very nice buzz words with complex looking charts. Don't be afraid to dive deep and ask questions they don't like such as "What did they do before Web3?" "What do they have to cover internal fraud?" "What insurances do they have?" "What happens to my assets if a regulator freezes your activity or shuts you down?" "Where do you store the private keys?" or even "What do I have to do to withdraw all of my funds and how can you stop me?"

The goal of asking all of these questions is to gather as much information as possible. As FTX among others has reminded us, you must remember that this isn't Wall Street and the government won't bail you out no matter how big you are. In this industry, there are no police, your only protection is your code and storage.

When using a custodian, you need to be aware of the inherent dangers, regardless of how big they are. Henceforth, here are some of the risk categories:

1) Custodian Risk:

   Regardless of who they are or how solid they may appear, you won't control your digital assets once they take them under custody. You no longer own, nor control your funds directly. Like with a bank, you may have US$1,000,000 in your account, it doesn't mean you can withdraw or spend them in one go. You have a title of ownership, but not tangible ownership. You have to ask the custodian to be able to move your funds, and they need to give you their consent. If for some reason they decide not to, your funds will not be moved as you desire, this is not ownership. Whenever you place your digital assets with a custodian, you must acknowledge that you are no longer the true owner, and are giving these rights to the custodian. From the moment that your digital assets are with the custodian, you have to abide by their rules and protocols. You must be aware that you're simply moving back into the classical financial banking system, but with far less security and insurance.

2) Hack Risk:

   If you place your digital assets under the custody of an entity, generally speaking it's because you trust them more than yourself to safeguard the assets. This is where you're also trusting the technology holding your placed funds too. The Web3 world boasts some of the most intelligent and talented hackers the world has to offer. Your chosen custodian may even explain that they've spent millions of dollars or even hundreds of millions of dollars on the technology they use to safeguard funds, this doesn't mean it's unhackable. Nothing in this world is unhackable, it all depends on how much time, effort, and money you're willing to pay to hack something. If hackers have hacked government entities and some of the largest banks in the world who spend billions of dollars and entertain a large portfolio of hundreds if not thousands of experts every year, believe me, they can hack a Web3 custodian. As stipulated, this is a real and constant risk so you need to understand the mechanics of what the technology layer used to safeguard your funds is and how it works.

3) Protocol Risk:

Within the internal company structure of every custodian are steps of which both yourself and the employees must abide by. These procedural rules are designed by the custodian and are very hard to by-pass no matter who you are. When you sign an agreement with the custodian, you also state that you will respect and abide by the protocol designed by the custodian. For instance, a protocol may be that to initiate a transfer of funds you will have to:

– Step 1: Place a formal request on a specific platform.

– Step 2: The custodian has three days to respond.

– Step 3: The custodian will send you a sheet you must fill in and return within two days.

- Step 4: The custodian has two days to accept or deny the request to move your funds.

- Step 5: After receiving a signed approval by the custodian, you may transfer your funds.

In this example, all of these steps are non-negotiable and must be followed every time you wish to transfer funds. Of course, the protocols of custodians will inevitably differ, but make yourself aware of all of them so there aren't any surprises and you may adapt your business strategy accordingly. The last thing you want is to be pressed to execute a transfer and find out all of the loopholes you have to jump through, ultimately penalizing your business operations.

4) Regulatory Risk:

Due to the young nature of the entire Web3 environment, countries and states have not been able to find true common ground, even if the European Union is trying. The custodians operating today in this industry must juggle constantly with changing laws and governmental friction. They may try hard to keep on top of them, and may very well be doing a good job; however, regulatory uncertainty and changes are very real. If the winds of regulation change and intensify suddenly, your custodian is required to do the same at the same time. If, for some reason, the custodian isn't able to keep on the right regulatory track, legal ramifications may be next on the menu. You must remember that you can't beat a government and they're fully capable of freezing and/or seizing all assets held by the custodian.

5) Third Party Risk:

Depending on how your custodian operates, there may be some third parties involved in their ecosystem. The implication of third parties may differ heavily depending on the tasks they're given. Some may be simple service providers, others may have a capital role to play with the architecture or security of the custodian, hence your funds. It may be the case that the custodian delegates the storage or a portion of a split private key. By dispatching these tasks, it is true that the custodian is mitigating risk to some degree by not keeping all of their eggs in one basket; however, the risk of that custodian is added, and all of the risk points we're enumerating here repeat themselves again for each and every third party involved. For every third party involved, it is your duty to take this into consideration and discuss all of these risk vulnerabilities with each third party to the best possible extent. If something happens to your funds because of one of the third parties used by the custodian, your investors won't care that it wasn't directly your fault, to everyone's eyes, you and only you are responsible. Plus, you must find out beforehand the procedure put in place by the custodian in such an event and make sure it is indeed a tangible plan.

6) Internal Fraud Risk:

Every custodian has employees or at least one physical, analog person behind the curtains running the show. For each individual involved in the custodian's company, there is an extra layer of risk we will refer to as "Internal fraud risk." What happens in the event a contracted individual steals your funds and disappears? What employees have access to your funds? What security measures are put in place to prevent employees stealing your funds? And more importantly, how do you recover your funds in such an event and what's the expected time frame? Furthermore, make sure you review the contracts for reclaiming your funds for this particular case. Knowing beforehand what the entailed terms and conditions are could be capital to actually recovering your funds if this misfortune strikes. Reviewing the document prior to placing your funds under their custody will give you perspective on what awaits you legally and how you can reclaim your funds; you also have time to negotiate amendments in the document if not satisfactory. One of the worst things that can happen is to overlook such details, place your funds with the custodian, then an employee steals them and they have no refund policies in place.

7) Insurance Risk:

If your custodian does have insurance, it doesn't mean that it's a green light to go ahead blindly. As we've all experienced at least once, insurance companies are designed to not pay out the funds even if you have a rightful claim, their goal is to make money. Make sure you're aware of which insurance company they're working with and review a copy of their insurance terms and conditions. You may not be able to amend or negotiate this contract, but it will give you peace of mind of if it really is possible to have the insurance company refund your placement and under what specific conditions. A lot of custodians take out cheap insurance that doesn't cover much, but they can market it like there's no tomorrow. Don't be sold on buzzwords and brand awareness. Make sure the insurance they claim to have will actually be useful and tangible if worse comes to worse. Moreover, obtaining a refund from an insurance company can take a very long time in the Web2 world, in the world of crypto, it could easily take longer, so the refund time must be taken into consideration for advancing with the custodian. Don't think that just because they have insurance if something happens you'll carry on your business as usual. This couldn't be further from the truth as the funds you would have lost could be out of your ecosystem for a while so you'll have to plan to do without for maybe even years. This could result in not building out the missing pieces of your product, missing the bull run, or not having enough liquidity provisions to pay for centralized exchange listings. Furthermore, seldom will insurance cover the full amount, think about your car insurance, even if you're fully insured, the insurance company will never refund you the full value of your car so why would it be any different with crypto?

8) Geopolitical Risk:

By nature, custodians are centralized companies owned by real people while being physically domiciled in a specific country and jurisdiction. With each one of these characteristics comes geopolitical status and implications, whether they be direct or indirect. If the custodian company is legally and fiscally domiciled in a country that decides to go to war, there can be embargos, seizing of assets, and political pressure. The country doesn't even have to go to war for the geopolitical risk to be real, there could even be fiscal pressures exerted by other countries for that company to be more stringent on tax evasion or crypto regulation, or even unprovoked inflation of a country's native currency like we've seen in 2024 in Nigeria due to the cheaper solutions for money transfers provided by Binance's Nigerian branch (Binance: Nigeria orders cryptocurrency firm to pay $10 billion (bbc.com)). If you placed your funds in one of your wallets on Binance's Nigerian branch this year, the chances are your funds will be frozen because of the geopolitical pressure applied by the Nigerian government upon Binance. It's not necessarily Binance's fault but nevertheless you can't access your funds and don't know when you'll be able to. It's important to take into consideration such factors as if the country your custodian is domiciled in is unstable or under political pressure from other larger countries, there is a chance it will eventually affect the custodian and the funds withheld.

9) Default Risk:

Just like any company, the goal of a custodian is to be profitable. If that's not the case or they've just started their business, there's a chance they can default. In the traditional world, when a company declares bankruptcy, there are insurances and protocols put in place to help and assist any clients. In the young world of Web3, this isn't yet the case and only the very large defaults of the industry such as FTX will get somewhat of this professional assistance. During a default in Web3, arguably the majority of the companies will simply just disappear with the funds overnight. Just like with any interaction with a company, you need to check their history and if possible, their financial status such as how much funds did they raise and when? Or what's their monthly burn rate? By gathering as much information as possible and performing a due diligence or even an audit on the custodian, you should be able to determine if they have a high, medium, or low default risk. This comes down to personal choice but if you find out they raised US$2,000,000 four years ago, have 25 employees and seven clients, either they're extremely expensive to use or they don't have a lot of funds left to keep the company running, which translates to a high default rate.

10) Management Risk:

All custodians manage digital assets, even if it's just storing them. The C-levels in the company in charge of their storage and/or security have tremendous responsibility. They are the individuals you need to perform due diligence on and understand who they are, their previous companies, and success stories. As we saw with FTX, the exchange defaulted because C-levels misplaced client funds purposely, resulting in the collapse of the entire company. They had all of the external indications of an extremely successful and trustworthy company, but many individuals lost a lot of money because they bought into the marketing and brand awareness without actually looking behind the curtains. Executing on such a task isn't easy, granted, for it may be virtually impossible for a normal trader; however, you have the duty and the right to make your own assessment on if the C-levels of the company are trustworthy. If you can obtain tangible proof of previous successful endeavors of which you can cross-reference with corroborating evidence, it's a good start. If you can find nothing on the founders or no real history, it may be viewed as a bit of a red flag. There are many custodians out there so do be picky and if you have a doubt, don't take the risk. Also, be wary of the custodians that have very recently established themselves no matter how saturated the industry is with their names, remember, it's only marketing.

11)   Access Risk:

This is another very overlooked risk point by project founders in the industry. You may remember one of the first centralized exchanges actually had this exact problem, access to the company wallets. QuadrigaCX was Canada's largest centralized exchange at one point with hundreds of millions of dollars' worth of digital assets under custody. Unfortunately, the founder passed away, taking with him the sole access to almost US$200,000,000 worth of digital assets belonging to people from across the globe (Quadriga founder dies, leaving $190 million in cryptocurrency locked – The Washington Post). This is a very real risk and has had devastating effects on the lives of many people. Make sure that the custodian explains how the access to your funds is possible, even if something happens to them or anybody else in the company.

12) Technology Risk:

Every custodian will use technology to some degree
in order to onboard, store, and move your funds.
The custodian is only as good as the underlying
technology within their structure. Regardless of the
millions of dollars they may have spent on their digital
architecture and infrastructure, technology needs
updates, maintenance, and can have bugs. Every time
engineers will tweak or verify the technology, they open
the possibility of modifying something they shouldn't
by accident, creating a bug in the system. If you need
to access your funds urgently and you can't because of
a bug or maintenance, it could result in big losses for
your business. If there is a bug in the system they can't
seem to fix, this may even lead to you not being able
to access your funds for a longer period of time than
expected, resulting in greater losses for your business.
Another interesting possibility is that the cost relative
to using the custodian may increase suddenly because
they need more funds to update their tech stack. If this
is the case, because you're already fully merged with
their ecosystem, it can be quite challenging to change
custodian swiftly, leaving you with no other choice
than to pay a much higher monthly fee than originally
expected and provisioned in your budget allocations.

13) Operational Risk:

As the custodian generally employs individuals to keep
the company running and functioning normally, some
tasks may be manual on the backend. If you need to
transfer some of your funds rapidly, you may need to

ask an employee to start the process. What happens if that employee is away on their lunch break or late in the office? What happens if you need client support and it's the middle of the night? Again, your business could suffer real consequences if you're dependent on human beings to validate or action something just so you may use your funds the way you wish to use them. When enquiring about using a custodian's service, ask if any of the tasks on their side will be done manually by an internal employee or if every single desired action on your side will be executed in a digital fashion from the backend of the automated segment of the custodian's infrastructure. Also ask about how and when you can get hold of someone to help you if needed. Especially in the early days of using a custodian, you may need someone to guide you from time to time on their platform so it's useful to know who to contact and when they're available.

14) Transparency Risk:

From the second you place your funds under the custody of any entity, your visibility is extremely limited. You will only see what the custodian wants you to see. Even if they have dashboards or analytic reports, you're trusting them to provide you with accurate information. The problem here is that you have to trust the humans behind the scenes to be faithful and honest, even if there may be something they'd rather not show. As goes the old adage, "Eyes that do not see, do not cry," if something very bad has happened and they feel they can resolve it before you'll notice, they can provide false information on your screen to make it appear as everything is well and fine while they try to repair the mishap. If they're not able to resolve the problem within the time they bought through providing you with fake analytics, by the time you find out, the problem may have amplified resulting in further complications making it very hard to recover. Also, you may have planned your token strategy in correlation with information you believe is true, when in fact it is not. This carries a very heavy impact on your entire business yet again. It's very hard to prevent or even minimize this risk as you are depending on them 100% to provide you with accurate information that usually only they have access to. Depending on how their custodian storage works, something you can do is to monitor the wallet addresses they use. It can be a manually laborious task, but checking their public wallet addresses every couple of days or so could be made part of your operational checklist. Try to find as many decentralized cross-reference points as possible so you may correlate the information they're providing you with with unbiased, pure analytics. By making such tasks part of an internal checklist, you could notice a distortion between your findings and their analytics then revert to them for answers, potentially saving you from a scandal.

Many more forms of risk may be enumerated as the more you dive into details, the more risk sub-categories you can find. The above are simply the main risk forms you will find in the majority of custodians and of which you must be wary of. Many project founders overlook all of these because of clever marketing and buzz words, many of them have witnessed first-hand the troubles and problems caused once a single point of risk becomes reality. You're responsible for the digital assets and must do appropriate research with a risk mitigation mindset to assess your next move with caution.

Segment 2 – Non-custodians

After having reviewed the more centralized approach for storing your digital assets, now it's time we looked into the more decentralized method. This option is the complete opposite of a custodian and echoes the freedom of what Bitcoin was designed for. True non-custodial storage points are when you and you only have full control and ownership of your digital assets. These forms of storage can come in all shapes and sizes, but more importantly, they can come in as either hot wallets (Glossary 48) or cold wallets (Glossary 49), on chain or off chain such as the Cyber Wallet, which is on chain, or a paper cold wallet like Icynote all the way up to the infamous digital cousin, a Ledger device. Use cases for both hot and cold wallets differ heavily, as does the security. For example, if you're a Web3 VC, you actively invest in projects and need a storage tool that remains extremely secure, as you'll likely have a few million dollars' worth of digital currencies in there, but it also needs to be easy and quick to validate transactions with. If, on the other hand, you're a wealthy individual and just want to lock away 50 Bitcoins you bought a while back, you'll need a device that does just that one thing, store securely. Depending on your needs, you will require different wallets for different use cases. As a project founder, a blend of both hot and cold wallets is probably necessary due to the fact that you can lock away the bulk of your funds you don't need to use immediately in a very secure manner, while having some hot wallets on stand-by to cover daily expenses. Hot and cold wallets also exist in custodian forms of storage too; however, the particularities of them will have a much greater impact on you in the non-custodial format. Due to the fact that here, you take full accountability of the storage and transfers of your digital assets and will be required to manually execute the steps and tasks necessary to accomplish them. The goal of using these forms of storage is to minimize risk by taking full accountability for the digital assets you're storing. However, there is still always a form of custody as you're entrusting your funds with hardware or technology built by someone else. Even if you build your own non-custodial form of storage, you still place your digital assets within that environment, hence the tool used to store them is a custodian to a certain degree. The goal is how decentralized that custodian is. For context and the sake of clarity, we will still refer to these much more decentralized forms of custody as non-custodial. Bringing further comprehension to the distinction between the custodian forms we discussed in the first segment of this chapter and the non-custodial forms we're about to discuss, we will draw the line in the sand where someone else can stop a transfer of your digital assets. True custodians can stop you from transferring your digital assets, true non-custodians can't stop you from transferring your digital assets.

Non-custodian forms of storage may represent the very essence of cryptocurrencies, but they also possess their own unique forms of inherent risk. To cut to the chase, here are a few:

1) Accountability Risk

   We've all heard stories of individuals who purchased large amounts of Bitcoin years ago, today the few thousand dollars' worth of Bitcoin they bought initially is worth millions of dollars. Unfortunately for some, they either misplaced the private keys, forgot the seed-phrase, or simply lost the device storing their digital assets (https://www.bbc.co.uk/news/av/uk-wales-55667622). Non-custodial forms of storage enable you to take full custody of your assets, but this doesn't come without responsibility. You and you only are responsible for the digital assets' safe-keeping.

There isn't a helpline you can call, no account manager
to assist, a company to blame, or an insurance claim
to place. It is solely up to you to know where all of
the details to access the digital assets are stored.
Furthermore, you're human and can forget or misplace
objects, such as James Howells, who threw away his
hard drive years ago which contained 7500 BTC. As
goes the famous saying, if you forget your seed phrase,
misplace your device, or can't find your private keys, it's
game over.

2)   Device Risk

If you'll be taking personal responsibility and
ownership of your digital assets on a non-custodial cold
wallet, you will also be responsible for the cold wallet.
Where and how you safeguard this device is another
question, do you leave it in a draw under your laptop?
Do you hide it somewhere in the attic? Or do you place
it in a safe box in the vault of a bank? These are just
some possibilities of where to store it, of course some
being more secure than others. Wherever you store
your cold wallet, you can't be too clever as this may
lead to you actually forgetting the whereabouts of it
altogether! You also can't be too careful; what happens
in the event of a robbery or a house fire or even a
water leak in your residence? As many eventualities
as possible must be taken into consideration as
anything could happen. By owning full responsibility
of your assets and the device holding the assets, you're
vulnerable on all angles, therefore must perform very
thorough risk mitigation beforehand, ensuring your
device is as secure as could possibly be.

3) Technology Risk

Whether you choose to use a cold or hot non-custodial wallet, you have the same risk segment as a custodian which is the technology powering your wallet. If you use a hot wallet which is decentralized, someone somewhere has made the tech stack behind it. Like all technology, everything evolves over time. In just over 30 years, we've witnessed video tapes, then DVDs, all the way up to streaming services. Nobody uses videos or DVDs today, even if that technology was considered great at the time. The wallets of today could become completely obsolete in the next couple of years, creating potential bugs in the technology of your device. Another problem here is what happens if you purchase a faulty wallet? If it happens with products from the biggest companies in the world, it can happen to the much smaller wallet providers of Web3. If you do choose this method, don't transfer everything all at once, do it by tranches to start with, making sure that your digital asset has been received on your new wallet. Also, be careful of brands you don't know, if using one, you may want to keep an air gap between that receiving wallet and the sender wallet as it could potentially be a virus designed to scrape your wallet at first contact. To minimize this, use a virgin intermediate wallet to act as the middleman, transfer a small amount of digital assets from your sender wallet to your intermediate wallet, then from your intermediate wallet to your new non-custodial wallet. This way you never jeopardize the full amount of your digital assets.

4) Durability

No piece of hardware is designed to last forever,
not the biggest ships sailing the ocean to the tallest
buildings in the world. Everything has an expiration
date. Often, the capacity of a non-custodial wallet to
retain the information (digital asset keys) can vary
depending on the humidity levels, temperature,
light exposure, among others. These must be taken
into consideration when you're shopping around for
your perfect non-custodial wallet. Your geographical
location can influence these decisions too, for example,
if you live in Singapore, they have an extremely high
humidity rate and it's very warm. On the other hand,
if you live in Siberia, chances are it's extremely cold
with snow. Different types of non-custodial wallets
will be more adapted to different areas of the world,
predetermining some necessary characteristics you'll
need to look out for when making your purchase. If
you use an unadapted non-custodial wallet for your
circumstances, this could result in a disastrous loss at
your expense.

In appearance it may seem that there's far less risk in using a non-custodial form of storage for your digital assets; this is most definitely not the case as even just one point of risk is the potential to lose your digital assets. Non-custodial forms of storage have their own unique risk points which are not to be taken lightly, but are to be considered. Being aware of such risks are capital for you to be able to formulate your own risk aversion strategy when opting for this specific type of storage. Without such awareness, it can leave you making silly mistakes such as misplacing your wallet or having it stolen, when all of the above could have been easily avoided.

Segment 3 – Security Traits Needed

Custodian or non-custodian, at the end of the day there are pros and cons for both. Regardless of how much research or mitigation you put in the process, there will always be risk to some degree, it's all about how much you can reduce this risk. In the wise words of the famous economist Thomas Sowell, "It's all about compromise." You can't have the best of both worlds. For instance, if you place your funds within a custodian's structure, you can't expect to move them freely at any given time of the day without passing through some security protocol checks. On the other hand, you don't need to worry that your cold wallet may be damaged and digital assets lost because your house had a water leak. It's all about compromise.

Finding the perfect balance between risk exposure, simplicity of use, and safeguarding of your assets can be very tricky. Not only because you need to perform deep due diligence on every option you have but you must also understand and anticipate the environment you'll be operating within from day one to a few years down the road. If you sign a 12-month contract with a custodian, you can't simply retract after seven months because your business requirements have evolved, you need to project yourself, token and business for at least 2 years. Painting a mental roadmap of how your business requirements will evolve will help you plan the storage of your assets. If your company is designed to generate US$15,000,000 worth of profits in the first 12 months, you can't simply store these funds in a kitchen cupboard on a Ledger device. Anticipating and planning the growth of your company is also a crucial component to structuring your storage of digital assets. Most definitely, you can pivot and adapt as you go along, changing or even combining different forms of storage is a possibility too. Usually, the larger your company, the more storage combinations you have, blending institutional grade custodians with clever non-custodial hot wallets, then some large cold wallets held in safe boxes of tier 1 banks across the globe can be a fantastic strategy when you start to scale. When you've just raised your first funds, however, you don't need to take it that far of course. Akin to the very nature of start-ups, your storage strategy must correlate with the stage of your fundraise and project. Think of it as the same process of fiscal optimization, when you start to generate a lot of revenue, your fiscal teams will create more and more elaborate structures, just like Amazon. At the beginning, Jeff Bezos not only didn't have the budget for this, he also didn't have the need. The same may be said for your storage of digital assets. You don't need a tank to protect a dollar, but you also don't want a wooden shield to protect ten million dollars.

As you start fundraising, a non-custodial cold wallet is more than enough. Seldom will you be doing multiple transactions per day as you don't have a lot of departments in your company, nor unexpected payments to be made daily originating from these departments; you're not yet a multinational. For the few, generally curated and anticipated payments you must make to finalize building your product, you have the bandwidth to spend some time to manually issue these transfers. Plus, security wise, as long as you don't tell anyone that you keep your digital assets hidden under a pillow on your bed, you should be fine. Even better is to use a non-custodial hot wallet such as the cyber wallet as the other co-founders and yourself can program a multi-signature mechanism, plus it's stored in cyberspace. If your house catches fire, your assets won't be lost. Another interesting component to look at is the fact that by using a digital non-custodial hot wallet, nobody can physically steal it from you. Using such a form of custody for your initial stages of fundraising is cost-efficient, swift, and controlled by you and the team, it's a great compromise and hassle-free as you'll have more than enough on your plate as you start to build your project.

Once you have raised a few initial hundred thousand dollars and started to build out your project, you'll be raising your next level of funds to hire team members and bulk up your company. Here, we're usually talking about a few million dollars. Using the same mechanism as above is actually still a great and efficient form of storage as funds can only be moved if all invited parties sign off on it, and you can still manually do the transfers when needed. If you place a portion of the funds raised on a fully decentralized cold wallet, it could cause problems as the person charged with safeguarding this non-custodial cold wallet could simply disappear and you'd never see it again. By aligning incentives and annulling any potential vulnerability of access to the funds, you have a strong storage strategy. Furthermore, non-custodial cold wallets are generally used by individuals for their own personal funds simply because they can access their own digital assets without any external validation. This ideology is counterproductive to most Web3 company structures, especially when you have partners and co-founders who need to have equal access to the funds raised. What better way to create this collaborative effort than to be sharing the same access and fused rights of transfer. This is not only a strong form of custody, but also an interesting democratic way of sharing the power and control of the company. Without this shared right of access and validation of transactions, they who possess these features are the ultimate deciders of what happens with the funds.

When you start to really scale the company, generate revenue, and increase the team sizes and departments, manually managing transfers of your raised funds can be tricky and extremely time-consuming. A multitude of options are possible here and starting to explore custodian venues is very interesting. Depending on your custodian, having access to a nice, clear management platform can make your life much easier. However, don't entrust the entirety of your funds with them. Only place what expenses you will need to cover every month within their custody. Not only will this immensely limit your losses if something happens to the custodian, but it will also give you a good sense of the cash flow of your company. If you calculate a burn rate of approx. US$95,000 per month and place that exact amount on the custodian's platform and realize at the end of the month you have some left over, either you made a mistake or spent less than expected that month. This will be a great supplementary indicator that you will visually see every time you execute on the transfers for salaries and other monthly expenses. The same goes for if you didn't transfer enough, obviously you have extra expenses. If you have an extra expense of even just US$100, if you're making multiple transfers from a wallet with US$6,000,000 in it, you probably won't think twice; here, using this monthly top up system, you will see it as you will need to top up the difference. Now your project is starting to scale, a storage system herein described can start to make sense and enhance your money management process.

Finally, when you become a very large company, generating millions of dollars in revenue every month and have raised US$20,000,000 in your series A round, you need to take the previous system to the next level. Transferring some of your digital asset funds into fiat currencies and opening bank accounts is a very important landmark too. This is a great indicator of your success as a Web3 venture also; by transitioning some of the currencies and custody from the crypto realm into the traditional banking system can bring a new level of security and sustainability to your company. By placing a portion of your funds in multiple, different Web3 custodians can also be useful. Using one custodian to safeguard the funds for the next six months of salaries, another custodian for future development of your company, one more as your war chest, and even another for receiving the revenue, for example. By segregating the different departments and verticals in your company financially, you are mitigating the risk of losing your funds if a custodian defaults while simultaneously keeping all of your departments financially independent and organized. You know which department needs what to function and can quickly tell if there's a problem. Also, you may organize multisignature mechanisms to each one of these custodian platforms and have the directors of each department be the initiators of this, helping you save valuable time. Finally, always keep a non-custodial cold wallet with the majority of funds you won't need for at least 12 months in a safe box in a AAA bank in a stable country. Make sure that you and the other important team members have access to this in the event you get into a car accident or another such unfortunate event, plus structure how to prevent one of the team simply walking into the bank and taking everything then disappearing without a trace.

Keeping the funds you need to operate with close by is important, but you don't need more than you know you're going to spend. Every time your digital assets are anywhere but in a cold wallet, they're exposed to hacks. Create air gaps where possible to minimize risk of exposure and be sure to place nothing over one year's worth of expenses on chain. By doing this and using different custodians for different departments, different non-custodial hot and cold wallets, plus leveraging the digital and analog banking system, you create a very extensive safety net for your entire operation the day that something goes wrong. Always remember to structure the custody of digital assets after thorough due diligence and development of a strategic plan. It's all about compromise.

CHAPTER 9

Market Making

Segment 1 – What Is Market Making?

Once you've started to transform your prodigious idea into a tangible, financially backed concept and started to structure the layout of actually going to market, you'll need to plan your technical liquid market too. Launching a token isn't just hard strategically, it can actually be quite a complex technical task too. Throughout the different markets, sizes, volumes, and price action you will encounter once your token is live, there are certain pre-arrangements you must make to ensure the viability of your token launch. Planning in advance your liquid market strategy means you need to find and agree upon terms and conditions with a market maker. Before we delve into how we discern a good deal from a bad deal or some other useful tips and hacks, let's first understand what exactly a liquid crypto market is.

Any publicly tradable token needs a liquid market, in short, every successful token needs a vast quantity of buyers and sellers. Not having enough buyers or sellers can be a problem as you won't be able to liquidate your tokens seamlessly. Besides building a great product, your goal is to make money, let's not forget this. If you have only ten people buying and ten people selling, it's highly unlikely you'll be able to sell off US$400,000 worth of your team's token allocation. On the other hand, if you have one hundred thousand buyers and only five hundred sellers, you should have very good conditions to liquidate your tokens. Having

© Alexander Rees-Evans 2024
A. Rees-Evans, *How to Launch a Token*, https://doi.org/10.1007/979-8-8688-0533-2_9

more buyers than sellers, both in large quantities is key to a healthy liquid market. However, prior to obtaining hundreds of thousands of people buying and selling your tokens, you'll more than likely have a few hundred or thousand if you've done a good job on your marketing.

One of the major problems individuals and other trading entities have is fulfilling their orders. For example, if I place an order to buy 10,000 tokens of "SunnyCoin" at US$1.75 each, I may have to wait some time to fulfill my order if not a lot of people are selling. The opposite works too, if I'm an early investor and want to liquidate some of my tokens in accordance with my vesting schedule but there's no immediate people placing buy orders, I could wait a very long time to sell my tokens.

For the project "SunnyCoin Inc" the team members themselves would have their own problems too, such as how can they liquidate their team's allocation tokens without damaging the price per token? And what will the community do if they try to buy or sell but have to wait weeks for their order to be fulfilled?

Another fragmented complexity is the different markets your token will be listed on. You may have your token at US$1.75 on Binance, but maybe it's also at US$1.68 on Pancakeswap. In these scenarios, clever traders will exploit such arbitrage opportunities and buy where it's cheapest, then sell on the exchange with the higher price, thus making a profit from the spread (Glossary 51).

One more important occurring problem is the spread itself on the same exchange. If individuals wish to buy and sell at very different prices, it can take a while for the orders to be fulfilled, but it can also create a very messy price chart (Glossary 52). If you have big steep differences in the chart of your token, you will not interest good traders, nor will you create a bullish sentiment around your token, encouraging more individuals to trade on your token.

There are many more problems that can occur, but by enumerating the few cited above, it should provide you with some more depth and understanding of such complexities. Anyhow, in all of these cases and others, you, as an esteemed team member of the project, will have to try and resolve them all. This is where a market maker comes in useful. Succinctly, a market maker helps fulfill orders and keeps the spreads tight, while in most cases, also manages arbitrage across exchanges.

Prior to your launch, you will provide them with a specific amount of your native tokens and of the chosen cryptocurrency you wish to receive payment in, such as USDT. These two cryptocurrencies together make what we call a trading pair (Glossary 53). By supplying beforehand your market maker with provisions in both cryptocurrencies, it will allow them to step in the market and fulfill orders that are waiting in a clever way.

If someone places an order to buy at US$1.76 but someone's selling at US$1.78, the market maker can come in and buy, then sell to the other person, immediately satisfying both traders and losing only US$0.01 in the process. It's a very small price to pay to keep all of your traders happy. It's important to note that in crypto, your market maker can actually make you some money too while they perform these transactions. If they know you will be doing a powerful marketing campaign the next day, the chances are your token price will increase that very day. Armed with this knowledge, they can buy tokens from the current market with your liquidity provisions, then sell strategically back to the traders at a higher price once you start marketing. There are many other ways market makers can make you money, but the majority of them are questionable from an ethics standpoint, including the one cited above.

Another use case of having a market maker is to help you liquidate your own tokens! If you start selling large tranches from your team allocation as one big chunk as soon as your vesting schedule allows, you will be shooting yourself in the foot. By selling a large amount of your tokens in one go will increase the total circulating supply massively and dilute heavily the price per token. If you sell a very large portion of your tokens all at once, it can even lead to starting a Fear, Uncertainty, and Doubt (FUD) movement, leading all holders to start selling as they saw an initial dip on the price chart. This can lead to the complete dump of your token and send your whole project spiralling into the abyss of the crypto graveyard of lost tokens. By selling your tokens through your market maker, they won't sell it as one big chunk, they will strategically sell tokens drop by drop to not damage the token price or chart, completely withdrawing any possible FUD action from your traders or community. They will take into consideration the entire market sentiment, buying pressure, and selling pressure to gradually offload your desired amount of tokens over a period of time.

Arbitrage across all exchanges your token's listed on is also a very important task a complete market maker will manage for you. Due to different orders with different price requirements on completely independent exchanges, be they centralized or decentralized for that matter, each exchange will have a slightly different price for your token. Generally speaking, if on Binance your token is at US$1.75 but at US$1.68 on Pancackeswap, traders will pick up on this straight away and buy where it's cheapest to sell where the price is higher. This will bring the prices to equilibrium organically; however, traders are making money off this delta plus having a large price delta between exchanges isn't healthy for your liquidity or token narrative as traders will solely focus on trading the spread to make quick profits and not holding it long term. Your market maker will be doing these buys and sells between the exchanges, outstripping all of the traders, forcing the narrative of your token to not be one of exploitation. Due to your market maker doing these buys and sells, they will not only bring the price to an equilibrium across exchanges but they will also be profiting from these trades. Usually these profits are split between the market maker and the project.

Market makers can also reveal to be very powerful at helping paint a very seductive price chart for traders. Instead of leaving your token's chart to be wildly crafted by the fluctuating winds of the public market, with a good market maker, you can actually influence and sculpt your price chart in a very attractive way. By providing extra liquidity provisions, your market maker can even buy and sell them to themselves at a high rate with an upwards trend, thus creating a stable, bearish chart for all to see. It's possible for the market maker to try and reproduce some well-known signals that could trigger Fear Of Missing Out (FOMO) in the minds of established traders such as the following candlestick chart patterns (How to Read Crypto Charts – A Beginner's Guide):

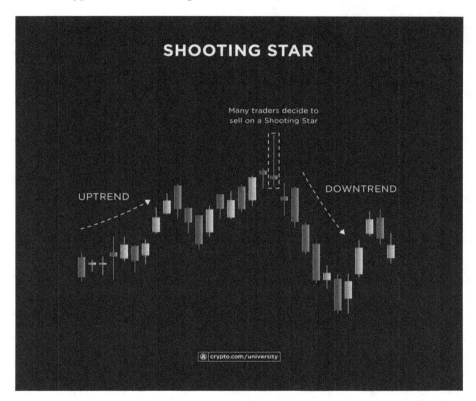

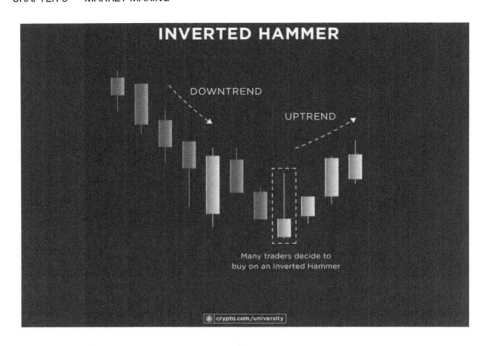

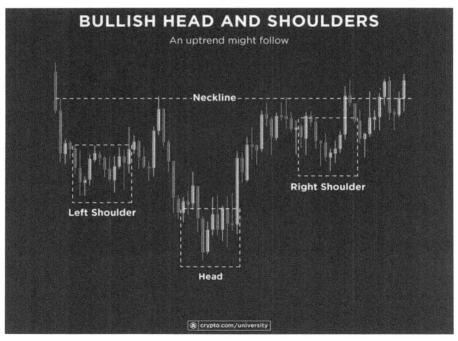

186

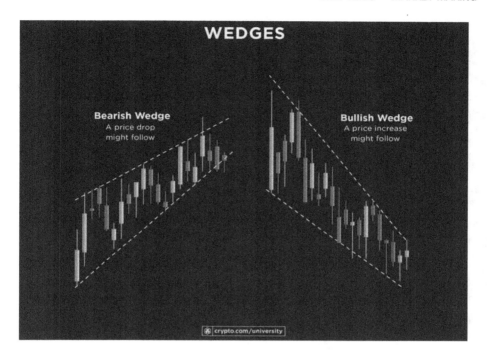

As your market maker has more or less the monopoly of the market for your native token, they carry huge influence and weight they use to leverage certain positions in your favor. By facilitating trades in a swift manner, keeping the order book tidy, limiting negative price fluctuations, helping you get the best price for tokens you liquidate, arbitrage between exchanges and keeping the spreads tight, your market maker can be an excellent ally. Market makers are very powerful partners and, depending on your choice, they will either be your best friends or your worst nightmare.

Segment 2 – What to Look Out for in Market Makers

Searching for the right market maker can be somewhat like searching for a needle in a haystack. Again, the majority of them boast big brand awareness and put a lot of money into marketing to stay in the spotlight. But what's actually under the hood? Just how efficient is their technology and how exactly are they making money? Yes, all market makers are in it for the money and have different ways of making it. If you don't pay attention to the fine prints or understand how they're making their money, it can turn around and bite you further on down the line.

In this segment, we're going to start by looking at the different types of commercial models generally proposed by market makers and what to look out for. Each model has its own risk/reward benefits, but some do so more than others:

1) Profit Share Model:

This model means that you share the revenue generated from the arbitrage, volume, and basically any money made from the active trading of your token. The profit share model is one of the most deceiving models you can opt for. The name itself sounds actually quite enticing and resonates with fairness; however, this couldn't be further from the truth. Very often, the way market makers pitch this model to you is by making it sound as if they will do a lot of work, hence bringing a lot of volume, leverage certain positions and only get paid if they do a good job. It sounds very good and very fair. The problems here arise from the incentive model residing within the commercials. Instead of your market maker doing their job and solely focusing on keeping your spreads tight and fulfilling the orders, they have full focus on making money by any means necessary.

For example, if they start increasing the volume so there's more room to liquidate tokens they will get a large cut from, they will do so; however, how exactly do they increase the volume? They will ask you for more liquidity provisions every week or so with vague explanations on the reason they need them for. They will then inject your liquidity into the market to create more volume, then ask for more liquidity of your tokens so they can liquidate them as now there's some volume in the market that can absorb the tokens destined to be sold. They will then sell the tokens you just gave them and buy them with the USDT or pair funds you provided with them just before. Yes, they basically sell you your own tokens without you even knowing! Because market makers providing such details usually provide you with little to no visibility on what's actually going on or what they're doing with your liquidity provisions, you will never know until it's too late and they've drained all of your liquidity provisions.

Regarding the arbitrage, again, they will actually keep a deliberate but constant spread between all exchanges that they can exploit on a regular basis. Instead of just keeping the token price delta between exchanges to a minimum, or even a zero, they will leave it in place. Sometimes they will even ask you for more liquidity provisions so they can influence the price more to grow the token price delta between exchanges, so they can exploit it and make more money. If they do the right thing and close that price delta as much as possible, it means they won't be profiting from it. Because they only get paid "If they do a good job," they will exploit and leverage every single delta between exchanges. You may say to yourself, "but if they're making some money from the arbitrage, so will I"; this is only partially true. They will be using your own liquidity provisions to either create, or enhance these spreads. Again, the positions they'll be exploiting will be artificially created or maintained by your own funds. The extracted finances declared as "profits" will simply be a small portion of your own funds they will return to you after losing a portion on gas fees and taking their cut.

Another common practice of market makers pushing this model is to sniper (Glossary 54) or frontrun (Glossary 55) your own token to either create more volume to sell your tokens in, or to steal your liquidity. Often, the second you launch a market maker using this model, they will actually sniper your project themselves without you knowing it's them. Because they have the monopoly of the market due to the amount of tokens they have, they can pump your price with their own funds behind your back, then sell off the tokens they bought before they sell yours, they control the market and it's up to them to sell off the tokens you entrust them with. Frontrunning your retail traders trying to buy tokens isn't uncommon either. When one of your community members will place an order of US$100 to buy 100 tokens at US$1.00 each, they will only receive 80 tokens instead of their full 100. Not only will they feel cheated, the market maker would have taken the 20 tokens missing and can keep them for themselves to sell off without you knowing, making more money.

Some of the market makers proposing this model may even promise to provide you US$500,000T of liquidity, out of their own pockets! Here, the problem is if they're putting half a million dollars worth of USDT in to buy your native tokens because "they believe in your project and token," how and when will they retrieve their funds? Generally speaking what happens in these cases is they will buy half a million dollars of your tokens, but only when the price is cheap or favorable by selling a large portion of your tokens you entrusted them with to dilute the market and bring the price per token down. Once they have purchased your native tokens at a discount, because they have the monopoly of the entire market as they control the majority of your native tokens, they can stop liquidating your tokens to create scarcity, or even just buy up a large portion of the circulating tokens with some of the USDT reserves you gave them as part of your liquidity provisions to pump the price up. Once the token price starts to rise, they will simply privilege liquidating the tokens they bought with their own funds before liquidating your tokens you need to build up your treasury. Always remember, if they're putting money in, their main priority will be fighting to get it back with a profit, not create a pretty trading chart for you.

2) Loan Model:

This particular model is much more discreet and slightly more honorable than the profit share model, but still is quite a double-edged sword. In short, they will sign a contract with you, enabling them to buy a large quantity of native tokens you lent them as liquidity provisions at a predetermined set price six months down the line. As an example, they can borrow 20,000,000 of your tokens at US$0.01 per token, once the time period of the contract permits, say after six months, they can buy back the same amount of tokens from you regardless of the current market price. The problem here is that the tokens they will buy back at let's say, for example, US$0.01 will actually be worth far more than that on the current trading markets. Topping that, there will also be no vesting meaning that they can sell virtually all of those tokens into the market all at once if they wish to. This can not only potentially damage your token price chart, it can also create FUD, leading all of your community to start selling their tokens too, resulting in the crash of your project. And again, because they have the monopoly of the market as they control all of your tokens, they will anticipate and push the market upwards with your liquidity provisions to increase the price per token. This way, once they buy back your tokens with a very large discount, the price of each token will be worth much more as they influence the market to drive the token price upwards. Now they have created a very high token price, they can sell all of their tokens and make tremendous profits. Even if there isn't a lot of organic trading volume to liquidate these tokens, they can simply use some of the USDT liquidity provisions you entrusted them with to buy the tokens they will sell into the market.

With this model, it can turn around and bite you when you least expect it. Anticipating market cycles such as time frames for Bear markets and Bull runs can play a major part in deciding if this model is for you. You may be thirteen months into a Bull market when you launch, but your market maker will buy back the tokens six months down the line at a very cheap price. The chances are that by the time they buy back your tokens, you will be in a Bear market. Taking into consideration the bigger picture will provide you with an idea of feasibility because if you launch at the end of the Bear market, by not having a heavy monthly fee or profit share model will save you immediate expenses and by the time your market maker will buy back your tokens, you will most likely be in the Bull run which means more organic liquidity and volume. Under these circumstances, you save money when you need it most, and there should be enough organic volume for you to absorb the selling pressure from your market maker when they dump your tokens.

3)   Retainer:

> One of the most simplistic and transparent commercial models proposed, is the retainer model. They take a simple flat fee every month and sometimes a small percentage of tokens you ask them to liquidate for you. In contrast with the profit share model, you know exactly how they make their money, it's very transparent. Secondly, they have no incentives to create volume for no reason other than to make money, nor do they have any incentive to keep a large token price delta across exchanges as they can't profit from it. Compared to the loan model, they have no possibility to dump tokens, hence making them a profit either.

With the retainer model, the only thing the market maker is focused on is actually doing their job, keeping the spreads tight and fulfilling orders. Just because they don't make profits from the arbitrage or other leverage points doesn't mean you won't. They will still make profits for you from the arbitrage trading; however, they will also keep the token price delta to a minimum. For liquidating your tokens, as it requires more work from them, they will take a small percentage, but their incentives are aligned with yours, to keep the token price healthy. Finally, they will actually implement a real strategy, beneficial for your token longevity and token price chart. If they don't do a good job, you can simply stop working with them and they won't get paid, that's where their incentive lies.

One more advantage a market maker can provide you value wise that can be part of any of the above models is an analytics dashboard. Not only will this provide you with full transparency so you may see the balance in the trading accounts, you will also see how many trades the market maker did with your liquidity provisions, all the way up to knowing how many real, living breathing people actually bought and sold your tokens. Such information can be extremely important for your business and marketing operations as you can see the direct correlation between a marketing campaign and your token adoption. Knowing at all times how many organic users are trading your token can be vital for the sustainability of your entire project.

The following dashboards came from Kaizen Finance's market-making department and illustrate just how powerful having such tools can be not only for transparency but for your entire business prosperity:

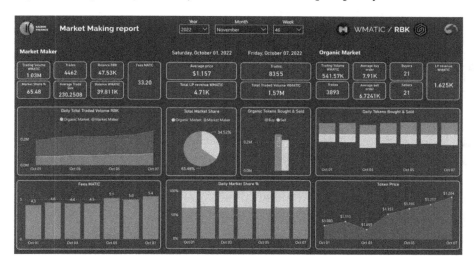

DEX analytics market making dashboard

CEX analytics market making dashboard

An important factor to consider when deciding upon which commercial market-making offer is the best fit for yourself is to always understand how the market maker is making money. It may appear that because you don't have a high monthly flat fee, a profit share or loan model will work out cheaper. In almost every other case, you will end up paying extraordinarily high fees through the liquidity they will either drain, leverage, or dump. What may cost you US$60,000 per year on a flat fee, would probably cost you a lot more from the other models. Reason being they have to make money somehow and there's zero transparency on what profits they're actually making. By taking a small slice of every possible leveraged position for the profit share model, or buying US$5,000,000 worth of your tokens for only US$500,000 then selling them like in the loan model, it will net that market maker US$4,500,000 in almost half the same period of time.

When you're making these decisions, take all options into consideration, but make sure that your chosen market maker will be incentivized to keep the spreads tight and fulfill the order book.

Segment 3 – How to Negotiate with Market Makers

As you start exploring your market maker options, you'll soon find that like with every single stage of launching your token, there are some hacks and useful strategies that can be used to get a more favorable deal. Regardless of the model you chose, be that retainer, profit share, or loan model, there's always a way to bring down the final price. Also, without knowing the industry standards for market making prices, you're putting yourself at risk of being exploited. Remember, the majority of advisors in this industry will simply refer you to whichever market maker will give them the most commission, not because that particular market maker is good.

Far too often, the lack of general industry knowledge can leave chinks in your armor as you negotiate, so it's best to ask around different, separated connections in the industry to get as impartial a feedback as possible. To give you an idea, generally speaking, here's the average prices per type of market maker:

Profit Share Model:

– 15% of the revenue generated from the trade profits

– US$1500 per month per exchange

– 3% of tokens to be liquidated by the market maker

Loan model:

– 1.5% of the total token supply

– Possibility to buy back the 1.5% of your total token supply without any vesting at 1/5 of the price per token six months after signing the contract

– 5% of the revenue generated from the trade profits

Retainer Model:

– US$2000 per DEX and per month

– US$3000 per CEX and per month

– 2.5% of tokens to be liquidated by the market maker

These numbers and terms vary depending on the market sentiment, reputation, and jurisdiction of where the market maker is based, among other parameters. For example, if you chose a Swiss regulated market maker such as G20 in the middle of a Bull run, it's very likely that their prices will be higher than in a Bear market and vice versa.

An interesting fact which correlates with one of the narratives in this book is that it's not because your market maker is big, such as GSR or Wintermute that they are actually better than some smaller, lesser-known ones such as Enflux, for example. The bigger market makers are usually just very expensive for no particular reason and can actually be way worse than some smaller ones as they're very slow to react. Depending on the jurisdiction of your market maker such as Switzerland, you won't be able to do any wash trading (Glossary 56), hence creating a very nice price chart and incentive for organic buyers to join in. Even if this is illegal, the majority of tradable tokens all do this by using market makers from more tolerant jurisdictions. This can actually be a negotiation tactic you may use while negotiating with larger, more institutional market makers. By pointing out that they can't do something another market maker's proposing to you, it can bring some extra leverage to the table and lower the initial commercials.

In any case, like with investors, you need to make yourself as attractive as possible by having big backers on your capitalization table (cap table), some tier 1 marketing agency and accelerator with sensible tokenomics. If you can get a high tier 2 to tier 1 exchange to agree to list your token too, you will have a lot of weight on your side when approaching market makers.

You may even find that one of your investors or the exchanges you're speaking with recommend market makers to you also. This doesn't always mean that the market maker will be good, but usually is a good start to your negotiations.

One of the most convoluted dilemmas you'll face during the process of structuring your token launch will be "What do I do first?" You need a good investor and exchange to get a good market maker, but you also need a good exchange and community to get a good investor!

The best way to go about it if you're not sure is in the exact order stipulated in this book as per chapters. Unless you're Netflix, no tier 1 exchange will even consider you for a listing if you don't have great investors and market makers backing you. Once you're backed by some great investors, you can, however, approach the high tier 2 and tier 1 exchanges to start discussions on what metrics you need to meet in order to be granted a listing with them. Simply having such conversations with some big exchanges allows you to inform your market maker that you're in discussions with very big exchanges. Sharing such information with your potential market maker will immediately make you look big and grant you more credibility. The bigger you make your project appear, the more the market makers will want to work with you. Not just for the money but to increase their reputation too! There have even been cases where a C-level of a marketmaking firm took a flight just to meet with a very large project that was about to launch and gave them really acceptable commercial terms just so they would use them as market makers. The bigger you make your project, the more flexible the commercials with your market maker will be.

Once you've made your project as big and attractive as possible, do some research on projects the market maker you're about to have a call with has launched. Try to find some messy token launches they participated in so you can use these examples as a reason why you're not thinking of going with that market maker, play hard to get. Show them that you know your stuff and are not a new kid on the block they can take advantage of. Ask direct questions such as "Who has access to the trading accounts?" or "How do you make money?" The goal is for you to come off as a serious project that knows a lot about how everything works in this industry. If you're able, end the first call leaving this impression; on your next call they should bring one of their experts in to try and answer your questions, this way, they're not thinking "How can we increase the commercials?" they're thinking "How can we retain this client?" Depending on the impression you leave after your first call will dictate the state of mind and approach the salesperson of the market-making company will take with you.

Once you've had a few calls with different market makers, don't get on another call with them for at least ten business days. This way, the sales person will try following up with you a few times and after several days, think that they've lost your business. When you send a message asking for a follow-up call after the salesperson lost hope, be sure to mention you were busy speaking with other market makers too. This little piece of information will sound an alarm bell in the salesperson's head, while indicating to them that competition may have provided you with really good commercials. When you get on that second call, the only thing that sales person is thinking is to close you whatever the cost, even giving drastic price reductions so as not to lose your business. When they ask what pricing the other market makers gave you, don't give any numbers, simply say something along the lines of "I don't wish to disclose this information as I'm comparing honest prices of each market maker, the best one will get our business." Implementing this negotiation strategy will put the sales person on the spot, there's no room for negotiating or trying to increase prices, it's now the opposite. The salesperson will feel like they have one shot and one shot only to get your business. They know that you're serious as it was very hard for them to get you back on a call, plus they know that all of their competitors will be giving you really good commercials as they want your business too.

By combining both the ten-day wait and direct but secretive approach on pricing, the salesperson now has to send you the best possible commercial proposal they can. They neither have room nor time to try and win you over on the relation side, nor do they have the luxury of sending a base proposal with inflated prices they may or may not reduce once you negotiate after receiving it. They must slash their prices to the absolute limit straight away. Using this strategy will not only save you money, it will also save you a lot of valuable time you may use elsewhere. Of course, this negotiation duo can be used in other areas, but only use it for the most flexible entities you can negotiate with, such as market makers, marketing agencies, and tech suppliers.

CHAPTER 10

DEXs and CEXs

Segment 1 – What Are Exchanges

One of the most crucial steps of launching your own token is to make sure that it reaches the eyes of millions of organic traders. Just like a traditional stock exchange, the stocks need a marketplace where traders can buy and sell those very stocks. As we've understood in the previous chapter, the market maker will simply fulfill all of the buy and sell orders in a timely and professional manner, trying to keep a streamline flow of trades. In the traditional financial world, there isn't just one stock exchange acting as the main marketplace, there's an entire plethora of them. Every corner of the world has their very own myriad of them ranging from the infamous New York Stock Exchange (NYSE) or NASDAQ in the United States, all the way up to the Hong Kong Stock Exchange (HKSE) in, you guessed it, Hong Kong. There are indeed many others around the globe and they all differ in tiers, clientele, traders, and the assets they trade.

The larger exchanges we just cited are without a doubt tier one. This means that they are at the top of the food chain when it comes to exchanges, technically speaking, they have the largest market capitalizations. To provide you with some depth here, as of 2024, the market cap of the NYSE is US$28.42 trillion (`https://www.statista.com/statistics/270126/largest-stock-exchange-operators-by-market-capitalization-of-listed-companies/`) which is more than the Gross Domestic Product (GDP) of most countries. We could of course add some

A. Rees-Evans, *How to Launch a Token*, https://doi.org/10.1007/979-8-8688-0533-2_10

more tier one stock exchanges such as Euronext out of Amsterdam or the Shanghai Stock Exchange (SSE) to the list, but you get the point we're trying to make here. Tier one exchanges hold inconceivable financial power that not only shape the financial markets within their respective countries, but actually influence, regulate and alter the global financial markets due to the amount of traders and global outreach.

Following suit, traditional tier two exchanges such as the London Stock Exchange (LSE) or the Tokyo Stock Exchange (TSE) still hold tremendous global influence and financial power, they just don't have the same trading volume as the larger, tier one exchanges. The vast majority of them also meet the same regulatory and legal requirements as their larger twins do, so they are on par with tier ones in certain aspects.

When it comes to tier three exchanges, we do start to see some notable differences between the tier one and high end tier two exchanges from many angles. Often, they don't have large market caps, lack serious numbers of traders, have little or no global influence while abiding by their own rules and regulations. To state some tier three exchanges in the traditional financial world today we can without a doubt cite the Colombo Stock Exchange (CSE) out of Sri Lanka, the Jamaica Stock Exchange (JSE) or even the Zimbabwe Stock Exchange (ZSE) from one of the most prone to hyperinflation countries on the planet, Zimbabwe.

Another big differentiator between exchanges is the type of assets that are actually available for trade. For example, different exchanges will specialize in trading very different assets such as stocks, bonds, metals, oil, derivatives, or even agricultural commodities!

In the world of DeFi, these tiers and asset class differences also exist, but with many more intricacies and complexities than their corporate brothers. In many ways, crypto exchanges are digital twins, there's assets, market makers, a marketplace, international traders, and regulations. Even if we just change the tradable asset class from a stock or a bond and replace it with a cryptocurrency, most people would just think it's an exact replica of any ordinary corporate exchange; this, however, could not be further from the truth. One word, entailing all of these differences, dominates the crypto exchanges but somewhat seems to shy away from the corporate twins, and that word is risk. Of course traditional financial exchanges from the corporate world share to some degree the pain of this word, however, risk in crypto exchanges is far, far greater.

The reasons for this highly volatile environment are plentiful, even more so, this high risk environment is what enables high returns, hence attracting a very different type of trader. The majority of the volume throughout all crypto exchanges doesn't come from professional traders, but more from normal everyday individuals trying to turn US$20 into US$2000 overnight. It may seem completely stark raving mad for the general population to even conceive such an insane concept; however, these feats have actually been accomplished before for a very small percentage of crypto traders. Due to these exploits, the majority of retail traders do believe that if it happened to someone else, it can happen to them. Little do they know that the exit liquidity for every single token, is the retail community. This is the harsh reality of this industry, the chances of investing in the right token at the right time and making millions of dollars is extremely unlikely, not impossible, just extremely unlikely. For it is this possibility of making generational wealth some pocket change that drives the majority of the retail investors. On the other hand, whether you or they like it or not, the exit liquidity for your token will be coming from the very same people, although maybe a handful of them will indeed make a profit.

Risk is an important word here, but not just for the bad. Due to regulatory uncertainty and a complete lack of compliance on behalf of the bulk of crypto exchanges, virtually anybody in the world with access to the Internet can actively participate in trading digital assets. The worldwide unbanked population can invest and grow their wealth thanks to crypto exchanges. They now have a place to store value without requiring an ID card, fixed residency, or a stable job. Every single individual around the world can now store, trade, and manage their finances without the need of a bank account, it's absolutely revolutionary. Another very attractive angle is the barrier of entry. There's no longer a need to have a few hundred dollars available to buy and trade assets, due to the highly fractionalized nature of crypto assets, anybody can join in. From the slums of Brazil to the low income households in the Philippines, they can all start trading with just a few dollars worth of crypto. Crypto exchanges have given real financial prospects not just to the trendy degens or new rebellious college graduates but to all of the underprivileged people in the world. When we think of crypto exchanges, all of the bad stories like with FTX and QuadrigaCX seem to pop up, yet what we must understand is that you can't take the good without the bad. The global financial freedom, prosperity, and hope crypto exchanges have given, far supersedes all of the bad incidents in my books.

Another side of the coin here still remains how your token can benefit from crypto exchanges. Now that we've understood the basics, one of the key points that has a direct correlation with your token price is the number of organic traders on that platform. The more organic traders, the more buying pressure your token should have. Finding out exactly how many organic users are in a given crypto exchange can be quite some task. There are usually two rating metrics to help paint that picture, both of which can be obtained via two publicly available tools, Coin Market Cap and Coingecko. In our case, we will use both of these analytics tools in very different ways, then overlap the information to help us understand which exchanges would be best fit for your token.

First on the list is Coin Market Cap (CMC), like how a Blockchain explorer helps us track, explore, and analyze transactions on the Blockchain, tools like Coin Market Cap and Coingecko allow us to analyze all information about tokens and crypto exchanges such as the volume, rankings, and more. The following document from CMC illustrates the performance of the exchanges based upon some specific metrics. (https://coinmarketcap.com/rankings/exchanges/)

Top Cryptocurrency Spot Exchanges

CoinMarketCap ranks and scores exchanges based on traffic, liquidity, trading volumes, and confidence in the legitimacy of trading volumes reported. Read More

Spot   Derivatives   DEX   Lending

# ⯆	Exchange	Score ⓘ	Trading volume(24h)	Avg. Liquidity	Weekly Visits	# Markets	# Coins	Fiat Supported	Volume Graph (7d)
1	Binance	9.9	$16,047,106,035	889	13,274,841	1633	415	EUR, GBP, BRL and +8 more ⓘ	
2	Coinbase Exchange	3.2	$2,179,848,587	765	70,079	402	249	USD, EUR, GBP	
3	Bybit	7.4	$3,734,657,718	608	6,027,807	903	636	USD, EUR, GBP and +3 more ⓘ	
4	OKX	7.6	$2,345,244,711	624	5,889,924	737	329	AED, ARS, AUD and +43 more ⓘ	
5	Upbit	7.4	$861,458,405	534	2,137,292	312	196	KRW	
6	Kraken	7.7	$616,295,031	755	1,360,433	818	268	USD, EUR, GBP and +4 more ⓘ	
7	KuCoin	6.6	$636,177,452	553	1,346,433	1352	819	USD, AED, ARS and +45 more ⓘ	

In this chart from Coin Market Cap, we can clearly see that Binance dwarfs all of the other exchanges by the trading volume, average liquidity, weekly visits, and markets. Another interesting category on this chart is the "Average liquidity." This defines how easy it is to sell a token and is ranked from 0 to 1000, 1000 being the best possible score you can obtain. When calculating the score, CMC takes into consideration a variety of factors such as the web traffic, average liquidity, volume and the legitimacy of that given volume. When indulging in the analytics provided by CMC, there is of course another component you need to be aware of, CMC actually belongs to Binance. To individuals who've been around in this industry for a while, they probably are aware of this but if this is indeed your first rodeo, you need to observe caution when dealing with all of the information they provide as these can be biased. This doesn't mean that their analytics aren't good, true, or useful, it simply means that when comparing competitors of Binance, you must cross-reference any information they provide with a non-affiliated entity. If not, solely by looking at this one page from CMC, the biggest and the best exchange is undoubtedly Binance. It's actually quite common for large KOLs and successful project or business founders to be stakeholders in some exchanges. For example, Justin Sun, founder of TRON Blockchain and the symbiotic TRON token, is actually a major stakeholder in the tier one exchange HTX (formally known as Huobi) and the tier two exchange Poloniex! Now if he owns a token, owns a Blockchain and exchanges, he will without a doubt be inclined to favor his token's and Blockchain's notoriety indirectly through the exchanges. This is a part of crypto you can't really do anything about, you just need to perform a real due diligence prior to making any token-related decisions.

Although Coin Market Cap does calculate to some extent how organic the volume of an exchange is from a neutral perspecive, in order to fully understand which exchanges have the most organic volume and more, we need to look at the second analytics tool, Coingecko. This analytics platform was founded in 2014 by TM Lee, Bobby Ong, and Dirk Dijk (`https://pitchbook.com/profiles/company/277284-07#overview`) with the goal of providing unbiased analytics for everything Blockchain-related.

The following chart from Coingecko grades the legitimacy of the organic trading volume while also taking into consideration some extra factors such as the cyber security, the web traffic, the order book spread and trade frequency among others. (`https://www.coingecko.com/en/exchanges`)

Top Crypto Exchanges Ranked by Trust Score

As of today, we track 219 crypto exchanges with a total 24h trading volume of $74.7 Billion, a -10.92% change in the last 24 hours. Currently, the 3 largest cryptocurrency exchanges are Bybit, OKX, and Coinbase Exchange. Total tracked crypto exchange reserves currently stands at $207 Billion.

🏛 Crypto Exchanges	🪙 Decentralized Exchanges	📈 Derivatives				All Countries ⌄
# ▲	Exchange	Trust Score ⓘ	24h Volume (Normalized)	24h Volume	Monthly Visits ⓘ	Last 7 Days
1	Bybit	10/10	$3,153,667,522	$3,740,018,536	31 M	
2	OKX	10/10	$2,363,237,429	$2,363,237,429	24.1 M	
3	Coinbase Exchange	10/10	$2,180,773,509	$2,180,773,509	46.3 M	
4	MEXC	10/10	$1,316,145,767	$1,316,145,767	14.5 M	
5	Crypto.com Exchange	10/10	$643,007,710	$1,042,634,065	6.31 M	
6	KuCoin	10/10	$642,055,773	$642,055,773	7.5 M	
7	Kraken	10/10	$598,407,896	$598,407,896	9.7 M	

As we can see from this Coingecko chart, we see a very different picture than the one originally presented by CMC. This conflicting information doesn't mean that Binance doesn't have the volume CMC claims they have, it simply provides a score on just how organic and legitimate the volume each exchange claims to have is.

Strangely enough, Binance wasn't even in the top five for legitimacy on their organic volume as pointed out by Coingecko, but what exactly does all of this mean and how is it possible? In short, some exchanges work together with market makers to create the illusion of a higher organic trading volume by whitewashing and market manipulation. The reason for them doing this isn't as far-fetched as you'd think, like in any line of business, once you're at the top, the only place you can go is down. Due to the money at stake, exchanges fight with whatever means necessary to keep their top position and if one starts doing this, they will gain a publicity edge over their competitors. Even if a competitor exchange didn't want to start using these tactics, they feel obliged to since if they don't, the exchange using this technique will simply surpass them. You need to keep in mind that all of these exchanges are in wartime mode and will do whatever it takes to stay on top. Again, following the example of Binance, this doesn't mean that they don't have arguably the largest trading volume in the world, it simply means that some of that volume isn't organic. This is where the Coingecko trust score comes in handy as it gives an idea as to what extent the trading volume is fake.

If we keep scrolling down the Coingecko trust score page, we stumble upon Binance US and Binance way further down the line than you'd expect.

4	MEXC	10/10	$1,316,145,767	$1,316,145,767	14.5 M	
5	Crypto.com Exchange	10/10	$643,007,710	$1,042,634,065	6.31 M	
6	KuCoin	10/10	$642,055,773	$642,055,773	7.5 M	
7	Kraken	10/10	$598,407,896	$598,407,896	9.7 M	
8	Bitfinex	10/10	$123,431,369	$153,254,114	1.21 M	
9	WOO X	10/10	$33,355,018	$33,355,018	503 K	
10	HashKey Exchange	10/10	$21,624,245	$21,624,245	1.85 M	
11	Binance US	10/10	$9,744,678	$9,744,678	1.47 M	
12	Binance	9/10	$7,694,099,813	$16,028,406,298	75.3 M	
13	HTX	9/10	$1,785,078,606	$2,607,396,654	17.5 M	

If we take the time to dive in deeper here, you'll notice that Binance US does have a rust score of 10/10, but only has a volume of US$9,744,678.00. In comparison with the main branch, Binance boasts a whopping US$7,694,099,813.00, it's a delta of epic proportions! However, if we compare the trust scores, Binance has a 9/10 compared to Binance US's 10/10. The reason here is straightforward, no branches of Binance will attempt any form of market manipulation in US jurisdictions. This directly translates as to no market manipulation involved with Binance US, but you could come to the conclusion that there is indeed market manipulation with Binance.

Now just because I gave Binance as an example doesn't mean that the other exchanges aren't potentially using the same tactics Binance may use, if not more. The goal of this segment is to help you understand how exchanges are ranked and what to look out for when comparing them.

Furthermore, another very important component to take into consideration when comparing exchanges is where they are licensed to operate geographically. If the community of your token is based in the United States, you will as a matter of fact have to take this into consideration when choosing the right exchange. If this happens to be your case, then Binance US probably is your best bet and the same goes for other geographical communities that pair more with specific exchanges. For example if the majority of your community is based in Asia, you may want to target an asian exchange over a larger european one. This part is a direct outcome of your community building and marketing as they both play major roles in what exchanges are compatible with the community you've built. It does work both ways too, if your goal from the very start of your venture is to list on Binance, then the style of your community building and marketing will be adapted to the type of community able to use that particular exchange. More often than not, projects simply just avoid the US community altogether as the regulatory framework spearheaded by the SEC is just too complex, expensive, and time-consuming to navigate.

As we saw at the beginning of this chapter, traditional exchanges from the corporate world also differ from the assets they promote for trading. We saw that some exchanges trade metals, some oil and gas, while others can simply trade stocks, etc. Well, in the world of crypto, this can also be the case. Unquestionably, the crypto industry doesn't just have different types of tokens, but each token can have its own sub-category such as Meme coins, Real World Asset (RWA) tokens, securities, green tokens, NFTs, and many many more! For these reasons, there are some crypto exchanges that have decided to specialize in offering a specific sub-category of tokens such as ClimateTrade, tZERO, or even OpenFinance Network. Depending on your sub-category of token you plan to launch, doing your homework on some of the more specialized exchanges/marketplaces can be of exceptional value. However, specialized exchanges may be a good fit at the start of your token launch, but can also have little to no scalability.

When deciding on which exchange is the best fit for your token, without taking a specific budget into consideration you must always check the following factors:

1) Trading volume

2) Hype of the exchange

3) Compatibility with your community

4) Compatibility with your token

5) Regulatory issues

6) Hack issues

7) Coingecko trust score

8) CMC score

9) Reputation

10) Investors recommendations

11) The management quality of the exchange

12) Leverage your token may use from being listed

13) Token speciality of the exchange

14) Marketing roadmap of the exchange for the exchange

If you're able to cross-reference all of the above points during the preliminary conversations with any given exchange, you will start to have a very clear picture if the exchange is the right place for your token. Don't get sucked in by the buzzwords or pretty information decks, because at the end of the day, in order for your token to be successful, a clever sales pitch from one of their employees won't help.

Segment 2 – What Are Decentralized and Centralized Exchanges

Unlike the centralized exchanges from the traditional financial sector, the crypto industry has yet another spectacular difference, centralized and completely decentralized exchanges exist! As you start to research exchanges prior to listing your token, you will be faced with the nimiety of where to start and which ones are worth exploring. Adding to this complexity, you will be obliged to juggle between the endemic beast of the crypto landscape, the DEXs, and the much more obedient and docile CEXs. Just trying to choose between these two antipodes of the industry can be quite a quandary, often leading to a pinching dilemma. Not long after, you'll find yourself in an imbroglio among advisors, teammates, market makers, partners, and investors, resulting in a deadlock or circular conversation. It goes without saying that this is the last situation any project founder could possibly want as, if you do happen to wander down this path of preclusion, it could end in your token launch being postponed and delaying all other linked aspects. Before we get into the different utilities of DEXs and CEXs in the Web3 ecosystem and how you can leverage them differently, we need to take a step back and understand what fundamentally makes them both very different. At the very core, we must start by comprehending what exactly centralization and decentralization are.

Contrary to what you'd think, centralization plays a very large role in the crypto ecosystem. Not a lot of people like to admit this but we have lost the battle to be a completely new alternative to fiat currencies since AML and KYC protocols were integrated. Furthermore, every single person in Web3 uses one of the most centralized currencies of all, even more centralized than the US Dollar, USDT. Unlike fiat currencies, or many other cryptocurrencies, USDT can verily be frozen at the will of the founders! As Tether Ltd, the founding company of USDT now works with governments and banks, at the request of one of these entities, they will freeze your USDT, even if it's in your wallet. Even the most hardcore degen traders sometimes use USDT and the problem at heart is that it couldn't be any further from true decentralization. Centralization in crypto is the possibility to have a form of control over your digital assets. This is exactly what CEXs do. For example, if you struggle accessing your wallet on a CEX, they more than likely have a customer service or helpline you may call to help resolve your endeavor. Furthermore, the second you place your digital assets in the wallet of a CEX, you're placing them under the direct custody of the CEX. Even if you have access to them, if they wish to, they can move those assets anyhow they want without your consent. To some degree, centralization isn't necessarily a bad thing either as this is the way that literally every single individual in crypto today started. This form of centralization reassures most new to crypto individuals as it provides them with simple, easy-to-use interfaces and a lifeline if something goes wrong.

Decentralization, on the other hand, is the antithesis to centralization. In the context of crypto exchanges, this means that there's no client service, no regulations, no custody via exchange wallets nor AML/KYC. One of the biggest differences is exactly that, they're not custodians of your digital assets. In order to trade on DEXs, you need to connect a decentralized wallet such as Metamask or the Cyberwallet, do your trade, then upon completion of your trade, disconnect your wallet and leave. It's a marketplace with zero custody which attracts a lot of more experienced traders as they prefer to eliminate all risk linked to custodians. DEXs are the last bastions of decentralization in this space alongside DAOs. However, full decentralization comes with its own inherent problems such as accountability. If you mess up a trade, nobody will be able to help you and you have full responsibility for your own digital assets.

CEXs and DEXs don't just differ from the accountability/responsibility side either, their respective trading communities vary also. The liberty of DEXs attract a much more tech savvy and serious type of trader, often with a keen eye for following active trends and price charts. Due to the nature

212

of these traders, they're far more inclined to do research and monitor the price charts of tokens before they get involved in trading a new token. This is another reason why market making on DEXs is especially important as a nice, bullish price chart is your greatest ally! Once the DEX traders feel confident enough to get involved, depending on how well your chart presents itself, you will attract very good traders who won't just dump your token, but will trade it often looking to make profits through much more complex forms of trading such as yield aggregation (Glossary 57), liquid staking derivatives (Glossary 58), or flash loan arbitrage (Glossary 59) among others. DEXs offer unparalleled trading opportunities to all of the professional and degen traders in this ecosystem. Sure, on some CEXs they have introduced some deeper trading perspectives, but they somewhat lack the real freedom of activity that DEXs provide so very well.

Following suit, the origins of traders differ heavily also. On CEXs every single individual wishing to trade has to pass some form of KYC/AML, penalizing those from sanctioned or unfriendly countries. DEXs, on the other hand, require no form of KYC/AML, hence enabling individuals who aren't allowed to participate in digital asset trading because the rulers or regulators of a country decided so. This liberty allows traders from strict or corrupt political environments such as China, the United States, Russia, Rwanda, or Nigeria to still continue trading crypto and enhance their financial freedom. In detriment to immense freedom DEXs offer, the other side of the coin is that criminals can also use them as tools in their money laundering schemes. CEXs offer the opposite features, even if there still are some loopholes sly individuals are able to exploit.

Finally, one of the most important angles that concerns your token is the volume. Just like with CEXs, the key to unlocking the full value of your token is to have as many traders as possible engage with it. Once again, we will use the same tools as before being CMC and Coingecko, but click on the button to view the volume for DEXs.

With this said, here are the top DEXs ranked by CMC. (`https://coinmarketcap.com/rankings/exchanges/dex/`)

# ▾	Name	Trading volume(24h)	% Mkt Share	No. Markets	Type	Launched	Vol. Graph (7d)
1	Uniswap v3 (Ethereum)	$791,133,303	18.1271%	923	Swap	May 2021	
2	Raydium	$785,894,284	18.007%	1114	Swap	Feb 2021	
3	Jupiter	$505,322,478	11.5711%	1181		Oct 2021	
4	Uniswap v2	$290,641,531	6.6594%	1675	Swap	Nov 2018	
5	Orca	$205,236,381	4.7025%	950		Feb 2021	
6	Curve (Ethereum)	$201,788,935	4.6235%	136	Swap	Jan 2020	
7	Uniswap v3 (Arbitrum)	$175,255,987	4.0156%	343		--	
8	PancakeSwap v2 (BSC)	$170,156,922	3.8988%	2957	Swap	--	
9	PancakeSwap v3 (BSC)	$99,298,988	2.2752%	775		--	

As we can see, the main differences between the data provided for CEXs is that the DEXs show their trading volume and market share. Also, it's important to note that PancakeSwap indirectly belongs to Binance too. Nevertheless, by shedding some light on the market share each DEX has, we can actually see that some DEXs we don't really hear about such as Raydium, Jupiter, or Orcua appear.

Furthermore, we can see the phenomenal differences between the volume on CEXs and DEXs. If we recall correctly, the highest trading volume we saw on CEXs came from Binance with an astonishing volume of over US$16 billion. Even if the Coingecko score is a 9/10, it's highly probable only a small portion of that given volume may not be organic. With the DEXs, however, the largest trading volume goes to Uniswap V3 with just shy of US$800 million. The difference between the trading volume between DEXs and CEXs is staggering and must be taken into consideration when choosing which exchange you wish to list on.

Once more, this chart from Coingecko undeniably proves this thesis, there is far more trading volume on CEXs than DEXs. Having said that, the Coingecko ranking does provide us with some extra insight as to exactly what's going on between the different DEXs.

https://www.coingecko.com/en/exchanges/decentralized

#	Exchange	24h Volume	% Market Share by Volume	# Coins / # Pairs	Monthly Visits ⓘ	Most Traded Pair
1	Uniswap V3 (Ethereum)	$840,506,447	20.4%	1,164 / 2,063	13,131,375.0	WETH/0XA0B... $286,985,879.20
2	Jupiter	$591,444,576	14.4%	1,247 / 14,205	10,378,468.0	USDC/SO11... $173,634,030.70
3	Raydium	$269,675,634	6.6%	1,297 / 27,388	4,831,933.0	MOTHER/SO1... $45,881,851.81
4	Orca	$258,907,618	6.3%	417 / 1,190	736,897.0	SOL/EPJFWD... $30,035,373.75
5	Uniswap V2 (Ethereum)	$208,042,810	5.1%	2,751 / 6,993	13,131,375.0	MAGA/0XC02... $73,143,684.96
6	Curve (Ethereum)	$201,008,644	4.9%	146 / 310	298,504.0	USDC/0XDAC... $39,377,403.76
7	Uniswap V3 (Arbitrum One)	$174,637,507	4.2%	241 / 627	13,131,375.0	USDC/0X82A... $61,829,672.54
8	Pancakeswap V3 (BSC)	$116,549,102	2.8%	488 / 1,185	4,853,293.0	BSC·USD/0X... $32,773,330.97

A very useful category of ranking found on this chart that isn't available on the chart from CMC is the "# coins / # pairs" category. This unique perspective allows you to understand not only which trading pairs are the most efficient per exchange, but which tokens are the most liquid across the board. By understanding which tokens are the most used in trading pairs across all exchanges, it can give you indications as to which tokens could be the most efficient to pair with your token to help insure a more liquid market when you launch.

Demonstrated by all of the information provided by two of the largest analytical tools in crypto, it is clear that even tier two CEXs generously offer far more trading volume than the tier one DEXs. CEXs also provide a direct on/off ramp to the fiat world, helping create extremely liquid markets for traders of all levels to enjoy.

DEXs provide absolute trading liberty, attracting many individuals from the United States and other complex countries to participate in trading activities while also retaining a large quantity of technical traders. Furthermore, if you do decide to list on a DEX, setting up and securing your liquidity pools (Glossary 60) will be necessary to ensure a fluid and liquid market. To ensure secure and functional liquidity pools, it's always best to use a reputable third party such as Kaizen Finance as if your liquidity pools get hacked and drained, it will have a negative ripple effect flowing from the DEXs to the CEXs, heavily damaging your token's health. Henceforth, the following piece will illustrate the direct advantages and disadvantages of CEXs and DEXs to help provide you with more depth when making listing decisions:

1. CEX

    Advantages:

    –   High liquidity

    –   High trading volume

    –   On/off ramp possibilities

    –   Internal support for traders

    –   Wallet generation for every user

    –   Easy to use

    –   Marketing support

    –   Specific communities

    –   Possibility of listing specific tokens

    Disadvantages:

    –   Listing fees

    –   Regulatory risk

    –   Hack risk

    –   Centralization risk

    –   Management risk

    –   Fraud risk

-   No privacy

-   KYC/AML protocols

2. DEX

   Advantages:

   -   No listing fees

   -   No KYC/AML protocols

   -   Experienced trader community

   -   A large spectrum of trading styles

   -   Global community

   -   Inclusive

   Disadvantages:

   -   Complex to use

   -   Small trading volumes

   -   Small liquidity

   -   Frontrunners/MEV bots

   -   Sniper bots

   -   No assistance

   -   No marketing support

   -   Liquidity pool vulnerabilities

With these direct comparisons, we fully understand the intricacies with listing your token on DEXs and CEXs. More often than not, a blend of both can carry the scalability of your token a very long way. By listing your token on one of each, you can get the liberty and more complex trading possibilities offered by DEXs, while simultaneously reaping the benefits of a smooth on/off ramp, high volume, marketing support, and customer help provided by CEXs. If you're able to combine the two, you will achieve a much more liquid market for your token, enabling you to sell off more of your tokens as more traders will be engaged. However, if you do decide to opt for this strategy, you will need more liquidity provisions from the very start as your market maker won't only require liquidity for a CEX, they will also require liquidity for your DEX.

Segment 3 – How to Negotiate with Exchanges

Once you've compared all strategic analytics between possible exchanges to list your token on, a final element before deciding will remain; needless to say, we're talking about the price. Apart from the liquidity you would need to provide, DEXs are free to list your token upon. Yet as we've seen, if you want your token to be successful, you need high volume and liquidity. CEXs are the dominating exchanges here, powerlifting your token from the abyss and straight into the spotlight of an immense number of traders. Just like a performer on stage, for some extra budget they can help centralize this spotlight on your token to really push their traders to get engaged. CEXs are non-negotiable if you wish for your token to get in front of millions of users in a targeted manner, unfortunately, this comes at a price. If, however, you choose the right exchange with the right go-to-market strategy, the funds spent on a CEX listing can easily be recovered so you will have nothing but profits from there onwards. Before we get into the nitty gritty of how to get the best price for your CEX listing, it's important to understand what makes them tick. If you start negotiating your listing price without placing yourself in the best possible position, or simply try to negotiate the price without any leverage, it will be a lost cause. It's all about making the exchanges need you more than you need them.

First of all, we need to comprehend how exactly CEXs make money. By understanding these financial mechanics, you will learn where the source of their funds come from and how you can use this information to your advantage. Aligning your token with their business model is the right way to go and the list below will walk you through those very sources of revenue:

1) Listing Fees | Tier 2 CEX price range = US$50, 000–US$250,000 | Tier 1 CEX price range = US$250, 000–US$2,500,000

   As we touched upon the above, the listing fees are a major part of fresh revenue for CEXs. Every token that wishes to list on a CEX must pay an up-front fee in stablecoins; in some cases you can even pay a percentage in your on native tokens. There is a very big warning sign around paying a portion in your native tokens though. The CEX won't pay salaries to their employees in your native token, so they're forced to liquidate those tokens as soon as possible to the detriment of your token price and health. You must remember that when there won't be any vesting for the tokens you give to the CEX, even if they insist they won't dump them and will liquidate them gradually, seldom is that the case. No matter how nice your interlocutor is, it's almost a guarantee that the second your token goes live on their exchange, they will sell them.

   When they do this, it eats up a chunk of the liquidity you were hoping to extract from the market by selling off your own tokens. This can lead to big treasury problems on your backend as you won't be able to liquidate the quantity of tokens required to build up your liquidity for market making. Adding to insult is the negative effect such a dump can have on your token price directly. If your token price starts to grow, once they begin selling your native tokens, the circulating supply of your tokens will increase, hence each token will go down in value. If this selling pressure is too aggressive, not only can it decrease the price of your token, it can also crash it. A sharp, negative drop on your price chart can trigger a FUD effect throughout the trading community. If they feel that the drop in your price chart is too steep, a selling frenzy will occur, leading to the total demise of your token, hours after launching.

Plus, if your token starts to pump, the tokens you gave the exchange to liquidate will go up in value meaning that you paid a far greater price than the CEX originally requested. If you gave the CEX US$60,000 worth of your tokens to help cover the listing fee, just a simple 2x from your listing price will transform that into US$120,000! Not only have you just given a tremendous amount of money to the CEX for free, you've also shot yourself in the foot as you will now suffer a selling pressure of US$120,000 instead of US$60,000. Such mistakes can lead to serious problems because you're more than likely to do better than a 2x on the day of your listing. The chances are you will hit a 5x if you've got good marketing and built a powerful community, every x you hit, you only increase the selling pressure from the CEX, further damaging your token price health.

2) Marketing:

It goes without saying that you don't approach a CEX to help you start building your community in the early days of your venture. It's also true that CEXs aren't marketing experts and don't have the possibility to help build your Discord community. This said, CEXs propose different forms of paid marketing or co-marketing activities for tokens about to list or already listed on their exchange. To provide some depth to all of this, when you approach a CEX to discuss listing possibilities, it's more than likely that they will have different listing packages, each with different content and pricing. The content in these different packages is mainly composed of different marketing and co-marketing activities they can provide you with on top of your basic token listing. The price delta between all of these packages can be quite consequential too, sometimes more than tripling your basic token listing fee! Anywhere from placing your token on the main advertisement banner of their website, X (formally Twitter) announcements, AMAs, Podcasts, all the way up to trading and staking competitions. These engaging opportunities can have quite the pay off if done correctly and with the proper timing, but once again, come with a price.

For pure marketing such as the AMAs and podcasts, etc., you should be required to pay the fee in fiat. As regards specific pricing, it differs remarkably between CEXs and there's no exact science. For the co-marketing activities, automatically they will ask for a portion in fiat and in your native tokens. Reason being, the

221

rewards to the winning traders from these activities will be paid out in your native token. Depending on the CEX you're conversing with, there may be a fixed number of your tokens you are obliged to provide them with beforehand so they may do some airdrops to kick start their community's engagement levels. Often they will ask for a sizable amount of your tokens that they distribute gradually across their community so don't be surprised when they quote you for this.

Among the marketing and co-marketing activities they provide, imagine that the day of your listing you pay for announcements on their social accounts, the banner, and a trading competition, you've spent a lot of money but probably already reached the peak of possible engagement with the social announcements and the banner alone. You didn't need to pay for the trading competition on the first day of your launch as just with the first two marketing stunts, you caught the attention of as many traders as possible that will probably trade your token just from that awareness. Trading activities are actually very dangerous for your token's health, especially in the beginning. It's not rare to witness steep engagement curves during these competitions, then a large disengagement curve in the trading of your token once the competition is over. Also, the winners of that competition will most likely be awarded a prize in your native tokens, which can only add to your selling pressure. The best value for money here comes nearly always with the banners and announcements from their social media accounts.

3)   Withdrawal Fees:

Whenever a trader withdraws either fiat or their digital assets from their custodial wallet on the CEX to a wallet or bank account outside of the CEX, often the CEX takes a small fee. Even if these fees are generally so small they're ignored by the majority of traders, when you start to see just how many traders withdraw their digital assets on a regular basis, the small, individual fees start to add up creating a very interesting stream of revenue for CEXs. These fees range anywhere from US$0 to over US$30 in some rare cases (`https://withdrawalfees.com/exchanges`) but on average they gravitate around the US$3 mark. Whether a degen trader simply uses a CEX as a swift on/off ramp for converting their crypto gains into fiat money, or a loyal retail trader wishes to transfer some crypto to their newly downloaded Cyberwallet, the exchange takes a share. This business model used by CEXs enables them to capture funds from a very large market, even those who do everything possible to stay away from the centralization aspect in Web3. One of the main use cases actually of CEXs by the much more degen community is simply to be a gateway from crypto to the analog world of currencies. Without such financial bridges, the world of crypto would be completely isolated from the real world, making operating in Web3 far too complicated for most people. Knowing just how utilized by the entire crypto community this bridge is, CEXs place themselves strategically to ensure they get a slice of everything that transits through there. Even if they use third parties for such operations in the crypto to fiat operations, they usually have a revenue share agreement with that third party service provider. When a CEX has hundreds of thousands or even millions of users withdrawing on a regular basis, these sums become astronomical, proving to be an incredibly important revenue stream for all CEXs alike.

4) IEOs:

Although we've touched upon IEOs earlier in this book, we must still acknowledge the financial value they provide to CEXs. Since 2017, IEOs have raised hundreds of millions if not billions of dollars for projects (`https://cryptopotato.com/the-icos-comeback-ieos-raised-262-million-in-6-months/`). Some of the largest CEXs alone have raised staggering numbers for their clients through their IEO platforms. It goes without saying that the CEXs don't offer this service to just any project, nor free of charge. As the IEO platform of the exchanges are live, the results of the raise act as a testament to the CEXs status and reputation. You could say that the results of IEOs orchestrated by exchanges are a window into how good the exchange is. Even if fundraising results don't necessarily reflect the quality of the trading volume or liquidity, they do, however, showcase to some extent the buying power of their traders. For this reason, CEXs have very stringent rules to which projects may be eligible to use their IEO service. Here, it's not just about the money, even if CEXs generally charge 10% of the funds raised, and in some cases add an up-front fee in fiat, they won't risk their reputation for this. Plus, just because your token was accepted to be listed on a CEX doesn't mean that your token met the standard to have an IEO with them. Generally speaking, the higher the tier exchange, the more stringent the rules for an IEO are. Prices and percentages from the raise can vary too depending on a multitude of factors such as market conditions, the size of your community, and the grading score of your project. With such tight guidelines, CEXs don't host IEOs on a regular basis so the revenue earned from successful IEOs is usually considered as a cherry on top for them.

5)   Margin Trading:

You may be thinking that this sounds like something that an experienced trader on DEXs would do, but that couldn' be further from the truth. Margin trading is simply a fancy word for saying "They provide loans to traders." If an experienced trader on the CEX has a good hunch on a position, they can apply to the CEX for a loan that they will then use to strengthen their trading position. In return, the CEX either takes a percentage off the volume they generate as interest, plus the return of the initial loaned capital, or simply returns the capital with interest at a mutually agreed upon date. This line of revenue inherently projects a higher risk exposure to the exchange, but for those who have funds to spare, what better way to turn a profit than betting on your top traders. Now the CEX does try to take some form of insurance from the trader applying for margin trading to help mitigate their risk and this is usually done under the form of a collateral that is locked up until the debt has been reimbursed. On some of the larger CEXs, they also provide classic loans in crypto too, of which the funds aren't destined to be traded but used by the individual for something completely different. As this form of loan isn't available on most CEXs, the main revenue stream out of the two does come from margin trading where they charge anywhere from 0.3% to just over 1% of the entire loan requested.

6)   Trading Fees:

The bulk of CEXs' revenues arises from this one category of revenue streams. More than the listing fees, more than the marketing fees alike, the trading fees are the oxygen of all CEXs and without them, they wouldn't survive. Every single transaction that takes place on the exchange passes through the order book of the CEX, which is managed by the management team of the CEX itself. Contrary to DEXs, CEXs don't have gas fees, they have what we call "maker/taker fees." In short, the CEX takes a tiny slice from every crypto that a trader buys, and a tiny slice from every crypto that a trader sells. They take a percentage of every single transaction that happens within the walls of their exchange. This is the reason why trading fees are the most important category of revenue for a CEX. Not only does it bring in an incredible amount of funds, it does this on a constant basis. On average, CEXs take anywhere from 0.1% to 1% of a trade (`https://www.tastycrypto.com/blog/cex-vs-dex/`) but either way, they're still making a profit off every single transaction. Unlike a listing fee, once it's paid for, that revenue stream closes down, then the CEX has to wait for one of their BDs to close a deal for a listing with a new project. This is a very unpredictable, segmented, and manual task. Trading fees, on the other hand, are recurring and literally stream revenue every second into the accounts of the CEX. Binance, arguably the largest CEX in the world today, generates over 90% of its total revenue from trading fees, representing billions of dollars worth of profits (`https://www.coindesk.com/business/2022/12/07/binance-generates-90-of-revenue-from-transaction-fees-changpeng-zhao-says/`). Furthermore, it's predictable to some degree as you can create statistics and, thanks to the frequency and volume, have a live visual representation of what's happening and when. As this data will be coming from hundreds of thousands if not millions of individuals simultaneously, it's possible to track potential movements and patterns, just like you can with a flock of swallows. The power of this constantly streamed liquidity is unmatched when it comes to revenue comparisons, making this line of revenue the most important for all CEXs.

After diving into the fundamentals of CEXs' lines of revenue, it's obvious what CEXs are interested in, trading fees. No matter what the exchange, this will always be a key factor they will consider when you apply for a listing with them. If you're able to increase the amount of users on their platform, they will earn more profits from their trading fees. This is why your community is always such an important factor when it comes to negotiating listings with CEXs. They aren't interested that your token will revolutionize the world as we know it, they're interested in making money. CEXs are big, powerful businesses and are driven by profit. They want to list tokens that will bring new, real traders to their platform that will actually start trading on their platform.

Now we've identified their weakness, you need to structure your community accordingly as they have grading procedures for every new applicant. These procedures vary from CEX to CEX but all have one goal, determine how big, active, and engaged your community is. They will have a dedicated due diligence team run tests on your social media channels to check the amount of people there in correlation with the amount of likes, actions, and comments to check the engagement ratio. If you have a community of 100,000 people on your X account, they will try to find out if this number is composed of bots or real people. For this, they prefer at least an engagement rate of 5%. In this case if you tweet a post on X with a 100,000 community, you should get at a minimum 5000 comments, likes, retweets, and even the quality of them all. The higher your engagement rate is, the more inclined to reduce the listing price a CEX will be. On the other hand, a large community with a low engagement rate can actually be counterproductive as the due diligence team from the CEX will simply imagine you have paid for bots to create the illusion that you have a large social media following. It's all about finding that perfect balance between a large community and a quality community. The bigger and better quality community you have, the easier and cheaper losing with a top CEX will be.

As you may have noticed, we have only mentioned the tier 1 and tier 2 CEXs to list your token on. Leaving out the tier 3 exchanges was intentional as, more often than not, they will damage the price of your token instead of helping it grow. One of the best ways to do just that is by listing on a good tier 2 CEX and a nice DEX shortly after so you can keep costs down, build up your treasury and your token's price chart. With some good market making helping you create volume on the DEXs and mitigate the spread from the arbitrage, you can build up your token's value while crafting a very seductive price chart over a few weeks or months. Simultaneously, your social media accounts should be growing alongside your engagement levels too, enhancing your attractiveness for the tier 1 CEXs. Once you've been able to keep your token and community growing in a sustainable manner and have already listed on a top tier 2 CEX and a good DEX, you'll be ready for the big league. Only with such a palmares will tier 1 CEXs not only take you seriously, but also drop the listing price from millions of dollars to a few hundred thousand dollars in the best cases. It is also possible to list on some other high tier 2 CEXs before approaching a tier 1 as the bigger and more engaged your community will be, the more CEXs will reduce the listing fees. Put yourself in a position where they need you more than you need them.

CHAPTER 11

How to Prepare for Your Launch Day

Segment 1 – What Is Your Launch Date Composed Of?

Congratulations! You've successfully waded your way through all of the challenges leading up to this very special day, the day your token will go live on an exchange. All of that hard work you and your team have put in for the past months or maybe even years is about to finally pay off. Forthcoming will be extreme visibility, reputational evolution, financial success, and the gratifying motion that you have successfully launched your very own token. You may also think that this is when you can start to put your feet up and finally start relaxing as you relish the fruits of your labor. This, however, could not be further from the truth. The official day of your token launch, often known as your Token Generation Event (TGE) (Glossary 61) will be far from a walk in the park. This is your "Make it or break it day." In hindsight, all of the work you've put in, is all to ensure the success of this one day. If you play your cards right, your token could very well become the next biggest hype since PEPE coin, if you play them wrong, on the other hand, this could very well lead to the complete and

© Alexander Rees-Evans 2024
A. Rees-Evans, *How to Launch a Token*, https://doi.org/10.1007/979-8-8688-0533-2_11

utter annihilation of your team, product, token, and reputation. If you had to pick one day where you'll need to be all hands on deck, this would be it.

You may have thought that all of the partnerships, exchanges, market-making agreements, advisors, and other entities you've included in this very special day will all do their jobs and your launch will go swimmingly well. You very well may have also thought that because you're only working with a tier 1 team and partners, nothing can go wrong. You couldn't have been further away from the truth. This is the one moment where you can't afford to take your eye off the ball by delegating or pre-celebrating. On this day, almost every single aspect from every single angle, can potentially go wrong. As goes the old adage "If you want something done right, you're never better served than yourself." In this chapter, we'll look into every main aspect that you need to watch over, prepare for and in short, how to ensure that you can indeed celebrate an extremely successful token launch. Without further ado, let us take a step back and understand what your launch date will be composed of:

1)   Pre-launch Announcements:

It goes without saying that you've been able to build up a solid community with at least a 5% engagement rate on your social media posts. Furthermore, you probably have built up hype around your TGE and your community is eager to start trading your token. It's at this cross-over that you must strategically plan with all of your KOLs and partners when and what they should announce on the day of your TGE. If you don't pre-plan in the utmost of meticulous fashions the content, publication times, and on what social media platforms they should post, you can end up with a really, really big bubble of confusion within your community. For example, if one of your KOLs misspells the token ticker in their tweet, this can very well create a snowball effect leading to mass confusion. Imagine for one second that the KOL has around half a million followers, each and everyone of them will end up searching for a token ticker that doesn't exist and worst of all, you may very well see one or two scam tokens that will try to steal your brand and community. If your token ticker is FYTER, there may be some ill-intentioned individuals who create a similar token with the ticker FYTERE. For large projects, this is quite common as there will always be a small portion of your community that will buy that token thinking it's yours. Although you can't prevent the scammers from doing this, you can nevertheless be as clear as possible through your messaging. Make sure that your marketing team and/or copywriting team review and validate any and all posts from all of your KOLs and partners prior to them being posted. Don't allow announcements from third parties to be made on auto-pilot mode, make it extremely clear that they can't publish without your green light and I guarantee you, you will always find something wrong with at least one of them. In some cases, it's also possible for you to review the future posts the day before your TGE, this way, you're not in a rush and will have more bandwidth on d-day.

2) Exchange Preparation:

If you're listing on a CEX, you need to be aware that you're directly entrusting that CEX to open the trading of your token. Indirectly, you're trusting the employees of that exchange with multiple tasks which accumulated, resulting in the listing of your token on the CEX. Human error is a fatal factor for this component as even tier 2 CEXs often have many departments and personnel working together for the listing of your token. It's completely possible that they list your token a decimal above or below your actual listing price, purely out of employee negligence and if you have a lot of decimals, the chances of them not getting it right are extremely high. The same may be said for your listing pairs, token description, name, logo and ticker. Depending on the CEX you'll be listing on, they can leave the uploading of some of the above information until only a short while before your token goes live. Even if you get along well and trust your account manager from that CEX, make sure you double-check everything because if your token lists at US$0.000012 instead of US$0.00012, you will have a serious problem on your hands. This problem won't only affect your retail community, but will especially affect your investors. Before you know it, you'll be getting calls from every single one of your livid investors screaming and shouting orders at you to rectify the price. Interestingly enough, if a similar scenario does happen and your token price crashes, the CEX won't be held liable. Although this would be far from being directly your fault, at the end of the day, you will be represented as the sole owner of your token's demise.

One more capital component you must monitor to perfection is the exact time of your token listing. If the CEX lists your token a few minutes behind schedule, the damage shouldn't be too bad as all impatient traders simply wait a couple of minutes. If however the

CEX opens the trading of your token one hour before the agreed time, this can be catastrophic as you may only have some early bird investors selling their tokens while your retail community won't be on par. This will result in tremendous selling pressure with little to no buying pressure there to help offset it. This same principle applies to the distribution of your tokens by launchpads if you've used them. You must double-check everything and get specific written confirmation (if it's on Telegram that's perfectly fine) from your account manager at the CEX of every single step and time for what will happen. Again, make sure all of this is grandma clear and that your account manager cross-references all of this information with every internal party involved from the CEX.

3)   Market Maker:

Having a good, solid market maker on board can really have a positive impact on your token on your launch day. Their goal is to keep your token price positive and the price chart seductive. You may indeed have had multiple calls with your market maker, but once again, this day can afford no mistakes for if your market maker's scripts aren't synchronized or they arrive late to the dance, your token will suffer the fullest on winds of the market. Here, make sure that they have access to the trading accounts of the CEX, sufficient liquidity provisions, all of their scripts are synchronized with the Application Program Interfaces (API) (Glossary 62) of the CEX, then that their scripts are on stand-by to be synchronized with your token, and finally, that they're aware of the exact date and time your token will be going live. It's a shame to say this but often, this poorly coordinated market making can result in a drastically fluctuating price chart, discouraging many traders from engaging, ending with the dump of your token. The same principle as point number 2 is applicable here. Send a grandma clear, written message in your market maker Telegram group so all of the market maker's team members can see it and cross-reference accordingly. Furthermore, make sure that they're aware of what percentage of your tokens they should liquidate too. Even if all is going according to plan on the CEX trading side of this venture, there can still be some problems from your internal strategy. If you ask them to liquidate US$100,000 worth of your tokens in the first hour of trading, make sure that they're aware of this and have developed a plan to do so. If you've convinced your investors to liquidate their tokens through your market maker too, you need to make sure that all is in place to facilitate this as the contrary will make your investors very displeased and create unneeded friction in your relationship with them.

4) Post-Launch Announcements:

There's a very big difference from the type of marketing and announcements you'll be doing just before, and just after the launch of your token. Here, we will solely be discussing the marketing announcements taking immediate effect after your launch. Compared to the pre-launch announcements we discussed earlier, these announcements will take place within the first couple of hours after your token goes live. It's fantastic that your token is performing great, but even when this

happens, you can't get caught in the moment. Without
a doubt you need to leverage this success as much as
possible so you can make the most of this short but
juicy event. By immediately sharing the stellar success
of your token on social media and through KOLs, it will
only enhance the buying pressure. By pre-designing
posts for your social media accounts, you will be ready
to publish them by the click of a button. No matter how
busy you get on this prominent day, you will still be
able to share these posts at the right time throughout
the day. If you don't take advantage of this position,
you may not create the intended snowball effect-
enhancing hype around your token. It definitely helps
to have already made some announcements on the
success of your token launch prior to it going live and
you can even design batches of them for different
scenarios!

The final part of this segment revolves around you and your team.
Much like a seasoned captain, you need to hold the ship's wheel and
steer with precision. You must be aware of absolutely everything going
on between your company and third parties. To a certain degree, you
will need to delegate some important tasks to your teammates as you
can't do everything by yourself, it's physically impossible. Be a strong
leader and implement a very direct form of communication for this day.
Whether a captain of a ship or a general in the army, both have something
in common, when they give an order, their subordinates execute without
questioning. You can't afford to spend time explaining to your team the
intricate details of why you're asking them to tweak a specific task as time
will be your enemy. Your team must obey your every command, and you
must get every command right as you will not have the luxury of trying
different solutions,

Segment 2 – How to Organize and Structure This Day

Now, we know the main third parties and formalities to look out for on the day of your launch, but just where do you start? Do you start with announcements? Do you start by double-checking if your CEX listing is ready? Or do you start by tweaking details with your market maker? There are many more questions that will enter your mind when you awaken on that splendid day, but the most important concern is the foundation of your token listing. Some parts of what we discussed in the earlier segment are more important than the others. Depending on which ones default or get delayed for a number of reasons, certain of them will cause greater damage to your token than others. For this reason, you must organize your day like a soldier would as he delicately shines his rifle and laces his boots before he's sent to the war zone for the first time. Both of you will be somewhat stepping into the unknown, this twilight zone separating imagination from reality. You will be joining a level where only the most elite of mortals can survive and return as victors. It's quite an interesting analogy as in both of these domains, to my heart's greatest distress, only a select few will make it. Nobody can guarantee for sure those who will. Although there may be a stroke of luck needed, those with the most training and preparation drastically increase their chances. This is what you're doing right here, right now.

Just like that soldier, the morning you wake up before the official launch of your token, you must be prepared. One of the most efficient ways to structure your plan for this day is by crafting a stringent checklist. This will be your interactive roadmap for the day, providing you with the rigorous direction much needed on this key day. Without further ado, the following piece will provide you with all of the steps and intricacies that your checklist must contain:

1) Morning wake up:

   Assuming your alarm just went off, before reaching
   for your phone to check messages, take a few minutes
   for yourself. Spend five minutes just thinking about all
   the stamps that led you to this moment of launching
   your token. Remember all of the hardships you went
   through, then think of how you overcame them. Take
   a few of these minutes to relax and relativize on all
   you've accomplished up to this point. Energize yourself
   on these thoughts and once you feel that you're in the
   zone, you can check your messages. The state of mind
   you're in will heavily impact how you will proceed
   going forward throughout your day so make sure you
   don't wake up on the wrong side of the bed. Don't wake
   up kiddy like a kid on Christmas day, and certainly
   don't wake up scared. Take your time to get in the right
   state of mind.

   Once you're in the zone and have checked your
   messages, go and take a cold shower to stimulate your
   body. This will accelerate your heart beat and contract
   blood vessels, ensuring your brain and muscles are well
   oxygenated. When you're finished, get dressed then
   have breakfast as usual.

2) Team meeting:

   Just before you and your team start following
   through and making sure all components are in
   place and ready to go, have a call with them. Start
   by thanking them for all of their hard work and how
   much you appreciate everything they've done so far.
   This will make them all feel valued and listen to your

next every word. This is when you double-check every team member is aware of what's happening, when the different events will take place and the roles, responsibilities, and tasks of each individual. Don't be fearful of going over the obvious, it can only solidify the point you're making everyone is aware of. As you come to the end of your team meeting, finish with a bang! Give a small pep talk and once again tell them how much you appreciate the time and effort they've put in to bring your project up to this point. Even if you're not much of a speaker and more of an introvert, it doesn't matter. Your team knows this and will in turn, appreciate and respect you even more for doing something they know you're not comfortable with. This pep talk will be their energizing wake up call, ensuring that you're all 100% motivated and giving them that extra boost so they will go the extra mile if needed. When they will be checking the content for announcements, organizing other segments of the day, thanks to this motivational drive, they won't take any shortcuts and pay more attention to details in everything they'll do. Without the right state of mind in your team, if one of them has to review a content piece before publishing, they may just skim through it briefly then validate without noticing a mistake. Spend a few minutes getting your whole team in the same motivated, calm, and dedicated mindset as yourself. It's more than worth it.

3) Exchange Listing:

One of the classic mistakes made is relaying the wrong information to all of the third parties. For this reason, we'll start at the top of the pyramid. The CEX you'll be listing your token on is the element of which every other aspect of your day will revolve around. This is why we need to start here for if you relay one piece of wrong information from your exchange, it will tremendously confuse all of your other third parties. When checking in with your account manager from the CEX, send him a message as follows:

"Hi John, Please can you confirm and double-check with all personnel involved on your side the following 6 points for my token launch today:

1) Token name: Fyters inferno

2) Token ticker: FYTER

3) Pair n°1=FYTER & ETH, Pair n°2=FYTER & USDT

4) Listing price: US$0,00012 (Three zeros after the comma)

5) Listing time: 17h30mins UTC+2

6) Listing date: 16/06/2024 (Today)

Please double-check with your backend if all of them confirm all of this information too.

Thanks in advance,

Alex."

Now some of these points may seem very obvious and not necessary to double-check, but remember, if just one individual in that CEX get's one wrong, your entire project could crash. It's better to be safe than sorry so don't be afraid to confirm the obvious.

4) Market Maker:

Once you have confirmed all vital information regarding the launch of your token with the CEX, you can start to cross-reference, relay, and contact the other third parties starting with your market maker. This is the second most important third party after your CEX and must always be near the top of your priorities before, during, and after your listing. As of now, you need to not only exchange messages but get on a video call with them too. You must remember that market makers are working on hundreds of tokens simultaneously and even if they're replying to you in the Telegram group, they could very well be trying to tweak several different components of several different tokens at the same time. Just because they replied via text, it doesn't mean they're actually paying attention to what you're sending. The best way to get their full attention is to hop on a call with them. Once they're in front of you and are visible from your screen, you know that you have their attention. This is the time where firstly, you can confirm that they have the exact same information as you for the CEX listing, then move on to double-checking if their backend is ready to run the scripts, they have moved your liquidity provisions into the trading accounts of the CEX and that they have

242

the metrics concerning which amount of your and/ or investors' tokens they need to sell. Once they've confirmed all of the above, you can move on to your next step of the launch day.

5)   KOLs:

The KOLs and influencers you've contracted to enhance your visibility comes next on your list. These, however, are the KOLs you subcontracted independently from your marketing agency. Beforehand, make sure that your marketing agency is aware of which KOLs you have alongside your plan, strategy, and timeline for announcements so you both may synchronize all announcements to consolidate your joint efforts and maximize the efficiency. Getting back to your own KOLs, assuming you already have a carefully crafted plan with them, do make sure that all of their messages and content are pre-approved as discussed before. Keep in mind that your KOLs' goal is to sell your native tokens to their own communities, this means selling pressure. They all need to post and share that your token is launching at the specific time and what CEX it will be tradable on to build up hype and excitement within their respective communities. Once your token is tradable on the CEX, you need to coordinate with them beforehand to discuss the time that each KOL should post on their socials so they don't all do the announcements at the same time. If not, when your token is live, it will likely create a spike in the price chart followed by a sharp dump as all of the KOLs will swell what they can. It may not crash your project but your chart won't look great. If possible, and depending on how many KOLs you have for this day, try to activate their social announcements one after another, not simultaneously. Let's imagine you have ten KOLs for the launch day and you'll be launching at 17h00mins UTC+2, if you can orchestrate your KOLs to start posting about your token one after the other with a 30-minute window in between, your token price action will be much healthier. For this reason, double-check the program and timelines for their social announcements and make sure there's not really any overlap between them.

By sticking to the corpus and organization of this checklist, it will place priority within your day and a good idea of what you need to do and when. The corpus of the checklist is of course subject to modification; however, you shouldn't try to modify the order in which they're placed as this is the capital component of your checklist. If you abide by this priority of affairs, you will be on top of all major segments composing your launch day, so please do use it.

Segment 3 – What to Pay Extra Attention to on Your Launch Day

Now that we know what needs to be done and in what order, it's time to have a look at some minute details you'll need to pay extra attention to on your launch day. Even if all of the above goes according to plan, there's still so many variables that can go wrong, you need to be aware of at the very least a few of them. These are going to be events that aren't under your control directly, but can tremendously impact your launch ranging from price fluctuation to unexpected dumps. These small details aren't really conceived by the average founder as potential problems. This is where if you're not expecting the unexpected and it hits, you'll more than likely be taken by surprise and so flabbergasted, you won't react in time to reduce damage. That's right, now we're not talking about prevention, we're talking about damage control.

One of the most common, uncontrollable defaults that can happen during your launch day is that your vesting distribution doesn't go according to plan. Often, your investors require that you use a third party to handle your vesting and distribution as they're supposed to be a neutral third party, without any possible favoritism in mind. As you remember, we went through the intricacies of what you need to keep in mind when choosing a custodian, because here, you will be using a custodian. Due to the fact that they will be holding all of your tokens destined to be distributed, they are in charge of the full distribution. Although they're blessed with this task and being paid in some form to do so, seldom will they be held responsible if something goes wrong. As they may take some heat, all of the attention will be on you, plus you're the captain of this ship and responsible for everything. It has happened in past token launches that the vesting and distribution did malfunction, either not releasing enough tokens, or the worst of the two, releasing too many tokens. If either happens, it's usually straight out of the blue and if you're not prepared for such a misfortunate event, it will only make matters worse.

To best prepare yourself for such an event, make sure you have an excel spreadsheet on hand with all of the wallet addresses, including which amount of tokens should be sent to what wallet addresses. This way, if not enough tokens have been distributed and you start receiving complaints, you can cross-reference with your vesting and distribution partner until you find the concerned wallet address then simply send what's missing.

If, however, a wallet address has received a much larger portion of tokens than it was supposed to, you need to have this same sheet and cross- reference to make sure they got more tokens than originally intended. Once you're sure, the only possible solution, unless you know who that wallet belongs to and they've returned the surplus of tokens to you, is to contact your market maker immediately. As your market maker controls the order book to some extent, they also have the fine power of blacklisting wallets. It may not be the most ethical of solutions to block that wallet, but it's either you do it before they're able to sell all of their tokens and save your price chart and token health, or you let them carry on and potentially crash your token price. There's no easy way around this, but at the end of the day, you need to think about your community and what's best for them. If you do find yourself in this situation, you have to act extremely fast as you never know when that individual will sell all of your tokens. The first sign indicating this may be the case is to see a large chunk of your tokens being sold at once. Because you've arranged for your market maker to liquidate the tokens for your investors and maybe your KOLs, this dump will most likely come from the private round so this is where you'll need to place your focus. By the time you cross-reference the problematic wallet with your excel spreadsheet and request your market maker to blacklist it until you can resolve the problem, the chances are you'll be too late. Make sure that you're observing that price chart all day so you can react as swiftly as possible to give yourself the best possible chance of salvaging the situation.

The second big pain point during your launch could be your market maker. Assuming you didn't take the loan or profit share model, but went for the retainer model, you may find out as your token becomes tradable that they're just not doing a good job. The orders may be taking far too long to be completed and the price chart may start to look really bad. This can turn out to be quite a nasty situation for you as your market maker is god almighty for your token. They have the monopoly and are in control of more or less everything happening to your token in the CEX's ecosystem. We did also discuss how a market maker isn't a magician in the market maker chapter of this book, but that doesn't mean to say they're not influencing either positively or negatively your token's health, trader's satisfaction, and price chart. If you do indeed realize that your market maker just isn't doing a good job, once again you need to practice damage control until you can find a replacement. For this reason, it's actually good to have two market makers. If one isn't good, you can simply ask them to stop and step aside, letting your second market maker take full and sole control. If you don't have this luxury, you're for sure in a bit of a pickle and the first thing you must do is double-check with that market maker that everything is working properly at their end and that all concords with your prior checks. Doing this may result in finding that they did forget something on that checklist and that they may be running the wrong scripts. If that still doesn't revolve it, simply ask them to change the script to the auto-rebalancing of the accounts. What this means is that market makers can tweak or change their scripts to specific trading styles. When a market maker uses their scripts to rebalance the accounts, this translates into them simply moving their scripts into an efficiency mode where they will try to take a little bit of profit from every buy or sell order they fulfill and place it in their treasury. Now why is this important? As you bring in your new replacement market maker, it's most likely that they'll need more liquidity provisions to recover from the mess your first market maker created. Instead of inciting your initial market maker to use your liquidity provisions to try to recover the mess they're creating, the chances are that if you allow them to do this, they will also mess it up and deplete your liquidity provisions. If you think that your market maker just isn't up to par, don't risk your position anymore. By asking your investors or partners, you can find a replacement market maker and have them take over within a few hours. By this time, your liquidity provisions should still be high and they can use them to rectify the wrong doings of the first market maker. When you start this transition, try to be very gentle as you inform your first market maker that you need them to stop as they still have access to your trading accounts of the CEX and might decide to send the tokens elsewhere or simply dump them out of rage. Inform them that they'll still get paid for the month's work and that it's not you forcing this decision, but your investors. This way they can't really argue with you about them, you're not the one making this decision. However you do it, do your best not to make them angry as they can still retaliate by negatively impacting your token's health and price chart.

For the remaining minute details that can go wrong on your launch day, there's not much you can do apart from paying special attention to your price chart, announcements, and staking portal. If one of these components does default or starts to look bad, it won't be catastrophic, but you still need to amend as fast as possible. Keep your team, third parties, and yourself sharp, especially from a few hours before your launch to a few hours after. Once your token has kept a very healthy, positive price chart for at least four hours from the time your token went live, you can start to take your feet off a little bit. This whole concept of launching a token resembles greatly the concept of building your own classic car from some spare parts, old parts, and imported parts. You spend years building it, meticulously assembling the core, modifying the motor until it hums, then finally polishing the beautiful lines. At the point you take it for a spin, you listen to all sounds potentially signalling a loose bolt, and symbiotically feel the way she drives and handles the road. This is the same as when your token goes live on the CEX, you put in all of that hard work and pray to god everything works as it should, carefully monitoring absolutely everything.

Much like the car, the real stress test is when you hit the motorway and travel for a few hours. It may not be the same intensity as Le Mans, but driving at high speed for a few hours will definitely expose any faults and if there are too many defective parts, the car will simply break down. If, on the other hand, your car holds strong for a few hours at that pace, the chances are that it will hold for much longer. It's exactly the same for your token launch. If you successfully make it through the first couple of hours, the chances are it will stay that way for a while. This doesn't mean that after four hours you should stop monitoring and stay out until the break of dawn, it simply means that you've done it. You've successfully launched your token and are more than entitled to a glass of champagne!

CHAPTER 12

Token Health, Longevity, and Final Words

Segment 1 – What Is Token Health and Longevity?

During your time perusing this book, you'll have noticed that many a time the terms "token health" and "token longevity" have been cited. Almost all chapters cite them, but just what do they signify and to what extent are they important to your token? This chapter could indeed be reserved for a new book as we're no longer in the designated realm of launching your token; here we stride into the domain of what's to come. Although this doesn't directly concern your token launch, your token's life doesn't just stop once you've achieved your TGE. It isn't an automated robot for which, once built, only some minor maintenance is required every so often. Think of your token more as a child. Following this narrative, your token launch is in essence the successful birth of your newborn baby. For all of the parents out there, you know that this is only just the beginning of a wonderful new adventure. For those of you who aren't yet parents,

© Alexander Rees-Evans 2024
A. Rees-Evans, *How to Launch a Token*, https://doi.org/10.1007/979-8-8688-0533-2_12

you're in for a very big surprise! The birth of your child isn't when you stop becoming a parent, it's when you start. As your baby will start to grow, you'll need to adapt and facilitate their development. During this period of evolution, your worries, requirements, attention, and assistance won't disappear, but they will change. Your interaction and implication levels will evolve alongside your child. It's the exact same thing for your token, you will watch as your token matures and faces different challenges during its existence. One of the worst books that could exist would be on how to take care of a child, but ends after the first day your baby is brought to life. Given this reasonable analogy, it seems only right that we touch upon what awaits you after the birth of your token and how to take care of it.

Launching us into this segment is your token health. Just what exactly is it? We're going to dive into all of that right now! Your token's health is a term used to describe the general state of your token once it's live. To fully understand the state of your token's health, the following metrics will need to analyzed then compared to the initial metrics on your tokenomics:

1) Fully Diluted Valuation (FDV) (Glossary 64):

   This can also be referred to as the fully diluted market cap, as we discussed in tokenomics; it always defines the accumulated price of all of your tokens. It's the total market value of all of your tokens if they were all in circulation. The goal is for your FDV to grow with time, not decrease. If your FDV does decline over time, it negatively affects your token brand and can, depending on the decline, decrease your chances of fundraising a series A or B round. This said, there are many cases where the FDV of a project does decline due to market conditions and sentiment so your FDV will most likely increase during a bull run and decrease during a bear market. The goal is to have a higher FDV when compared to similar past market conditions.

2) Market Capitalization (MC) (Glossary 64):

Compared to your Initial Market Cap (IMC) (Glossary 65), your MC is the US dollar value of all of your tokens currently in circulation. Just like your FDV, as time goes by, you want to make your MC increase. Of course if your FDV has increased over time, then without a doubt your MC has too. The use for still checking this metric is it will give you another metric to compare with your initial tokenomics. In this case, you'll be comparing it with your IMC as this is the starting point of your expected growth.

3) Trading Volume (Glossary 64):

The trading volume of your token reflects the appetite of traders buying and selling it. It represents the dollar value that has transitioned through your token and is calculated on a 24h basis. For this metric, the higher the better, and this number should be in the millions for a solid project. If you have a low trading volume, it isn't a good sign. A great way to determine if your trading volume is good is to compare it with other similar tokens as yours on an analytic blockchain website like CMC or Coingecko. Try to compare it to tokens with similar tokenomics as yours also to get multiple points you can cross-reference.

4) Price Chart:

This may seem obvious but the price charts found on blockchain analytic websites such as the ones previously stated can provide great, quick visual insights on your token's health. To get the best idea of your token's overall health, check the price chart at least three times. One for 24h of trading, the second for one month of trading, and finally, since your token has been made tradable. Just like a triangle, you need three points of verification. Each time you check, take note of the visual trend and the color of the chart. Fluctuating between green and red, green being positive price action and red being the negative, you'll be able to paint yourself a detailed picture of your token's well-being.

5) Order Book Depth:

To find out your order book depth, instead of foraging through the given data on the exchange, you can simply ask your market maker to provide you with it. Once you have it, jot down how many buy and sell orders of your token there are for a given period of time. If possible, get the number of trades per week every week, starting from the day of your launch. This way, you can collect this data over time and see in detail how your native trading community evolves as your token does. As always, the more the better.

6) Bid-Ask Spread:

Essentially, the bid-ask spread is the price difference of someone willing to buy, and someone willing to sell your token. Again, you can ask your market maker to provide you with these details, or even better, provide you with the average bid-ask spread every week or so. In short, the smaller this price difference is, the more liquid is your token. If you start to see very large bid-ask spreads, this isn't a good sign of health for your token. The most popular tokens have exceptionally low bid-ask spreads as they have so many traders looking to buy and sell that there's always a trader willing to pay full price.

7)   Number of Users:

Don't confuse this with the number of holders, this is simply the number of wallets containing your token. This doesn't mean that those tokens can't be sold at any given time, it simply shows the amount of wallets that do contain your token at a given moment. Usually you can check the number of wallets containing your tokens by going on to a blockchain analytics website such as Etherscan or BSCscan, for example, and click on the "holders" tab, which will lead you to a secondary web page where you'll find the number of holders among other metrics. It's useful to gather this information every two weeks or so to help provide a clear view of evolution, even years down the line.

8)   Number of Stakers:

This is the part to look into the details of how many wallets have participated in staking your tokens. It's important to note the distinction between wallets and individuals here as one individual can have multiple wallets. To verify how many wallets sent tokens to be staked, the easiest way is to ask your staking platform provider to provide you with all of this data on a fortnightly basis once again. The more data you gather over time, the easier it will be to create helpful analytics.

9) Number of Transactions:

By researching the number of transactions on similar analytic websites as cited above, you will be able to see just how many buy and sell orders have actually taken place over a given period of time. Generally speaking, you don't have to jot down every two weeks or so the metrics of this but if you do, you'll have a better understanding of your token trades further down the line. If not, just check these numbers every time you start to do research for analytics.

10) Social Media Growth:

Over time, all of your social medias are supposed to grow. This is where sometimes, a few after the token's launch the marketing slows down, leading to disengagement on behalf of your community. To help keep you on track, every so often, check your social media following, number of comments and likes. It's important to check all of these metrics as often community members simply mute your channel/ group, or just never return to your X account after they clicked follow. If we consider your social media following, it must grow; as for your engagement rate, it should be around 5%, if possible.

11) Partnerships:

As your token evolves in the realm of trade, you need to keep adding more and more new partnerships. The reason is simple, without high quality partnerships with larger projects, you will always remain on the same level, as will your token's perceived value. Much like a company, by stagnating for a year or two with the same type of clientele, it can be harder to obtain a new type of clientele as you've associated yourself too much with a specific group. Because the world of crypto evolves so fast, this phenomenon of association sticks much quicker. If you only partner up with tier 2 or tier 3 projects, then you automatically become one. Check the quality of partnerships you've built over time and make sure they're consistently getting better in quality. If that's not the case, rethink your partnership strategy and model.

12) Roadmap:

Be as true to your roadmap as possible, that's how you'll develop a trustful relationship with your community that can help you make it through bad times, so it's important to deliver on what you've promised. Also, as your roadmap has a timeline, if you're on par with it, it's a good indication that your project and token are healthy as there's been no major delays due to lack of liquidity or talent.

Your token's health is primarily composed of all of the above cited components. If you have the bandwidth enabling you to retrieve the data from these metrics every week or so, it will enhance the precision of your token's health. If you don't have the time to do this on a weekly basis, at a minimum you must do it every month. As all projects are different with different FDVs and MCs, we need to tailor the final calculation to create a percentage to define your token's health. That's why we need to attribute a value to each one of the 12 metrics needed to calculate your token's health. Determine the value of each metric by choosing a number defining how important they are on a scale of 0-1 The intrinsic value of all metrics must equal 1 as demonstrated below:

1) FDV = 0.1

2) MC = 0.1

3) Trading volume = 0.1

4) Price chart = 0.1

5) Order book depth = 0.1

6) Bid-Ask depth = 0.1

7) Number of users = 0.1

8) Number of stakers = 0.1

9) Number of transactions = 0.05

10) Social media growth = 0.05

11) Partnerships = 0.05

12) Roadmap = 0.05

Secondly, we need to determine the weight of each metric as follows:

To find the normalized value for the FDV, MC, Trading volume, Number of users, number of stakers, number of transactions, partnerships, social media growth, you must

‒ Compare the current value to an average or previous value

Example:

‒ If the FDV has increased 20% since last year, then your normalized value is 0.2 (always on a scale from 0 to 1).

In short, for every category, find the percentage of increase then normalize it from a scale of 0-1 by dividing your percentage by 100. When done correctly, in our example we have the following results:

1) FDV = 0.2

2) MC = 0.2

3) Trading volume = 0.7

4) Price chart = 0.6

5) Order book depth = 0.8

6) Bid-Ask depth = 0.7

7) Number of users = 0.9

8) Number of stakers = 0.7

9) Number of transactions = 0.8

10) Social media growth = 0.6

11) Partnerships = 0.7

12) Roadmap = 1

Now that we have the intrinsic values and normalized weight for each category, we must do the next calculation:

1) FDV: 0.1x0.2 = 0.02

2) MC: 0.1x0.2 = 0.02

3) Trading volume: 0.1x0.7 = 0.07

4) Price chart: 0.1x0.6 = 0.06

5) Order book depth: 0.1x0.8 = 0.08

6) Bid-Ask depth: 0.1x0.7 = 0.07

7) Number of users: 0.1x0.9 = 0.09

8) Number of stakers: 0.1x0.7 = 0.09

9) Number of transactions: 0.05x0.8 = 0.04

10) Social media growth: 0.05x0.6 = 0.03

11) Partnerships: 0.05x0.7 = 0.035

12) Roadmap: 0.05x1 = 0.05

Once we have the results, we simply need to add them together and multiply the result by 100:

Token health: (0.02+0.02+0.07+0.06+0.08+0.07+0.09+0.09+0.04
+0.03+0.035+0.05)x100 = 65.5%

We can now clearly see that the token's health is 65.5% which is OK. Because we have a mathematical understanding of what's going on, we can tweak our strategy for the lesser performing categories we saw initially such as the FDV, MC and the price chart. Also, by taking a few minutes out of your day once a month to do this calculation, you'll have a very interesting perspective of your token's health that you can keep track of!

As for your token's longevity, we do exactly the same calculations by slightly modifying the categories like this:

1) Number of users

2) TVL of the Blockchain

3) Number of Dapps on the Blockchain

4) Partnerships

5) Social media growth

6) Number of stakers

7) Token burn rate

8)   Security breaches

9)   Relevance of your sector

It goes without saying that your token's longevity is heavily determined by your tokenomics before your token goes live; with that in mind, the above factors are also variables that can influence the longevity. For example, if you launched an AI project when that was the trend, that sector may no longer be trendy a year down the line, hence the sector loses relevance and traction to a certain degree. Your token's health and longevity are capital metrics you should monitor at least once per month. Doing this will help you keep on top of any changes in the ecosystem and your token, allowing you to adjust any and all possible variables so you stay ahead of the changing winds of crypto!

Segment 2 – How to Maintain and Entertain Your Community

It's great to know the details of your token's health and longevity, but just what do you do if they aren't up to par? This is where in almost all cases it can be solved by increasing your community's engagement. The bottom line is that you'll seldom have more buying pressure than on your launch day, and if you've read this book attentively, it should go well. The upcoming problem, however, is the buying pressure usually drops either a few hours after your launch or the next day. Depending on the quality of CEX you'll be listing on also has an impact as the quality and buying power will be higher on large tier 1 CEXs, but it will start to die down eventually. It's at this moment that your token can start to lose traction and saunter off into the path of solitude, as taken by many a token. Possibly, it may simply be that there's a large change of narrative in the market and your token naturally starts to lose traction as members of your fellow traders and community switch their focus to another project and token. Or, maybe you notice that your buying pressure just gradually decreases slowly over time and need to fix it. Almost any and all possible scenarios can be fixed by a community, it's for this reason that weeks, months, or even years after your token launch you must still take dear care of your delicate community.

We mustn't forget what makes a community tick. Just why do they become a member of your community? It all boils down to that one simple thing, money. This is what's often forgotten by project founders once their token has been launched, their activities stop, airdrops stop, and all development revolving the token becomes almost nonexistent. This doesn't mean that you should replace or change the code of your token, it simply means that if your token's price or revolving ecosystem doesn't present future opportunities for financial growth, your community will cease to expand and become dormant. You may still have impressive numbers in your social media accounts, but that doesn't mean that they're still active. That's why we're now going to explore some engaging activities you can use on a regular basis to keep your community engaged and active:

USDT Giveaways:

As soon as you develop your tokenomics, try to increase the portion of your future treasury. Once you've been able to liquidate enough tokens to build up your treasury, you'll have a fair sum of USDT. By using some of this USDT as a reward for certain tasks performed within your token's ecosystem, you will hit the direct nerve of every single community member. When using USDT this way, you have to tailor the amount to the desired effect taking into consideration the bulk of your community. For example, if your community's mostly composed of individuals from developing countries, maybe a US1000T reward will be more than enough to engage them. On the other hand, if your community's mainly composed of members from developed countries, you will need to heavily increase this USDT reward to obtain the same level of engagement.

Token Airdrops:

Contrary to USDT giveaways, depending on how many of your native tokens you wish to give away, token airdrops can damage your token's price action and chart. Also, token airdrops aren't just destined to be used prior to your token going live on an exchange, even some of the most reputable tokens do airdrops months or even years after they launch to reward long term holders. With the technology available today, you can easily find which wallets have been holding most of your tokens. By making an exciting announcement about an upcoming airdrop of your native tokens, you can also require your community to re-engage with your social media to be eligible as a recipient. You can ask them to comment, like, and repost a tweet on X or your other social media accounts, thereby creating the illusion of a highly engaged community, turning into a snowball effect until you actually have revitalized your community.

NFT Drops:

NFT drops can be an interesting way to not only remind your community about your project but also give you the opportunity to engage with a new community if not yet done, the NFT community. This community is typically much more long-term orientated than a token community and are generally active in NFT Discord servers such as Neo Tokyo, Pudgy Alpha, Ape list, Cool Cats, and many many more. There are about 300 very good NFT communities in Discord and all of them are mostly safeguarded by their community members. This means that you'll have to put in some work beforehand to gain access to them, or you can delegate these tasks to companies like Infernolabs to save time.

Ambassador Program:

Some of your long-term community members do want to be actively involved with your project, so why not let them? A great ambassador program can grant this opportunity to some select members that will in turn, try to promote your project and token by their own means simply because they want your project to succeed and feel as if they're part of this success. It is quite rare, however, that they'll do this for free even if sometimes it can be the case. Measure the rewards based on their performance and be relatively generous. These individuals can help boost your community from the ground up and bring more new members on board if they're motivated enough. By giving them tasks such as onboarding new members to your community or commenting and sharing as much as possible on all of your posts in exchange for some tokens or whitelist spots for your next project, you can soon find yourself with a powerful army of believers in your project, all simultaneously pushing your brand awareness and visibility to new levels for minimum cost.

Merchandise:

Much like what Pudgy Penguins achieved with Walmart by placing their characters as fluffy, analog toys on shelves within their shops, it propelled them onto the global stage, outside of the Web3 community. This is a very powerful option, to take your community and project to the world of traditional commerce. Best of all, you don't have to have a powerful NFT collection to make this happen, all you need is the right contact in your network. If you're able to partner up with a large distributor of food or beverage commodities or comic books, for example, and place your logo or brand alongside theirs, you will automatically find yourself unlocking a new line of community reactivation, onboarding, and potential revenue stream.

Partnerships:

Far different from merchandise is your brand awareness promoted by other entities, not just in the realm of Web3. For this, you don't need to sell a physical asset, you simply need to show your community and the entire world that your brand is part of something big. A great idea is to partner up with musical artistes and have your brand in their music videos or even a film. This is what Omega did with the James Bond films featuring Daniel Craig. They had their brand become a desirable item used by the main character. Of course you can't get your token to be worn by an actor, but you can place your brand in the background or become part of the lyrics of a viral song. Once again, this will boost your current community's faith in your token and open new doors for outsider investment opportunities.

Sponsorships:

More and more we see Web3 companies sponsoring major sporting events such as football or F1 racing. The CEX Kraken actually did a brilliant job of sponsoring an F1 racer at major F1 competitions such as in Singapore. The visibility and brand awareness brought to them by paying a large fee was definitely worth it as they kept on doing it. If you don't have that type of budget, you can always start small by sponsoring university teams or crypto conferences. Depending on your goal, you will have to decide the type of subject you wish to sponsor as it can either be good or bad for your brand depending on what the outcome will be. Furthermore, you must think about the goal of this campaign, is it to simply increase your brand awareness and perceived value, or is it to obtain new traders and increase your volume? Depending on your answer, you will need to choose the most comprehensive prospect to achieve your specific goal.

- Events:

To stay in the very heart of the elite crypto
community, you can also decide to host your own
side event at a major crypto conference. By hosting
the most epic of all side events, all of the influential
individuals from Web3 will attend and generally
have a good time. In this setting, you can create
a great relationship with some top KOLs, traders,
and investors that you'll be able to set up business
meetings with later on that week and discuss a
potential collaboration withyour project. To add,
you can also hire a media team to cover your side
event providing you with tremendously valuable
media footage you can share on your social media
accounts, creating some buzz among your current
community.

- Celebrations:

For every achieved milestone of your roadmap
or major new features you add, make it known to
all of your community! Don't simply send out a
few tweets saying how good it is, make a party out
of it. For retail investors, they don't usually have
the opportunities to fly out to exotic conferences
or hang out at exclusive side events, this is where
you can fill the gap. By bringing the party to them
thanks to a big metaverse you've connected with,
you can create a very cool immersive experience
where your community can hang out altogether
and engage with each other on a more intimate
level. You can also hire a well-known DJ to make an
appearance and play some banging tunes too! Even

265

if you already have weekly hang outs in a metaverse, leverage the connections you have to host something memorable for every big announcement or achievement you have. Create some unique NFTs or skins for these occasions as giveaways for the attendees and don't forget to share all of the highlights on your socials, you can even do a special giveaway to the top 20 attendees who create and share their own best highlights.

Referral Programs:

As we know, your community is with you as they believe you, your project, and token will lead them to financial gain. What better way to help them than creating a referral link generator where each and everyone of your community members can have their own unique referral link at the click of a button. By providing them with this opportunity, they will be far more likely to push their friends, family, and own entourage to buy your token. This system is used in almost every single major traditional company for a very simple reason, it works. There's even some companies that have based their entire business model on this, such as the modern tupperware meetings, where they all try to get you to join their subscription program, then you can do the same with your friends and earn money from their purchases. Half of the time the products they're shilling are of really poor quality, but it works exceptionally well because they have a great referral program, and financial gain is the key incentive.

There's an endless list of possibilities to help ramp up your community's engagement levels and there will be even more by the time you've read this book. With the ten ideas given above, they have been tested and proven to work so are definitely a great place to start. Regardless of the method you'll choose to increase your token's longevity and health, you must always keep one basic factor when considering options: Will this provide financial growth to my community members? If the answer is yes, you're probably on the right track. If the answer happens to be a no or a maybe, go back to the drawing board and only execute on a plan that will work. Finally, try to keep a healthy balance between what financial value you'll be giving away and what you'll get back in return. If you're giving away US$50,000 worth of value, make sure the exposure and potential onboarding of new traders will cover that initial cost so your token's health and longevity will indeed increase.

Segment 3 – How to Develop a Long-Term Token Strategy

In this last chapter of our journey together, we'll be onboarding the vital strategic components that you must take into consideration from the development to the entirety of your token's lifespan. You will need to think about how you can create a clear vision for your token that by far transcends the dates of your roadmap. Solid tokenomics are for sure a good start, but they won't help you that much once your token supply is fully distributed and diluted, nor will they assist you as the market, trends, regulations, or ecosystem evolves. Just like the captain of a ship, they always integrate a security margin for the depth when the boat enters the port just in case the tide has changed. Classic tokenomics models don't usually have a margin of tokens just sitting in one corner, just in case you made an error or needed to absorb a shift in the market. Once your token's launched, there's no going back, they're set in stone. This is why the main components of any long-term strategy is split into two main parts which we'll explore now.

The first part of a great long term strategy for your token is based upon what is known as perceived value. Money is what all participants in the crypto industry are interested in. May they be from developed or underdeveloped countries, rich or poor, it doesn't matter, they're all participating for financial gain. This is why you need to make sure that your project remains an ideal candidate for them to place their funds in, hoping they prosper. But just why would they choose to invest in your token rather than the other thousands that are available? The correct answer is perceived value. Perceived value is what makes any community member believe that they will receive financial growth from investing in your token. Just as how value is to a certain degree a highly subjective matter, the perceived value is this exact subject. As an example, some women prefer Chanel handbags over Louis Vuitton, even if they're more or less the same price. Some men prefer to watch a match of football with their buddies as others would rather have a poker night. Each individual perceives value differently, that's why some high net worth individuals prefer to purchase a fancy penthouse in flamboyant Miami, while others a bastide among the lush olive trees in the south of France. Each individual is wired to desire one asset rather than the other and this is why we have such diverse marketplaces all around the world for almost every type of asset imaginable. They all, however, have a common denominator for defining value, this is the price. But what creates the price of a typical asset or commodity? It's the supply and demand ratio. In the world of crypto, this won't help you though as nearly every single crypto project has a capped supply, hence creating the illusion of scarcity. This is where we need to think a little beyond just the price as a determining factor of value and find an alternative, as the price of your token is purely speculative.

The only other factor that could replace the price as a determining factor for value is desire. The desire to learn, the desire to love, the desire to be loved. Human beings are simple creatures at heart and desire is the main driver for almost everything all individuals do. According to Nietzsche, this is the main fault in a Dionysiac lifestyle when compared to its antipode, the Apollonic lifestyle. Dionysiac being the art of complete self-indulgence in all of the fruits life has to offer, and Apollonic being the art of refusing to indulge in any of the fruits life has to offer if they don't serve your best long- and short-term interests. In Nietzsche's view, if you were able to transcend the life of a Dionysiac and follow that of an Apollonic style, the result would turn you into an "Ubermensch," translating as Superman. Luckily for us, the entire crypto industry is oriented much more toward a Dionysiac form of ecosystem rather than Apollonic. At the very core, the main difference between them both is the control of our inner desires, hence the hypothesis that desire is the ultimate component to make any individual tick. With regard to your project and token, while considering the above information, you need to make both of them as appealing as possible from the very start.

To take advantage of this Dionysiac ecosystem, you must enhance your desirability, leading to a higher perceived value of your project. For this part, there isn't an exact science. If there was, it would be the same equivalent of finding Nicolas Flamel's philosopher's stone, enabling you to create gold at will. Developing the highest possible perceived value is one of the most complicated challenges you will face and the only suggestion to help you here is to make yourself look as big as possible by only collaborating with the biggest entities in this space, starting with your cap table. Once again this is a tricky equation as you need to convince each and every one of your tier 1 partners to actually partner with you. Just like any old business, the easiest way to do this is to get introduced to them from a solid contact, then fly out to meet them and simply ensure that you have a good time. If they're going to watch the Olympics, go and join them. If they enjoy hiking, get yourself in shape and go hiking with them. Ensuring you create such a tight relationship with them can be costly and even take some time, but if you're able to do this with just two or three of these powerful tier 1 contacts, not only will they join you but they will bring more tier 1 partners on board by themselves. Before you know it, you will have a snowball effect of tier 1 partnerships appearing left, right, and center. If you're not a sociable person, send the most sociable and likeable person from your team to go and create this relationship for you. Even if you're the CEO and they're not a C-level, send them, and always remember, you do business with people, not companies.

The second and final main component to a successful long term strategy is letting your community win from time to time. If your community keeps on losing money, even if your token price keeps rising, they will more than likely stop investing and simply switch to another token. It really is that easy. If they lose money after replenishing their wallet a few times by trading your token, they'll get tired and just start trading on a completely different token the next day. Much like in a casino, if you go every day and every single time you play either roulette, blackjack, poker, or the slot machines you lose, after a few days or weeks, depending on your tolerance to loss, you'll just stop going. This is why the casinos do let you win from time to time. This is also why they showcase large amounts won by other, normal individuals, just like yourself in big letters on an even bigger board for all to see. It shows you that it's possible to win really big amounts of money. Now if you keep playing the slot machines and for every US$20 you put in, once in a while you win a couple of dollars until one hour later you win US$30, the chances are you're not going to quit and walk away with your US$10 gain, you'll remember the crazy amounts other normal people just like you won from the board in the middle of the casino and think, I can do it too. This is usually when you slowly start to go downhill and deplete your US$30 until you go all in with the remaining coins in your jar, that ultimately seals your fate. But the next day you'll go back, confident that you can do better and keep trying until three weeks later, you'll win US$380. At that moment you'll be ecstatic as you just spent US$20 and won US$380, netting you a profit of US$360! Now however, you'll have the impression that you can win even more during your next visit and probably up your budget to US$40 until you repeat the same scenario over and over and over again. The brilliance of the casino here is that although you netted a US$360 profit once, every day for the past three weeks you've spent hours winning then losing then winning and losing some more until, after a few hours every day, you've lost your initial US$20 each day for the past three weeks totaling a loss of US$420. Although you netted US$360, you're still actually at a global loss of US$60. The casinos make a tremendous amount of money by the sheer volume of individuals losing these small amounts over very long periods of time, and this is why they're successful, they let you win from time to time knowing that if they do, you'll keep coming back.

Your token business model and community may be compared to this scenario. If you keep liquidating your tokens every time your price chart increases, for sure you will make money, but when can your community have a win? Don't be too greedy with your token liquidations and allow your community to win from time to time because if you do, they'll keep coming back.

To conclude not only this chapter but also this book, I thank you dearly for the time spent perusing the accumulation of experience, knowledge, tips, and hacks found in these pages. May the information of this book ensure you a successful token launch, and your project, community, and reputation exceed all expectations, forging a path to financial freedom for all.

Glossary

Definitions from the Cambridge dictionary:

1) Token – A digital unit designed with utility in mind, providing access and use of a larger crypto economic system. Token Definition I CoinMarketCap

2) CEX – Centralized exchanges (CEXs) are a type of cryptocurrency exchange that is operated by a company that owns it in a centralized manner. Centralized Exchange (CEX) Definition I CoinMarketCap

3) DEX – A peer-to-peer exchange allowing users to trade cryptocurrency without the need for an intermediary. Decentralized Exchange (DEX) Definition I CoinMarketCap

4) Blockchain – A distributed ledger system. A sequence of blocks, or units of digital information, stored consecutively in a public database. The basis for cryptocurrencies. Blockchain Definition I CoinMarketCap

5) NFTs – Non-fungible tokens (NFTs) are cryptocurrencies that do not possess the property of fungibility. Non-Fungible Token (NFT) Definition I CoinMarketCap

© Alexander Rees-Evans 2024
A. Rees-Evans, *How to Launch a Token*, https://doi.org/10.1007/979-8-8688-0533-2

6) DAO – A decentralized autonomous organization (DAO) is founded upon and governed by a set of computer-defined rules and blockchain-based smart contracts. Decentralized Autonomous Organizations (DAO) Definition | CoinMarketCap

7) ICO – Short for Initial Coin Offering, an ICO is a type of crowdfunding, or crowdsale, using cryptocurrencies as a means of raising capital for early-stage companies. Initial Coin Offering (ICO) Definition | CoinMarketCap

8) Yield farming – Yield farming involves earning interest by investing crypto in decentralized finance markets. Yield Farming Definition | CoinMarketCap

9) Peg – A "peg" is a specified price for the rate of exchange between two assets. Peg Definition | CoinMarketCap

10) Degen – Shorthand for Degenerate. Degen trading or Degen mode is when a trader does trading without due diligence and research, aping into signals and FOMO into pumps. A Degen Trader does not know about metrics like FDV or TVL, nor do they care. They will buy because the asset logo looks cute, or because the slogan is memeable, or because some twit-famous anime girl on the Internet says she's looking into crypto and the first two shill comments gets more likes than others. Essentially, a degen trader buys into an asset not because they see value, rather they do so with the belief that others will join in after them and speculate on the price swings. Definition of Degen | CoinGecko

11) Liquidity mining – Liquidity mining is a mechanism or process in which participants supply cryptocurrencies into liquidity pools, and are rewarded with fees and tokens based on their share. Liquidity Mining Definition | CoinMarketCap

12) Staking – Staking is a form of participation in a proof-of-stake (PoS) system to put your tokens in to serve as a validator to the blockchain and receive rewards. Staking Definition | CoinMarketCap

13) Smart contracts – A smart contract is a computer protocol intended to facilitate, verify, or enforce a contract on the blockchain without third parties. Smart Contract Definition | CoinMarketCap

14) STO – A security token offering (STO) is a public offering where tokenized digital securities are sold. Security Token Offering Definition | CoinMarketCap

15) Tokenomics – Tokenomics is the science of token economy which consists of a set of rules that governs a cryptocurrency's launch and supply. Tokenomics Definition | CoinMarketCap

16) Roadmap – A roadmap is a high-level visual summary that helps map out the vision as well as the direction of a specific product. Roadmap Definition | CoinMarketCap

17) Vesting – Vesting periods, vesting schedules, token unlocks, and vested tokens. What exactly do these mean, and how do they affect the circulating supply of a cryptocurrency? Read on to fi

18) Cliff period – Cliffs are known as the period of time that must pass before the release of the tokens starts. The duration of the cliffs can vary depending on the purpose of an allocation. What Are Cliffs And Vesting, And Why Do They Matter? I by SIPHƎR I Medium

19) SAFT – A Simple Agreement for Future Token (SAFT) is a contractual agreement at the time of launch of a token creating ownership rights for token investors at a future date. Simple Agreement for Future Token (SAFT) Definition I CoinMarketCap

20) Bear market – When prices of assets in a market fall by 20% or more from recent highs, it is called a bear market. As a result, investor confidence is low, and the economy and market turn pessimistic. Bear Market Definition I CoinMarketCap

21) Bull market – A bull market in crypto and stock markets refers to a time during which the prices of assets grow dramatically. These markets act as a source of motivation for both investors and purchasers. Bull Market Definition I CoinMarketCap

22) ROI – Short for "Return on Investment," the ratio between the net profit and cost of investing. ROI Definition I CoinMarketCap

23) Protocol – The set of rules that define interactions on a network, usually involving consensus, transaction validation, and network participation on a blockchain. Protocol Definition I CoinMarketCap

24) Fork – Forks, or chain splits, create an alternate version of the blockchain, leaving two blockchains to run simultaneously. Fork (Blockchain) Definition | CoinMarketCap

25) Mint – Minting is the process of generating new coins using the proof-of-stake mechanism and adding them to the circulation to be traded. – Minting Definition | CoinMarketCap

26) Burn – Cryptocurrency tokens or coins are considered "burned" when they have been purposely and permanently removed from circulation. Burn/Burned Definition | CoinMarketCap

27) Fair launch – A fair launch refers to an equal distribution of a cryptocurrency token at launch. This means everyone will have an equal opportunity to acquire tokens from the beginning, preventing insider trading and price manipulation. – What Is a Fair Launch in Crypto? | CoinGecko

28) Block – A file containing information on transactions completed during a given time period. Blocks are the constituent parts of a blockchain. Block Definition | CoinMarketCap

29) FOMO – An acronym that stands for "Fear of Missing Out." – – FOMO Definition | CoinMarketCap

30) Dump – A sudden sell-off of digital assets. – Dump Definition | CoinMarketCap

31) Pump – In cryptocurrency trading, pump refers to the price of a digital asset increasing, often at a faster pace or in larger moves than normal. – Pump Definition | Decryptopedia™ by BabyPips.com

32) Proof of work (POW) – A blockchain consensus mechanism involving solving of computationally intensive puzzles to validate transactions and create new blocks. *see Proof-of-Stake (PoS). – Proof-of-Work (PoW) Definition | CoinMarketCap

33) Whale – A term used to describe investors who have uncommonly large amounts of crypto, especially those with enough funds to manipulate the market. – Whale Definition | CoinMarketCap

34) Loan to value – The loan-to-value (LTV) ratio is an assessment of lending risk that financial institutions and other lenders examine before approving a mortgage. – Loan-to-Value (LTV) Ratio: What It Is, How to Calculate, Example (investopedia.com)

35) KOL – In the cryptocurrency space, KOLs may be individuals or organizations that have a strong following and influence over the opinions and actions of cryptocurrency enthusiasts and investors. KOLs may include popular crypto influencers, analysts, and thought revaluable leaders who have a ut providation for and analysis on cryptocurrency projects and market trends. – What Does KOL Stand for in Crypto? How Are KOLs Different From Influencers? – Bitkan.com

36) SEO – SEO stands for "**Search Engine Optimization**." It's the practice of optimizing your web pages to make them reach a high position in the search results of

Google and other search engines. In other words:
People will be more likely to see your website when
they search online. SEO focuses on improving the
rankings in the organic (a.k.a. non-paid) – What is SEO?
• SEO for beginners • Yoast

37) Non-disclosure agreement – A non-disclosure
agreement (NDA) is a legally binding contract that
establishes a confidential relationship between two
parties: one that holds sensitive information and the
other that will receive that sensitive information. The
latter agrees that the sensitive information they receive
will not be made available to others. An NDA may also
be referred to as a confidentiality agreement. Non-
Disclosure Agreement (NDA) Explained, With Pros and
Cons (investopedia.com)

38) Proof of concept – In the context of **blockchain**
projects, PoC is undertaken to demonstrate that
the blockchain-based solution would meet the
stakeholders' business and technical expectations.
What Is a Blockchain Proof of Concept?-
Phemex Academy

39) Minimum viable product – a product that has enough
features to interest early adopters and validate the idea
in the early development stages. What is Minimum
Viable Product (MVP)? Definition & Meaning | Crypto
Wiki (bitdegree.org)

40) Transactions per second – Transactions per second
(TPS) stands as a pivotal metric, reflecting the speed
and efficiency of a blockchain network. It's akin
to the horsepower in cars – a higher TPS indicates

a more powerful network, capable of handling a greater volume of transactions swiftly and smoothly. Understanding TPS is crucial for anyone involved in the crypto space, be it investors, developers, or enthusiasts. Transactions Per Second (TPS) I Bybit Learn

41) Real world assets – Real world assets (RWA) in crypto refers to the tokenization of tangible assets that exist in the physical world, that are brought on chain. They also include the growing issuance of capital market products on-chain, where digital securities are tokenized and offered to retail customers. What are Real World Assets (RWA) in Crypto? I CoinGecko

42) Liquidity provisions – Your runway is the amount of time your startup has to achieve profitability or another milestone, such as securing additional funding. Runway: What is it, types, calculation and formula, why track it (sturppy.com)

43) Angel investor – An angel investor is a wealthy individual who invests their personal funds into start-up companies or small businesses in exchange for equity ownership. They are usually entrepreneurs themselves, and have a strong interest in supporting new businesses, especially in their early stages of development. Unlike venture capital firms, angel investors invest their own money, rather than managing funds on behalf of other investors. Angel Investor Explained: Definition and In-Depth Insights (coinscan.com).

44) Venture capitalist – The concept of "Venture Capital" (VC) is a form of private financing aimed at early-stage companies and startups that have medium/long-term growth potential. Contrary to popular belief, venture capital is not just about financial contributions. This is because it can also include technical or managerial expertise (i.e., strategic advice regarding the management of the business). On the other hand, venture capitalists are typically high-net-worth individuals, investment banks, or other financial institutions. Indeed, we are not talking about a few thousand dollars of investment, but rather several millions, even hundreds of millions. What is a VC (Venture Capital) in crypto? (coinacademy.fr)

45) Hot wallet – A hot wallet is a cryptocurrency wallet that is always connected to the Internet and cryptocurrency network. Hot wallets are used to send and receive cryptocurrency, and they allow you to view how many tokens you have available to use. Hot Wallet: Definition, Types, Examples, and Safety Tips (investopedia.com)

46) Cold wallet – A cold wallet is a crypto wallet that does not connect to the Internet or interact with any smart contract. Since cold wallets don't connect to the Internet, they are immune to online threats like malware or spyware. Plus, isolating these accounts from smart contracts also protects them from malicious approvals. In short, they are simply for sending and receiving assets. What Is a Cold Wallet? | Ledger

47) Order book – The term order book refers to an electronic list of buy and sell orders for a specific security or financial instrument organized by price level.

An order book lists the number of shares being bid on or offered at each price point, or market depth. It also identifies the market participants behind the buy and sell orders, though some choose to remain anonymous. These lists help traders and also improve market transparency because they provide valuable trading information. What Is an Order Book? Definition, How It Works, and Key Parts (investopedia.com)

48) Spread – The spread is the difference between the buy and sell prices quoted for a cryptocurrency. What is Cryptocurrency Trading and How Does it Work? – IG | IG International

49) Crypto price chart – Crypto charts are graphical representations of historical price, volumes, and time intervals. The charts form patterns based on the past price movements of the digital currency and are used to spot investment opportunities. How to read Crypto charts? (moneycontrol.com)

50) Trading pair – They consist of two assets that can be traded with each other on an exchange and are also used to quote one crypto against the other. Crypto Trading Pairs Explained (coindesk.com)

51) Sniper bot – Sniper bots are automated software programmed for specific actions at predetermined times to find applications in online auctions, sales, and crypto trading, ensuring precise market transactions.

What are sniper bots, and how to stop token sniping exploits? (cointelegraph.com)

52) Frontrunner – Front running is the act of placing a transaction in a queue with the knowledge of a future transaction. Front running on a blockchain platform normally happens when a miner, who has access to information on pending transactions, places an order that would earn him a profit based on a pending trade. Front Running Definition | CoinMarketCap

53) Wash trading – Simply put, wash trading refers to the practice of buying and selling the same financial instruments to create a false representation of market activity. This seemingly deceptive tactic can have consequences for market integrity and fairness. In other words, wash trading involves an individual or entity acting as both the buyer and the seller in a trade, creating an illusion of genuine market activity. In most cases, the goal is not to derive profit from the trade itself but to manipulate market perceptions, such as boosting trading volume or influencing price trends. This practice is considered unethical and, in many jurisdictions, illegal. Wash Trading | Binance Academy

54) Yield aggregation – Yield aggregators essentially automate the process of staking and collecting the generated rewards on behalf of users, to optimize gas fee spending via different strategies [sometimes complex]. These strategies involve moving tokens around different platforms and maximizing yields via auto compounding. https://members.delphidigital.io/learn/yield-aggregator

55) Liquid staking derivatives – Liquid staking derivatives represent a user's staked assets and can be used in DeFi activities, enabling them to earn additional yield on top of their staking rewards. Liquid staking has grown to become one of the biggest narratives in crypto, dominating DeFi with a combined TVL of $21.6 billion and Lido alone reaching over $14 billion in TVL. `https://www.coingecko.com/learn/what-is-liquid-staking-liquid-staked-derivatives-you-need-to-know`

56) Flash loan arbitrage – A flash loan is a type of loan where a user borrows assets with no up-front collateral and returns the borrowed assets within the same blockchain transaction. `https://chain.link/education-hub/flash-loans`

57) Liquidity pool – A liquidity pool is a crowdsourced pool of cryptocurrencies or tokens locked in a smart contract that is used to facilitate trades between the assets on a decentralized exchange (DEX). Instead of traditional markets of buyers and sellers, many decentralized finance (DeFi) platforms use automated market makers (AMMs), which allow digital assets to be traded in an automatic and permissionless manner through the use of liquidity pools. `https://www.gemini.com/cryptopedia/what-is-a-liquidity-pool-crypto-market-liquidity`

58) TGE – Initially, the term "ICO," which refers to "initial coin offering," was used to refer to the initial release of cryptocurrency tokens to the public as a fund raising mechanism. However, due to regulatory concerns of ICO being modeled after IPO (Initial Public Offering) and its implication as an investment vehicle, some

projects began coining different naming convention. Token Generation Event (TGE) is one such convention. Definition of Token Generation Event (TGE) | CoinGecko

59) API – Application Programming Interface is a set of protocols or tools for setting up access to remote software application. API can help in integration of your own applications to CEX.IO functions (such as trading bots). API Setup guide | CEX.IO Help Centre

60) Fully diluted valuation (FDV) – Fully diluted valuation (FDV) is a measure of the total value of a cryptocurrency project, assuming all of its tokens are in circulation. It's a statistical representation of the maximum value of a cryptocurrency project, providing individuals with a view of the project beyond the given point. What is a Fully Diluted Valuation (FDV) in crypto? | Coinbase

61) Trading volume – Crypto trading volume is a measure of the total amount of money flowing in and out of a cryptocurrency market over a certain period of time. The trading volume combines all volumes on centralized exchanges and decentralized exchanges. Trading Volume Definition | CoinMarketCap

62) Bid-ask spread – A bid-ask spread is the amount by which the ask price exceeds the bid price for an asset in the market. The bid-ask spread is essentially the difference between the highest price that a buyer is willing to pay for an asset and the lowest price that a seller is willing to accept. An individual looking to sell will receive the bid price while one looking to buy will pay the ask price. What Is a Bid-Ask Spread, and How Does It Work in Trading? (investopedia.com)

Index

A

AIWorld, 52
Application Program Interfaces
    (API), 235, 285
Artificial Intelligence (AI),
    61, 76, 81
Ask Me Anything (AMAs), 91
Automated market makers
    (AMMs), 284

B

Bear market, 62, 65, 66, 276
Bitcoin, 67–69, 71
Blockchain, 6, 82, 273
Bull market, 276

C

Chief Technical Officer (CTO), 38
Cliffs, 276
Coin Market Cap (CMC), 204–206
Cold wallet, 281
Colombo Stock Exchange
    (CSE), 202
Community driven economies, 44
Conversion Rate (CR), 97

Conversion rate optimization
    (CRO), 96
Cryptocurrency, 2, 67, 158
Crypto projects
    audits, 14
    blockchain technology, 13
    community, 14
    compliance, 15
    effective governance
        structures, 15
    smart contracts, 13
Crypto project structure
    blockchain ecosystem, 26
    business model, 21
    colors, 33
    community and team, 19
    community engagement, 23
    contact information, 32
    continuous improvement, 24
    crafting, 39
    cryptocurrency, 34
    digital innovation and market
        uncertainties, 19
    entrepreneur, 38
    expert, 35
    fundraising wizard, 36, 37
    graphics, 33

T, U